ALSO BY AMERICA'S TEST KITCHEN

More Mediterranean

The Complete Plant-Based Cookbook

Cooking with Plant-Based Meat

Boards

The Savory Baker

The New Cooking School Cookbook: Fundamentals

The Complete Autumn and Winter Cookbook

One-Hour Comfort

Cook for Your Gut Health

Foolproof Fish

Five-Ingredient Dinners

The Ultimate Meal-Prep Cookbook

The Complete Salad Cookbook

The Chicken Bible

Meat Illustrated

Vegetables Illustrated

Cooking for One

The Complete One Pot

How Can It Be Gluten-Free Cookbook Collection

The Complete Summer Cookbook

Bowls

The Side Dish Bible

100 Techniques

Easy Everyday Keto

Everything Chocolate

The Perfect Cookie

The Perfect Pie

The Perfect Cake

How to Cocktail

Spiced

The Ultimate Burger

The New Essentials Cookbook

Dinner Illustrated

America's Test Kitchen Menu Cookbook

Cook's Illustrated Revolutionary Recipes

Tasting Italy: A Culinary Journey

Cooking at Home with Bridget and Julia

The Complete Mediterranean Cookbook

The Complete Vegetarian Cookbook

The Complete Cooking for Two Cookbook

The Complete Diabetes Cookbook

The Complete Slow Cooker

The Complete Make-Ahead Cookbook

Just Add Sauce

How to Braise Everything

How to Roast Everything

Nutritious Delicious

What Good Cooks Know

Cook's Science

The Science of Good Cooking

Bread Illustrated

Master of the Grill

Kitchen Smarts

Kitchen Hacks

100 Recipes

The New Family Cookbook

The Cook's Illustrated Baking Book

The Cook's Illustrated Cookbook

The America's Test Kitchen Family Baking Book

America's Test Kitchen Twentieth Anniversary TV Show Cookbook

The Best of America's Test Kitchen (2007–2022 Editions)

The Complete America's Test Kitchen TV Show Cookbook 2001–2022

Healthy Air Fryer

Healthy and Delicious Instant Pot

Toaster Oven Perfection

Mediterranean Instant Pot

Cook It in Your Dutch Oven

Vegan for Everybody

Sous Vide for Everybody

Air Fryer Perfection

Multicooker Perfection

Food Processor Perfection

Pressure Cooker Perfection

Instant Pot Ace Blender Cookbook

Naturally Sweet

Foolproof Preserving

Paleo Perfected

The Best Mexican Recipes

Slow Cooker Revolution Volume 2: The Easy-Prep Edition

Slow Cooker Revolution

The America's Test Kitchen D.I.Y. Cookbook

The Cook's Illustrated All-Time Best Series

All-Time Best Brunch

All-Time Best Dinners for Two

All-Time Best Sunday Suppers

All-Time Best Holiday Entertaining

All-Time Best Soups

Cook's Country Titles

Big Flavors from Italian America

One-Pan Wonders

Cook It in Cast Iron

Cook's Country Eats Local

The Complete Cook's Country TV Show Cookbook

For a Full Listing of All Our Books

CooksIllustrated.com

AmericasTestKitchen.com

PRAISE FOR AMERICA'S TEST KITCHEN TITLES

Selected as the Cookbook Award Winner of 2021 in the General Cookbook Category
International Association of Culinary Professionals (IACP) on *Meat Illustrated*

Selected as the Cookbook Award Winner of 2021 in the Health and Nutrition Category
International Association of Culinary Professionals (IACP) on *The Complete Plant-Based Cookbook*

"The book's depth, breadth, and practicality makes it a must-have for seafood lovers."
Publishers Weekly* (starred review) on *Foolproof Fish

"Another flawless entry in the America's Test Kitchen canon, *Bowls* guides readers of all culinary skill levels in composing one-bowl meals from a variety of cuisines."
BuzzFeed Books* on *Bowls

"This is a wonderful, useful guide to healthy eating."
Publishers Weekly* on *Nutritious Delicious

"*The Perfect Cookie* . . . is, in a word, perfect. This is an important and substantial cookbook. . . . If you love cookies, but have been a tad shy to bake on your own, all your fears will be dissipated. This is one book you can use for years with magnificently happy results."
The Huffington Post* on *The Perfect Cookie

"The book offers an impressive education for curious cake makers, new and experienced alike. A summation of 25 years of cake making at ATK, there are cakes for every taste."
The Wall Street Journal* on *The Perfect Cake

"True to its name, this smart and endlessly enlightening cookbook is about as definitive as it's possible to get in the modern vegetarian realm."
Men's Journal* on *The Complete Vegetarian Cookbook

"Here are the words just about any vegan would be happy to read: 'Why This Recipe Works.' Fans of America's Test Kitchen are used to seeing the phrase and now it applies to the growing collection of plant-based creations in *Vegan for Everybody*."
The Washington Post* on *Vegan for Everybody

"Offers a real option for a cook who just wants to learn some new ways to encourage family and friends to explore today's sometimes-daunting vegetable universe. This is one of the most valuable cooking resources for the home chef since Marian Morash's beloved classic *The Victory Garden Cookbook* (1982)."
Booklist* (starred review) on *Vegetables Illustrated

"A one-volume kitchen seminar, addressing in one smart chapter after another the sometimes surprising whys behind a cook's best practices. . . . You get the myth, the theory, the science, and the proof, all rigorously interrogated as only America's Test Kitchen can do."
NPR* on *The Science of Good Cooking

"The 21st-century *Fannie Farmer Cookbook* or *The Joy of Cooking*. If you had to have one cookbook and that's all you could have, this one would do it."
CBS San Francisco* on *The New Family Coookbook

"The go-to gift book for newlyweds, small families, or empty nesters."
Orlando Sentinel* on *The Complete Cooking for Two Cookbook

"Some books impress by the sheer audacity of their ambition. Backed by the magazine's famed mission to test every recipe relentlessly until it is the best it can be, this nearly 900-page volume lands with an authoritative wallop."
Chicago Tribune* on *The Cook's Illustrated Cookbook

"It might become your 'cooking school,' the only book you'll need to make you a proficient cook, recipes included. . . . You can master the 100 techniques with the easy-to-understand instructions, then apply the skill with the recipes that follow."
The Litchfield County Times* on *100 Techniques

"The America's Test Kitchen team elevates the humble side dish to center stage in this excellent collection of 1,001 recipes."
Publishers Weekly* on *The Side Dish Bible

"Filled with complete meals you can cook in your Instant Pot. Next time you're thinking of turning to takeout or convenience foods, prepare one of these one-pot meals instead."
NBC News* on *Mediterranean Instant Pot

THE
EVERYDAY ATHLETE
COOKBOOK

165 RECIPES TO BOOST ENERGY, PERFORMANCE, AND RECOVERY

AMERICA'S TEST KITCHEN

with **ALICIA A. ROMANO**
MS, RD, LDN, CNSC

Library of Congress Cataloging-in-Publication Data

Names: Romano, Alicia A., author. | America's Test Kitchen (Firm), issuing body.
Title: The everyday athlete cookbook : 165 recipes to boost energy, performance, and recovery / America's Test Kitchen with Alicia A. Romano, MS, RD, LDN, CNSC.
Description: First edition. | Boston, MA : America's Test Kitchen, [2022] | Includes index.
Identifiers: LCCN 2022004261 (print) | LCCN 2022004262 (ebook) | ISBN 9781954210042 (paperback) | ISBN 9781954210059 (ebook)
Subjects: LCSH: Athletes--Nutrition. | Physical fitness--Nutritional aspects. | Cooking. | LCGFT: Cookbooks.
Classification: LCC TX361.A8 E97 2022 (print) | LCC TX361.A8 (ebook) | DDC 613.2024796--dc23/eng/20220213
LC record available at https://lccn.loc.gov/2022004261
LC ebook record available at https://lccn.loc.gov/2022004262

America's Test Kitchen
21 Drydock Avenue, Boston, MA 02210

Printed in Canada
10 9 8 7 6 5 4 3 2 1

Distributed by
Penguin Random House Publisher Services
Tel: 800.733.3000

Pictured on front cover **Strawberry-Banana Smoothie** (page 252), **Chewy Granola Bars with Walnuts and Cranberries** (page 262), **Fattoush with Butternut Squash and Apple** (page 207), **Crispy Chicken with Cabbage Slaw and Tonkatsu Sauce** (page 121)

Pictured on back cover (clockwise from top left) **Black Bean Breakfast Burritos** (page 48), **Chia Pudding Cups with Fresh Berries** (page 225), **Penne with Cherry Tomatoes and Crispy Caper Crumbs** (page 227), **Salmon and Black Rice Salad with Snap Peas and Radishes** (page 171), **Strawberry Electrolyte Refresher** (page 239)

Editorial Director, Books **Adam Kowit**

Executive Food Editor **Dan Zuccarello**

Deputy Food Editor **Stephanie Pixley**

Senior Editors **Camila Chaparro, Leah Colins, Joseph Gitter, Sacha Madadian, Sara Mayer, and Russell Selander**

Associate Editors **Sam Block and Sarah Ewald**

Test Cook **Carmen Dongo**

Executive Managing Editor **Debra Hudak**

Project Editor **Nicole Konstantinakos**

Editor **Emily Rahravan**

Assistant Editor **Sara Zatopek**

Consulting Nutritionist **Alicia A. Romano, MS, RD, LDN, CNSC**

Design Director **Lindsey Timko Chandler**

Deputy Art Director **Allison Boales**

Photography Director **Julie Bozzo Cote**

Photography Producer **Meredith Mulcahy**

Senior Staff Photographers **Steve Klise and Daniel J. van Ackere**

Staff Photographer **Kevin White**

Additional Photography **Joseph Keller and Carl Tremblay**

Food Styling **Joy Howard, Catrine Kelty, Chantal Lambeth, Gina McCreadie, Kendra McNight, Ashley Moore, Christie Morrison, Marie Piraino, Elle Simone Scott, Kendra Smith, and Sally Staub**

Photoshoot Kitchen Team

Photo Team and Special Events Manager **Alli Berkey**

Lead Test Cook **Eric Haessler**

Test Cooks **Hannah Fenton, Jacqueline Gochenouer, and Gina McCreadie**

Assistant Test Cooks **Hisham Hassan and Christa West**

Senior Manager, Publishing Operations **Taylor Argenzio**

Imaging Manager **Lauren Robbins**

Production and Imaging Specialists **Tricia Neumyer, Dennis Noble, and Amanda Yong**

Copy Editor **Deri Reed**

Proofreader **Ann-Marie Imbornoni**

Indexer **Elizabeth Parson**

Chief Creative Officer **Jack Bishop**

Executive Editorial Directors **Julia Collin Davison and Bridget Lancaster**

CONTENTS

WELCOME TO AMERICA'S TEST KITCHEN

This book has been tested, written, and edited by the folks at America's Test Kitchen, where curious cooks become confident cooks. Located in Boston's Seaport District in the historic Innovation and Design Building, it features 15,000 square feet of kitchen space including multiple photography and video studios. It is the home of *Cook's Illustrated* magazine and *Cook's Country* magazine and is the workday destination for more than 60 test cooks, editors, and cookware specialists. Our mission is to empower and inspire confidence, community, and creativity in the kitchen.

We start the process of testing a recipe with a complete lack of preconceptions, which means that we accept no claim, no technique, and no recipe at face value. We simply assemble as many variations as possible, test a half-dozen of the most promising, and taste the results blind. We then construct our own recipe and continue to test it, varying ingredients, techniques, and cooking times until we reach a consensus. As we like to say in the test kitchen, "We make the mistakes so you don't have to." The result, we hope, is the best version of a particular recipe, but we realize that only you can be the final judge of our success (or failure). We use the same rigorous approach when we test equipment and taste ingredients.

All of this would not be possible without a belief that good cooking, much like good music, is based on a foundation of objective technique. Some people like spicy foods and others don't, but there is a right way to sauté, there is a best way to cook a pot roast, and there are measurable scientific principles involved in producing perfectly beaten, stable egg whites. Our ultimate goal is to investigate the fundamental principles of cooking to give you the techniques, tools, and ingredients you need to become a better cook. It is as simple as that.

To see what goes on behind the scenes at America's Test Kitchen, check out our social media channels for kitchen snapshots, exclusive content, video tips, and much more. You can watch us work (in our actual test kitchen) by tuning in to *America's Test Kitchen* or *Cook's Country* on public television or on our websites. Listen to *Proof*, *Mystery Recipe*, and *The Walk-In* (AmericasTestKitchen.com/podcasts), to hear engaging, complex stories about people and food. Want to hone your cooking skills or finally learn how to bake—with an America's Test Kitchen test cook? Enroll in one of our online cooking classes. And you can engage the next generation of home cooks with kid-tested recipes from America's Test Kitchen Kids.

Our community of home recipe testers provides valuable feedback on recipes under development by ensuring that they are foolproof. You can help us investigate the how and why behind successful recipes from your home kitchen. (Sign up at AmericasTestKitchen.com/recipe_testing.)

However you choose to visit us, we welcome you into our kitchen, where you can stand by our side as we test our way to the best recipes in America.

facebook.com/AmericasTestKitchen
instagram.com/TestKitchen
youtube.com/AmericasTestKitchen
tiktok.com/@TestKitchen
twitter.com/TestKitchen
pinterest.com/TestKitchen

AmericasTestKitchen.com
CooksIllustrated.com
CooksCountry.com
OnlineCookingSchool.com
AmericasTestKitchen.com/kids

EATING *FOR* EXERCISE

The team at America's Test Kitchen is, of course, surrounded by food all day. It not only fuels us to work in our 15,000-square-foot test kitchen, but also to bike to and from the office, take a yoga class, or work out in one of the nearby gyms. America's Test Kitchen is home to cooks, editors, and creatives of all kinds—and everyday athletes.

We use the term "everyday athlete" broadly, to cover a range people and their physical activity. No matter your age or ability, if you add an active element to the equation of your life a few or more times a week—swim laps, participate in a recreational league, take spin classes, or hit the weights after work—*you* are an everyday athlete. What's often missing from the everyday athlete's equation? Food.

Maybe you haven't factored your nutrition into how you feel after, or even before, exercise. But it could be the key to enjoying your activities and reaching your unique goals. Food *is* fuel—the most important fuel source for your workouts, the most powerful tool for boosting energy, and critical to recovering from exercise properly. If you find it hard to get going for your morning conditioning class, you might be running on empty—maybe you didn't eat right last night or you skipped a snack to get out the door. If you feel less ready to conquer tasks after a run and more ready for a nap, maybe you didn't eat an adequate meal after. Do you go to the gym with discipline but never increase stamina, perform better, or lift heavier? Take a look at what's on your plate.

With the *Everyday Athlete Cookbook, we* show that it's not just elite athletes who should pay attention to the makeup of their meals. And it doesn't take elite attention. Along with registered dietitian and nutritionist (and passionate athlete) Alicia Romano, we introduce you to the science-backed principles of sports nutrition; we fill your plate with abundant, delicious food; and we give you the tools to fit eating well into your day with the utmost ease. And if you already track your eating around exercise, you'll be thrilled at how much more deliciously you can be eating.

We were amazed at the dishes we developed for this book by working on flavor first, and then calibrating recipes to meet athletic needs. For starters, don't pay attention to social media or reality TV; there's no cutting carbs. In fact, carbohydrates should be your primary fuel source, and a generous amount is required to give you the fuel to perform, the support to recover, and restored energy for the next sweat session. You'll discover that the perfect plate features a 3:1 ratio of fueling carbohydrates to sustaining protein. But we've done all the work—no calculators at the dinner table. Sign us up for Pumpkin Spice Waffles (page 62) or meals like Turmeric Scallops with Mango Noodle Salad (page 173). To boot, they sustained our own extracurricular activities during testing.

Maybe you're already fueling properly, but in addition to *what* you eat, *when* you eat it matters tremendously. We explain the whens (and whys) of enjoying every recipe based on your workouts. Looking for a lunch to energize your afternoon spin class? Try Penne with Cherry Tomatoes and Crispy Caper Crumbs (page 227): It has quick-digesting carbs to rev your engines, while limiting hard-to-digest elements that can interfere with exercise. Other meals, such as Seared Flank Steak with Oat Berries, Zucchini, and Peppers (page 148), are great for after. It offers up fiberful grains, has the right amount of protein to grow and repair muscles, and incorporates healthy fat. And many of our meals are versatile enough to work both before and after exercise, or even on rest days to enhance your overall nutrition. What about in-between? Learn the art of snacking and make tasty bites, even an easy DIY electrolyte drink, to have on hand for energy boosts.

While this book is for anyone, tailor it to your lifestyle. There are dead-simple recipe modifications for those participating in endurance or strength and interval training. And while some fitness books can make planning for meals a workout in itself, every recipe here includes clear meal prep suggestions since we know you're busy. So try the make-ahead frittata bites recipe (see page 44); it makes 12 bites that are perfect for on-the-go mornings. Or how about Chicken Bun Cha Bowls (page 111)—great for dinner tonight, with leftovers for tomorrow's lunch. Feel your best while eating your best.

FUELING WITH FOOD

Of course, we have many reasons for eating and food has endless sensory appeal, but its core purpose is to provide our bodies with energy for living.

If you're an everyday athlete and expend a fair amount of that energy through working out, your body, unsurprisingly, requires extra fuel to complete those athletic tasks. To do this with the most gusto—achieving fitness goals, without tiring midway through, and with restored energy to go at it next time—you should pay attention not only to *how much* food for fuel, but also to the *type* and *timing* of that fuel.

For a minute, think of a car: A car requires fuel in order to run, and in some cases it needs a specific type of fuel to run its best. Now, if the car needs to drive a long distance, it's likely it will need to start with more fuel. And after a drive, it's important to fill the tank back up so the car can run the next time. If all of this happens, you avoid the dreaded flashing "empty" light, when the car doesn't have enough fuel to run altogether.

Our bodies are quite similar. Fuel from food and hydration provides the everyday athlete with the energy to run (literally), move, and contract muscles through an hour of moderate to intense activity. You need to fill yourself with enough food before and after exercise to fuel your tasks.

In this book, we cover specific nutrition strategies geared toward best fueling your engine for athletic activities. We guide you on the type of food to eat before you work out (and when), the food to eat after you work out, and the food to eat anytime. Following our guidance will boost energy levels, optimize performance during workouts, and give you an edge on your post-workout recovery.

But what do these achievements mean exactly?

Boost Energy
Are sluggish days leaving you unmotivated to get yourself to your favorite exercise class?

In order to avoid sharp inclines and declines in energy levels throughout the day, you have to, simply, eat and drink enough. But if you go further, by becoming aware of the composition of your meals, you have the opportunity to boost available energy for exercise. The recipes in this book are calibrated to provide the beneficial nutrients the body uses to create usable forms of energy that allow you to function.

Optimize Performance
Do you find yourself starting a workout strong, only to hit a wall halfway through? Do you have goals in mind with your fitness (a longer swim session, heavier weights) that feel tough to reach?

By properly timing well-composed meals, you can ensure that your body has access not only to enough energy to work out, but enough available reserved energy to release throughout your workout, setting you up to perform at a high level and hit your goals.

Improve Recovery
You may hit the gym hard or power through a 3-hour hike, but then what? Do you feel sapped?

Recovery is the process of refilling your energy tank, and it relies on a number of factors like rest between exercise sessions, adequate sleep, stress management, hydration, and what we call refueling. You want to pay attention to what and when you are eating after an exercise session in order to replenish your energy stores, rehydrate (especially after those super-sweaty sessions), repair lean muscle tissue, and aid in rebuilding muscle mass. We have recipes that are specially formulated for after your workout to aid recovery.

Every body has unique nutritional needs beyond exercise. This book is not a prescribed diet, but its teachings will help you achieve the above three goals and level up your athletic pursuits. And of course the test kitchen ensures great taste and variety.

THE THREE MACRONUTRIENTS

In order to understand sports nutrition, it's important to understand the fundamental roles that nutrients play in body functions. Take a dive into how the three influential macronutrients are used in your body through the stages of digestion.

Carbohydrates: Your #1 Fuel Source

Carbohydrates are the body's primary, preferred fuel source. A key function of carbohydrates is providing your body with available energy: that is, energy to fuel activity and movement. Carbohydrates are fast-acting and turn into energy as soon as they are ingested and digested, much quicker than your food's other energy source, fats. Additionally, they're the primary fuel source for your brain.

Stage 1: Glucose Becomes Available

Most of the carbohydrates you eat are digested and then broken down into a simple sugar called glucose before entering the bloodstream.

Digestion of carbohydrates begins right away in the mouth through chewing and mixing with saliva. Saliva contains an enzyme called amylase that breaks down more complex carbohydrates into smaller, simpler sugars. Once they reach the stomach, carbohydrates are mixed through peristalsis (muscle contractions of the stomach) into a more uniform mix called chyme; chyme is slowly released into the small intestine where digestion is completed and glucose becomes available for absorption into the bloodstream. Meanwhile, insulin is released into the blood upon eating and plays a critical role in transporting glucose to cells and tissues like the liver, muscle, and adipose tissue.

Stage 2: ATP Is Produced to Power the Body

When glucose is absorbed, it's used to produce a molecule called adenosine triphosphate (ATP), which is employed by the cells to power your body's tasks, including movement and exercise. Although ATP can be produced from both dietary carbohydrates and fats, the body prefers the faster process of using carbohydrates as its primary energy source to produce ATP.

DURING EXERCISE, YOUR BODY GETS ENERGY (ATP) FROM:

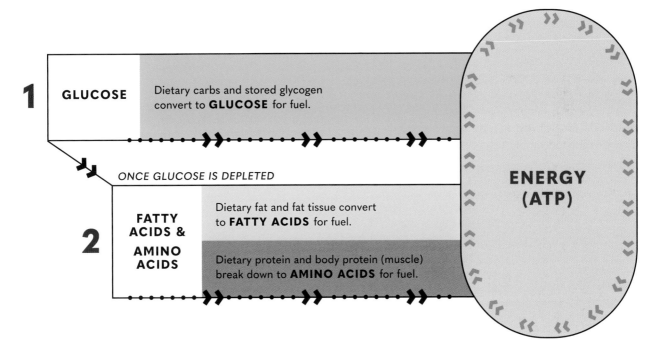

1 **GLUCOSE** — Dietary carbs and stored glycogen convert to **GLUCOSE** for fuel.

ONCE GLUCOSE IS DEPLETED

2 **FATTY ACIDS & AMINO ACIDS** — Dietary fat and fat tissue convert to **FATTY ACIDS** for fuel. Dietary protein and body protein (muscle) break down to **AMINO ACIDS** for fuel.

ENERGY (ATP)

DON'T CUT THE CARBS

When you've thought about building muscle, you probably thought about eating lots of protein. Protein will help with greater satiety and building lean muscle mass, but we invite you to reconsider the popular narrative that it is king, and consider the importance of carbohydrates in maximizing muscle building, repair, and maintenance.

Inadequate carbohydrate intake may deplete protein stores and muscle mass.
When the body isn't fueled with adequate carbohydrates during exercise, it will quickly deplete stored glycogen and scrounge for additional energy sources; these can be fatty acids or amino acids (protein). With prolonged low carbohydrate intake, this may result in the breakdown of your hard-earned muscle protein.

Carbohydrate intake can increase the rate of protein uptake in the muscle.
After a workout, our bodies recover what was lost (glycogen for the next workout) and repair what was broken down (muscle tissue). The body needs the right mix of carbs *with* protein to improve protein synthesis and prevent protein breakdown.

The body can't store an excess of protein.
When you eat more protein than you need for rebuilding muscle, any excess is used for energy or stored as fat, likely not what you're looking for.

Stage 3: Glycogen Is Stored to Fuel the Long Game
In many cases, the body may have enough glucose to fulfill its current needs. So what happens when you eat more carbohydrates than what your body needs for, say, your 45-minute moderate-intensity gym session? Excess glucose can be stored in both the liver and the muscle for later use; this storage form of glucose is called glycogen, and it's your energy reserve, ensuring the body has enough glucose for all of its functions. For the everyday athlete, glycogen stored in the muscle is especially important as it can be used by muscle cells to fuel longer periods and a higher intensity of exercise.

Thus, the body requires adequate carbohydrate intake to ensure stored energy is available—and available right away—during exercise. In the absence of adequate glucose, the body will turn to alternative forms of energy, fatty acids or protein, to fuel the workout. Fatty acids are less reliable and efficient in producing the energy you need, requiring more chemical reactions in the body and more oxygen (that you're expending during exercise) to burn. Protein generally becomes a fuel source in the absence of enough nutrients in the diet and its use will lead to muscle degradation.

Proteins: The Building Blocks of Life
Protein provides the building blocks for the body's cells; it is required for structure, function, and regulation of the body's tissues and organs, including our lean muscle mass. Here are the two stages of protein digestion:

Stage 1: Amino Acids Support Our Bodies
Proteins are made up of molecules called amino acids. During digestion, protein is broken down by digestive juices into amino acids, which are then absorbed across our small intestine and released into the bloodstream to be taken up by cells and used for a variety of important functions throughout the body.

Stage 2: Amino Acids Are Replenished
Amino acids need to be consistently replenished to meet various demands, such as production of hormones, antibodies, and enzymes; supporting immune function; and growth and repair of body tissue, including lean muscle mass—all important roles in maintaining a strong body.

It is important to note that protein is not the body's desired energy source. Rather, it is a supporting character to carbohydrates. In the presence of adequate energy from carbohydrates, protein is spared as an energy source, allowing the body to use protein as it intends: to build and repair lean muscle.

Fat: Our Secondary Energy Resource

The final macronutrient is fat, which is the most concentrated energy (calorie) source and used to fuel the body. You're going hard at your workout: Once carbohydrate storages are depleted, the body will turn to fat for energy burning. Here are the stages of fat digestion:

Stage 1: Fat Is Digested Slowly to Support Our Bodies

Fat digestion begins in the stomach and its process is delayed overall. Ingestion of fat stimulates the release of cholecystokinin (CCK), a hormone that in addition to suppressing your appetite, delays stomach emptying. This allows fats to enter the small intestine gradually, where they can be further broken down by digestive juices and eventually absorbed as a usable form of energy across the small intestine.

Fat plays an essential role throughout the entire body, as lipids are a part of every cell membrane, organ, and tissue in the body. Fats serve a number of functions for immune-related molecules, enhance absorption of fat-soluble vitamins (like vitamin D), and play a role in cholesterol production and heart health.

Stage 2: Fatty Acids Are Oxidized to Produce ATP

Fat is a fuel source for energy production and utilization. In the absence of adequate carbohydrates (glucose, stored glycogen), the body will turn to fat as a fuel source. Fatty acids produce ATP through a process called oxidative phosphorylation. As stated, in the presence of adequate carbohydrate fueling, this process typically occurs during long-duration exercise as it is not efficient. The body needs to utilize fat as fuel as training volume increases and access to fuel from carbohydrates decreases.

FLUID AS FUEL, TOO

Hydrating plays an equally important role as eating in our bodies' function and performance. Hydration, from water and other fluids, is crucial for a number of body processes including regulation of body temperature, delivery of nutrients to cells, organ function, joint lubrication, and more. For the everyday athlete, the benefits of adequate hydration include:

❯ Delay of physical fatigue

❯ Performance stamina

❯ Improvements in body heat regulation

❯ Enhanced recovery after exercise

❯ Decreased stress on the heart

❯ Improved cognition, which can aid in mental sharpness, agility, and reaction time

Fluid needs on a day to day basis and during exercise vary by individual and can be influenced by a number of factors including genetics, gender, age, environmental conditions (like temperature, altitude), intensity and duration of exercise, and fitness level. What is most important? That you maintain fluid intake throughout the day so you begin any activity well hydrated.

As a general rule of thumb, maintenance hydration is around half of your body weight (pounds), in ounces. For example, if you weigh 200 pounds, you should drink about 100 ounces of fluids throughout the day (1 cup is 8 ounces, so that's 12½ cups). How do you know if that's enough? You can gauge your overall hydration level by monitoring your urine output (it should be 6 to 8 times per day) and color (it should be clear to pale yellow), and by assessing factors that may influence the need for additional water (watch out for headaches, fatigue, light-headedness, and muscle cramps). Risk of dehydration increases when there are increased losses, such as during longer duration/high intensity exercise, or when in hot or humid conditions. In these situations, electrolyte beverages may be needed to replace sweat loss (these will contain carbohydrates and sodium and in some cases, potassium; see page 21). After exercise, it's essential to rehydrate the same way we refuel with food to optimize recovery and future performance.

TIMING MATTERS

Just as important as the contents of an exercise meal, the timing of eating it can have a great impact on your performance and recovery.

The Salmon and Black Rice Salad (see page 171) will have a different effect on your body and energy levels depending on whether you eat it before a workout, after a workout, or in the hours apart from working out. Eating before exercise should provide your body with enough fuel to sustain your energy levels through the workout. The black rice in the salmon bowl (along with some crunchy vegetables) gives you the carbohydrate boost you need for energy to work out. Eating after exercise should aid in recovery, refueling, building and repairing lean muscle, rehydration, and improving future performance. This is because after exercise there is increased blood flow and a variety of active metabolic processes available to help to facilitate glucose uptake, resynthesis of glycogen, and repair of lean muscle. The combination of carbohydrates and protein in the salmon recipe will bring you back to life and contribute to those strong muscles after exercising.

Let's take a more granular look at how your body uses food around activity time.

THE LIFECYCLE OF WORKOUT MEALS

1
Fuel Up
The food you eat in anticipation of a workout can take anywhere from 2 to 4 hours to completely empty from the stomach. It then completes digestion and absorption in the small intestine to be converted to immediately usable forms of energy, so you're now armed with the power to work out.

2
Use the Resulting Energy
As the duration and intensity of your exercise increases, your body will need more energy and begin to pull from stored glycogen to maintain energy production. If your glycogen stores run out (think with longer duration, higher intensity), your body will first turn to fatty acids, which will be oxidized to create ATP.

3
Rest and Recover
Food and fluid intake after exercise has the potential to refuel your body by replenishing glycogen stores, initiating muscle and tissue repair, decreasing the rate of protein breakdown (a normal post-exercise process), supporting the body's metabolic switch to muscle building, and adequately rehydrating the body to improve future performance.

WHEN TO EAT

Depending on the timing of your workout on a particular day, there are windows when your body most needs food for energy and most efficiently uses food for recovery. You don't want to be hungry before a workout, but you don't want to be full; you want to eat soon after a workout, but you can supplement with snacks when that's convenient. Here are the categories of meals (you'll see them in this book) and lessons on how to fit them into your day.

WHAT'S THE GLYCEMIC INDEX AND HOW CAN IT HELP?

The glycemic index (GI) is a system used to rank the blood glucose response to consuming a food containing carbohydrates against a reference food (glucose or white bread) containing the same amount of carbohydrates. Essentially, GI measures the rate at which blood glucose levels increase: A high-GI food will spike blood sugar more quickly, while a low-GI food will produce a slower increase in blood glucose levels.

Although there has been limited research on the use of the GI as it applies to athletes, studies show that utilizing the GI may be beneficial in both pre- and post-workout settings. For example, endurance athletes may benefit from eating low-GI carbohydrates before activity to enhance performance. With the slower increase in blood glucose levels, less insulin is released, which prevents dips in blood glucose (common when activity starts). In theory, lower insulin levels may encourage the use of fat as fuel, which may spare glycogen stores and increase the capacity for endurance activity.

On the flip side, research has also supported consumption of high-GI carbohydrates after prolonged exercise (in combination with protein foods) as high-GI foods may cause a greater spike in insulin resulting in a more rapid increase in glucose uptake (and therefore glycogen storage) post activity.

Although we cannot promise the GI index will play the most vital role in your performance and recovery, you may find that paying attention to it, especially before endurance exercise or after high-activity exercise, may give you a leg up on your fueling and recovery.

Pre-Workout Meals
(3 to 4 hours before working out)

Timing Eating 3 to 4 hours before a workout allows the body enough time to digest food and minimize gastrointestinal upset during exercise (individual tolerance may vary), and to absorb nutrients to fuel your workout. (For information on snacking, see page 10.)

Contents The focus of a pre-workout meal should be on carbohydrates sharing the plate with a modest amount of protein and low amounts of fat and fiber (and don't forget to hydrate). Spicy Basil Noodles with Tofu and Bok Choy (page 221), for example, is a great choice to rev your engines. The wide rice noodles are balanced with just enough seared tofu, and the dish features nutritious vegetables in a quantity that isn't too fiberful to digest. A general recommendation for fluid intake is 17 to 20 ounces of water with your pre-activity meal and about 8 ounces 20 to 30 minutes before you start exercising. Avoid gulping to minimize stomach sloshing.

WHAT TO AVOID BEFORE WORKING OUT

You shouldn't have foods that don't agree with you before working out. Look out for your red-flag foods; we recommend avoiding the following:

High Fiber and Fat Meals
These include dishes with high-fiber grains, large portions of raw vegetables, fried foods, fatty cuts of meat, and large portions of nut or seed butter, oils, or butter. These foods slow digestion and divert blood flow to the gut and could cause cramps, diarrhea, gas, or fullness during a workout.

Too Much Protein and Too Few Carbohydrates
Protein can slow digestion and cause gastrointestinal upset. And a prolonged focus on too much protein can limit energy reserves during exercise.

Carbonated or High-Sugar Beverages
These may result in cramping, bloating, burping, and diarrhea.

Post-Workout Meals
(within 2 hours after working out)

Timing Meals should be consumed within 2 hours after activity has ended. (Snacks can help when this isn't feasible.) At this point, the body is primed to utilize food and fluid to their maximum potential—something you should capitalize on.

Contents Post-workout choices should include a combination of carbohydrates, modest protein, and a little bit of fat. As you have learned, post-activity carbohydrate intake is still essential for refilling your energy tank for the next activity session (as well as everyday life), while protein intake is key for repair and regeneration of muscle. The amount of fat and fiber you can eat becomes greater than in pre-workout meals. Fat can inhibit the breakdown of glucose, ensuring that post-workout carbohydrates are directed to rebuilding glycogen stores in the muscles. Here's a place to add a colorful variety of antioxidant-rich foods that are perhaps higher in fat and fiber to support your entire body. If a recipe calls for a carbo-hydrate that comes in a whole-grain variety (say a pasta or bread product), it's wise to choose the whole grain for a post-workout meal since they are often excluded from pre-workout meals. Take the Mango Turkey Sloppy Joes (page 98): If you make them for eating after a workout, jump for the whole-wheat bun!

It is common to experience a lag time in appetite after your sweat session, as research suggests activity may suppress the release of ghrelin, the hunger hormone responsible for stimulating appetite. This may impact the amount or type of food that you choose to eat, and thus a snack or liquid-based meal could be your best immediate option.

Drinking about 8 ounces of water within 30 minutes after activity is ideal for initiating rehydration. The amount of total fluid you need and whether you need electrolyte replacement (see our electrolyte drink on page 239) depends on the duration of activity, the amount you sweat, how salty your sweat is (yes, we mean it), and more.

Maintenance Meals
(rest days, any meals more than 3 to 4 hours before or after activity)

Timing Performance fueling is not intended to be all or nothing: A strong nutrition foundation (the meals you eat anytime) along with balanced day-to-day habits should extend well beyond the fueling and recovery windows to maximize the benefits. In a way, we're always fueling, we're always recovering. Maintenance meals and snacks can be used in the time windows outside activity or on days of lower intensity activity (think leisure walking, light stretching, and the like).

Contents The foods and fluids in maintenance meals and snacks are intended to keep fueling and recovery goals going so you're powered for what's next, while also providing the body with a wide variety of nutrients required to fulfill daily processes. You should put a strong emphasis on a colorful variety of antioxidant-rich plant-based foods to support a number of body processes (e.g., organ function, digestion, immune function, anti-inflammatory action, cell repair, muscle repair, bone health, growth). Don't limit fiber or healthful fats. And don't worry about the ratio of carbohydrates to protein on your plate (for more information, see page 20).

THE ART OF SNACKING

Snacks aren't unnecessary indulgences—they're an essential part of your eating plan, regardless of your activity level. Snacks create an opportunity to honor your hunger between meals while stabilizing your energy levels, and they are also a great way to bridge nutritional gaps.

This may mean including colorful fruits and vegetables in your snacks, choosing some quality carbohydrates or healthful fats, or simply taking the opportunity to enjoy some of your favorite foods.

For the everyday athlete, an important part of nourishing your body includes leaning into snacks or mini-meals as a normal part of your day. Snacks give you the energy burst you may need when there's a long window between mealtime and exercise. In other cases, snacks offer a more easily digestible or feasible fueling option, whether you are on the go, short on time, or not quite ready to stomach a full meal, say, in the morning or after a workout.

If you're working out at night and lunch was at noon, you might be too hungry and not have enough energy to put in your best effort. A substantial snack of carbohydrates and protein, like an apple and some peanut butter, or a filling protein drink (page 241), consumed 1 to 2 hours before the gym could get you to a personal record.

If you're working out midday after breakfast and don't have the immediate energy you want to get physical, be prepared by sticking some quick-digesting simple carbs like rice cakes or a granola bar in your bag.

We've emphasized the importance of post-workout meals, but if there's a lag time between your workout and when you might get to make lunch or dinner, you'll want to snack here too to jump-start the recovery process.

Snacks can be as elaborate or as simple as your mood dictates. Grab packaged foods from your pantry, or reach for smaller half-portions of meals from this book (we indicate which recipes are good snack options on the recipe pages). For example, if you have leftovers from yesterday's make-ahead burritos (page 48), enjoy half of the leftover burrito for a quick post-workout snack. Additionally, we have a whole chapter of snacks (pages 236–281) with recipes calibrated perfectly for pre- and post-workout scenarios.

QUICK SNACK OPTIONS

Having effortless snacks is essential for your busy lifestyle. Store-bought is fine, although you're welcome to make your own. Below are some suggestions for quick snacks. There are two types of pre-workout snacks. The first might stand between meals, when mealtime is a long way from workout time: Snacks eaten 1 to 2 hours before a workout should be balanced, provide adequate carbohydrates, and prevent hunger. The second pre-workout snack is for fast fueling 30 to 60 minutes before working out. It should provide quick energy while minimizing potential for digestive distress (i.e., simple carbs without protein, fat, or fiber). It's for when you need an energy pick-me-up, didn't have time for full fueling, or can't stomach more to eat. Post-workout snacks, on the other hand, are meant to nourish and replenish so they should be substantial and include protein.

Pre-Workout
(1 to 2 hours before)
Carbohydrates can be complex but not with so much fiber that you experience unrest. Aim for approximately 30 grams of carbohydrates.

- Yogurt with granola or muesli (page 59)
- Fruit smoothie (pages 251–252)
- Cottage cheese with crackers
- Cheese stick and fruit
- Half a sandwich or wrap (we have several options)
- 1 cup cereal with dairy or plant-based milk
- 1 hard- or soft-boiled egg (see page 295) and 2 slices of toast
- 1 tablespoon nut butter on toast with ½ banana
- 1 cup oatmeal
- Rice cakes with 1 tablespoon nut butter and honey
- 1 apple with 1 tablespoon nut butter and raisins
- Simple chicken breast with rice
- Pitted dates with 1 tablespoon nut butter

Pre-Workout
(30 to 60 minutes before)
Quickly digesting carbohydrates that provide bursts of energy are essential.

- Granola bar (store-bought or homemade, page 262)
- Handful of crackers or pretzels
- Piece of toast or ½ English muffin with jelly
- Piece of fruit or 1 cup cut fruit
- Rice cakes
- Carbohydrate-containing sports drink (try our own electrolyte beverage on page 239)

Post-Workout
(within 1 hour)
Fat and fiber amounts can be higher here since activity has ceased.

- Low-fat chocolate milk
- Protein drink (page 241) and a banana
- 1–2 eggs cooked to your liking (see pages 292–295) with 2 slices toast
- Greek yogurt with granola and fruit
- Cottage cheese and fruit
- Half a sandwich or wrap
- Hummus (try our Sweet Potato Hummus, page 279) with pita bread and veggies
- Tuna and crackers
- Granola bar (store-bought or homemade, page 262) and yogurt

A DAY IN AN ACTIVE LIFE

The importance of eating—and eating enough—in conjunction with your workouts is clear. Realistically, however, we know you won't always have the time (or desire) to eat at exactly the right time, let alone the same time every day. Everyone's life is different, with busy schedules, unpredictable hours, tough commutes, last-minute commitments, and days that just don't go as planned. With this in mind, we've laid out eight scenarios showing how snacks and meals can fit around your workout time and preferences; maybe you'll see yourself in one of them.

1 THE RISE AND GRIND

For some of us, early morning is the only time we can consistently fit in activity. Rise and grind: You wake up, work out, and then head out for the day.

We suggest waking up and prioritizing hydration. If you're eating adequate post-workout and maintenance meals, you shouldn't wake up with zero energy storage. For a boost to get going, eat a small snack based on simple carbohydrates 30 to 60 minutes prior to exercise (think: a piece of fruit, a slice of toast, or crackers). Of course, pay attention to your digestion in the early hours; if you find that eating within 30 minutes prior to exercise doesn't serve you, drink water, plus some carbohydrate-based liquid.

Since you've only snacked, we suggest prioritizing a post-workout meal within just an hour (not a full 2 hours). If a meal isn't appealing or feasible right away, try having a snack immediately following activity, and then eating a meal. Below are two camps you might fall into.

HELPFUL HINTS: Since you may be leaving your house for the day in this scenario, you'll want to get comfortable with meal planning, that is, making snacks, breakfast, and lunch that you can carry with you. (For more information, see pages 24–25.) And make sure your previous days of eating were nutritionally supportive; otherwise working out on just water or a small snack might not energize you adequately.

Out the Door with a Snack

You wake up, work out, get ready for the day, and are out the door again. For you, the focus should be on appropriate snacks before and after activity, followed by a refueling meal once you have time to sit down.

6:00 am	Wake up and hydrate.
6:30 am	Eat a pre-workout simple snack (quick-digesting carbs and fluid) 30 to 60 minutes prior to activity (see ideas on page 11) for quick fuel.
7:00 am	Work out for 45 to 60 minutes.
8:30 am	Eat a post-workout snack within 60 minutes (ideally closer to 30) after activity to quickly reboost energy before your full meal.
9:30 am	Eat a post-workout meal (see page 9) within 2 hours of activity.
Beyond	Fill the rest of the day with maintenance meals (see page 9), snacks, and proper hydration.

Early Workout with Breakfast

You wake up, work out, and have enough time to eat a nourishing meal before you get on with your day.

5:30 am	Wake up and hydrate.
6:30 am	Work out for 45 to 60 minutes.
8:30 am	Eat a post-workout meal (see page 9) within 1 hour after activity (2 hours is pushing it without pre-workout fuel).
11:00 am	Eat a late morning snack as needed based on the duration and intensity of exercise and your hunger.
Beyond	Fill the rest of the day with maintenance meals (see page 9), snacks, and proper hydration.

2 THE NIGHT TRAINER

Morning workouts are *not* for everyone. For some, clocking a few extra hours of sleep is more important than getting up for a sweat session. For others, motivation and energy are greater in the evening.

Similar to other times of the day, it's important to focus on balanced maintenance meals in the distant time frames from your workout, while considering pre- and post-activity fueling within the hours surrounding your workout. If your lunch meal is more than 4 hours prior to your workout, we recommend considering a simple pre-workout snack in the hour prior to activity. See two possible ways of eating around an evening workout below.

HELPFUL HINT: Since dinner is extra-important for this scenario, you may want to plan for one of many dinners made from premade components so you don't have to hustle to cook elaborately after your workout and busy day.

Later Evening Workout

You've been up and at it all day and had your lunch well before your evening workout. In order to give you the appropriate energy prior to activity, we suggest adding a well-planned snack about an hour prior to exercise, followed by a post-workout meal within 60 minutes.

7:30 am	Wake up and hydrate.
8:00 am	Eat maintenance (see page 9) breakfast and morning snacks.
12:30 pm	Eat lunch more than 4 hours prior to activity following pre-workout (see page 8) or maintenance options (see page 9).
5:00 pm	Eat a pre-workout snack (see page 11) 1 to 2 hours prior to exercise.
6:00 pm	Work out for 45 to 60 minutes.
8:00 pm	Eat a post-workout (see page 9) dinner within 2 hours after activity (closer to 1 hour is most desirable here as you will be hungry).
Beyond	Eat an optional after-dinner snack depending on the duration and intensity of exercise and your hunger.

Earlier Evening Workout

If you opted for a late lunch or were able to start your activity earlier in the evening, it's not always necessary to include a snack prior to exercise. When there is less than 3 to 4 hours between your lunch and your evening workout, you can certainly go without a snack and focus on a fueling pre-workout meal for lunch. (Of course, listen to your body if you need a pick-me-up.) But if your commute from workout location to kitchen (and a finished dish) is more than 2 hours, eat a snack as soon as you can after your workout.

7:30 am	Wake up and hydrate.
8:30 am	Eat maintenance (see page 9) breakfast and morning snacks.
1:30 pm	Eat a pre-workout meal (see page 8) for lunch 3 to 4 hours prior to activity.
5:00 pm	Work out for 45 to 60 minutes
6:30 pm	Eat a snack as soon as you can to refuel before you can get to the dinner table.
9:00 pm	Eat a post-workout meal (see page 9) for dinner when you can.

3 THE LUNCH CHAMP

For some of us, life allows a lunch-break workout. This scenario requires a bit more food planning than the others, especially when considering the timing of your morning and breakfast in relation to your workout. If breakfast is within a 3- to 4-hour window before your workout time, then a pre-workout breakfast option (see pages 34–63) would be great, and a snack may not be necessary. However, if you are an early riser and more than 4 hours fall between your breakfast and your workout, you should consider a simple pre-workout snack (see page 11) for a quick energy boost. Let's walk through these two cases.

HELPFUL HINT: In both of these situations, in addition to snacks, it will be important to carry a more traditional packed lunch—optimized for exercise—as you'll want to eat pretty soon after returning from your workout.

Late Morning Workout

Maybe you sit down to breakfast but you cut it close to sitting at your desk. Once you get to work, you have only 3 hours until break time. Your breakfast, if nourishing enough, will fuel you—then you can come back with an appetite for your second meal.

6:45 am	Wake up and hydrate.
8:00 am	Eat a pre-workout breakfast (see pages 34–63) 3 to 4 hours prior to exercise.
11:00 am	Work out for 45 to 60 minutes.
1:00 pm	Eat a post-workout meal (see page 17) when you're back to work (likely within an hour).
3:00 pm	Eat a mid-afternoon snack as needed based on the duration and intensity of exercise, time between meals, and hunger.
Beyond	Eat a maintenance (see page 9) meal for dinner.

Lunchtime Workout

The time between breakfast at home, commuting, working on a deadline and, finally, taking an activity break, might be long. Even with a solid breakfast, you'll need a snack boost. Then you can come back and refuel with lunch as normal.

6:45 am	Wake up and hydrate.
7:30 am	Eat a maintenance (see page 9) or pre-workout (see page 8) meal for breakfast more than 3 to 4 hours prior to activity.
10:00 am	Eat a pre-workout snack (see page 11) within 2 hours prior to exercise.
12:00 pm	Workout for 45 to 60 minutes.
1:45 pm	Eat a post-workout (see page 8) lunch when you're back at work (likely within an hour).
3:00 pm	Eat a mid-afternoon snack as needed based on the duration and intensity of exercise, time between meals, and hunger.
Beyond	Eat a maintenance meal for dinner.

4 THE WEEKEND WARRIOR

For many, the weekend can be more flexible and allow for longer duration exercise, or more active days overall. It's equally important to prioritize well-considered meals and snacks to support increased movement during these times. A typical scenario may include a later start to the day followed by a late morning or early afternoon workout. Regardless of how and when you are choosing to move your body on the weekend, we suggest considering pre- and post-workout meals and snacks in the time frames surrounding your activity. Here are two weekend situations you might find yourself in.

HELPFUL HINT: Don't stress too much around weekend workouts. You may fit a short sweat session in on a day of fun; or you may take advantage of the extra time to go on an ultralong run or hike. Eat according to the guidelines you've learned and your hunger on these days.

Pre-Brunch Workout

Picture this: It's a beautiful Saturday morning and you can't wait to hit up your favorite late-morning outdoor strength and conditioning class. You have plans to grab an early afternoon brunch, but it won't be in the right time frame to refuel and recover from your workout. In this scenario (and unpredictable ones like it), we suggest leaning on pre- and post-workout snacks (see page 11) within the hour before and the hour after your activity followed by a satisfying brunch.

8:00 am	Wake up and hydrate.
9:00 am	Eat a pre-workout snack (see page 11) within 1 to 2 hours prior to activity.
10:30 am	Work out.
12:30 pm	Eat a post-workout snack (see page 11) within 1 hour after activity.
1:30 pm	Eat brunch within 2 hours of activity.
Beyond	Fill the rest of the day with maintenance meals (see page 9) and proper hydration.

Relaxed Early Afternoon Workout

There might not be any kind of day better than a lazy Sunday: You wake up without an alarm, put on a pot of coffee or tea, and have no plans for the morning. The day is beautiful, so you decide to go on a long hike with friends or family. This calls for a breakfast that will nourish your Sunday while providing fuel (cue the pancakes on page 61?). On these days, allow breakfast to be your pre-workout fuel and follow your activity with a snack or meal based on how your day goes.

9:30 am	Wake up and hydrate.
10:30 am	Eat a relaxed pre-workout breakfast (see pages 34–63) 3 to 4 hours prior to activity.
2:00 pm	Work out.
4:00 pm	Eat a post-workout snack (see page 9) or a post-workout meal (see page 11) preferably within 1 hour after activity.
Beyond	Fill the rest of the day with maintenance meals (see page 9) and proper hydration.

CALIBRATING YOUR FOOD FOR YOUR ACTIVITIES

No matter what kind of athlete you are or how much meal planning you'd like to do, the recipes in this book will benefit you—they were calibrated to do so.

Our inclusive definition of an everyday athlete: an individual who engages in regular physical activity of moderate to high intensity (probably 45 to 60 minutes) three or more days per week. You don't have to be training for an event or competing or playing team sports to be an everyday athlete; you can just be moving your body and seeking consistent joyful enhancement from physical activity. Whether you love a group fitness class or sessions with a personal trainer, or prefer outdoor activities like hiking or trail running, you can make any recipe knowing it will be good for you.

In addition to following the timing guidelines for optimal fueling for your workouts, it's important to understand that the recipes in this book have gone through careful calculations in the test kitchen. They meet the ratio of carbohydrates to protein that science has shown is optimal for someone moving their body at our defined level for the everyday athlete.

IT'S ALL ABOUT THE RATIOS

Let's recap the nutritional pillars that support you as an everyday athlete:

> You need to eat, and eat *enough*. Skipping meals or skimping on intake, especially around exercise, will only inhibit your performance.

> Carbohydrates are the body's preferred fuel source and should be incorporated into all meals and snacks, especially in the windows of time before and after moderate to intense activity. Inadequate carbohydrates mean inadequate fuel.

> Protein intake is important; however, it should not trump carbohydrate intake. Instead, the focus should be on incorporating protein with carbohydrates to optimize the replenishment of energy stores and to support the repairing and rebuilding of lean muscle mass.

> Hydrate, hydrate, hydrate: A well-hydrated body will function best. Period.

Now, when structuring our recipes around *how much* of these nutrients is best for the everyday athlete, we turned again to science and landed on carbohydrate-to-protein ratio—that is, the amount of carbohydrates (in grams) and protein (in grams) eaten in combination at a given time (meal or snack). Leading sports nutrition recommendations are to consume carbohydrates with proteins together in a **3:1 ratio** (3 grams of carbohydrate to 1 gram of protein) in the meals before and after moderate to intense activity for the most benefits for most athletes.

Here's a representation of a 3:1 ratio with a classic simple breakfast:

2 eggs (14g protein) **+**
2 slices of toast (30g carbohydrates) **+**
1 serving fruit (~12g carbohydrates)
42g carbohydrates : 14g protein = 3:1 ratio

WHY IS 3:1 BEST FOR FUELING?

Before a Workout
We already know that carbohydrates are the most necessary for—and the most efficient at—supporting adequate energy supplies and reserves prior to exercise. Protein intake prior to activity can play an essential role in amino acid availability for your muscle cells and has been linked to reduced post-activity muscle soreness. The ratio of 3:1 prioritizes carbohydrate intake with some, but not too much, protein (see Don't Cut the Carbs, page 4). The prioritization is important because carbs also stimulate insulin release, and insulin helps you better utilize the protein you eat.

It is important to note that as the time for activity gets closer (2 hours or less before the workout), the priority of meeting this ratio diminishes and is replaced with an emphasis on adequate quick-digesting carbohydrates.

After a Workout
The appropriate carbohydrate-protein intake is even more important with meals and snacks after activity. Research shows that when a 3:1 ratio is consumed within 1 to 2 hours after moderate- to high-intensity activity, your body's insulin response is nearly doubled, which results in more stored glycogen. This means the body's energy tank will be fuller for your next round of activity, and there will be greater availability of protein/amino acids to do their job of repairing and rebuilding lean muscle. While we need to eat enough protein to support muscle repair and building, and protein synthesis, once we meet what we need, the rest is just excess that will be oxidized, not utilized, and stored as fat.

Our Pomegranate Chicken with Farro and Cucumber Salad recipe (page 119) shows what a recipe with a 3:1 ratio of carbohydrates to protein looks like. Maybe it seems like there's a bit more farro than you'd normally eat, or a bit less chicken, but this optimal combination will satisfy you (and your taste buds) and make you an all-star at the gym.

3:1 ratio

PUT DOWN THE CALCULATOR

Did we mention we also want you to eat with enjoyment in mind? That means without the stress of calculating every morsel of food that goes into your body. That's where the test kitchen comes in. We took care of the dirty work and developed creative recipes with the 3:1 ratio as a top priority.

THE TAKE-HOME POINT

Adequate carbohydrate intake is essential to the everyday athlete. Carbohydrates and protein, ideally at a 3:1 ratio, is the most effective nutrient combination for meals/snacks after activity as well as meals/snacks prior to activity. The end goal is to eat in a way that lets you feel your best and get the most out of the activities you love.

CUSTOMIZING THE RATIOS FOR DIFFERENT WORKOUTS

For the majority of activities and eating schedules, a 3:1 ratio of carbohydrates to protein will best fulfill your pre-workout and post-workout nutritional needs. But there are some situations where additional protein or carbohydrates may provide a leg up for proper fueling and recovery. The recipes also feature meals that are best suited to endurance workouts (like long-distance running, hiking, or bike-riding) or strength or interval workouts (think: HIIT class, CrossFit, heavy

4:1 ratio

2:1 ratio

lifting). There are also plenty of suggestions for customizing the recipes to fit your specific needs, so nearly any recipe can be optimized for your preferred activities that day (for more about the recipes' "dashboards," see page 23).

Endurance Training

If you are an endurance athlete or someone who enjoys steady-state exercise longer than 60 to 90 minutes, higher carbohydrate consumption is necessary to fill and refill the tank, and thus a **4:1 ratio** will be more appropriate for you. In Fideos with Chickpeas and Goat Cheese (page 229), the noodles and chickpeas provide abundant satisfying carbohydrates.

Strength or Interval Training

The role of protein differs for endurance and strength-training athletes; endurance exercise places a greater demand on protein as an alternative fuel source, whereas strength training requires additional amino acids as the building blocks for muscle development. For the everyday athlete engaging in focused strength or interval training, or those working toward changing body composition (building lean muscle), a boost in protein intake, closer to a **2:1 ratio** of carbohydrates to protein, will provide the necessary mix of carbohydrates for replenishing glycogen plus additional protein intake for your muscles. This plate of Seared Flank Steak with Oat Berries, Zucchini, and Peppers (page 148) features a higher amount of lean protein and a slight decrease in carbohydrates to accommodate the body's needs after strength or interval training.

A chart of potential activity types and the ideal meal ratios associated with each follows. This might not look the same for you every day, and by no means captures all possible activities. But it can help guide your choices for fueling these activities and others like them. Many of the recipes in the book can be tweaked to meet any of these nutritional goals by making simple ingredient adjustments that we provide. And when in doubt, be assured that *any* recipe in this book is going to be supportive of your body; meal planning shouldn't be hard work.

Consider two scenarios that might apply to one person for navigating eating seamlessly: First, let's say you work out with a trainer 2 days a week for about 45 minutes. Your sessions are based on flexibility, mobility, and strength training without high intensity or conditioning work. On these days you choose to pump up the protein (eat in a 2:1 ratio) to aid in adequate refueling and post-strength muscle recovery.

Now, on the weekends, you can't wait to get outside. Your favorite way to move your body is through a long endurance trail run, usually lasting 90 minutes to 2 hours. You appropriately fuel with a pre-activity endurance meal and/or snack and make sure to boost the carbs (eat in a 4:1 ratio) after activity to properly replenish glycogen stores and aid in a full recovery.

EXERCISE TYPE	DURATION (MIN)	PLATE RATIO
Endurance		
Running (moderate intensity)	>60–90	4:1
Road cycling	>90	4:1
Hiking (moderate-high intensity)	>90	4:1
Swimming (moderate intensity)	>90	4:1
Trail running (high intensity)	>60–90	4:1
Strength or Interval		
Indoor cycling class	45–60	3:1
Boxing class	45–60	3:1
Track/mountain cycling	45–60	3:1
HIIT/interval training	30–45	2:1
HIIT/interval training	45–60	2:1–3:1
Strength training	30–45	2:1
Strength training	45–60	2:1–3:1
Everyday		
Low-intensity workout (walking, light yoga, stretching)	n/a	any
Outdoor running (moderate intensity)	45–60	3:1
Hiking (moderate intensity)	60–90	3:1
Swimming (moderate intensity)	60–90	3:1
Trail running (high intensity)	45–60	3:1
Team sports	90	3:1

EATING FOR EVERY BODY

All the recipes in this book, no matter what ratio they meet, are calibrated to meet the fueling and recovery needs of the everyday athlete and are aimed at supporting their energy and performance. However, some individuals reading this book may also wonder where body composition and weight-based goals come into play.

We have chosen to take a weight-neutral approach and to focus on the pillars of eating for the everyday athlete concerned about adequate nourishment to enrich activities. And it's important to note that by appropriately fueling your body, you are indeed supporting repair and regrowth of lean muscle mass. And so our message doesn't change: The right mix of carbohydrates and protein before and after a workout are a key factor in optimizing body composition goals (in most cases, this means increasing lean muscle mass and decreasing body fat percentage). Since carbohydrates are necessary for protein to complete its job of repairing muscle breakdown and building lean muscle, in the absence of an adequate amount, the body will oxidize fat and protein for energy leading to the loss of lean muscle mass—a hindrance to those body composition goals. For this reason, we wouldn't recommend reducing the carbohydrate-to-protein ratios of your meal beyond 2:1.

Building lean muscle mass is extremely protective for the body, and its benefits may extend to an individual's resting metabolic rate (metabolism)—that is, the more lean muscle mass you have, the faster your metabolic rate might be. It is important to note, however, that we are all unique individuals with unique body shapes and sizes, lifestyles, genetics, and needs. Thus fat metabolism can vary significantly from person to person. In addition to an individual's lean muscle mass, research suggests that age, genetics, gender at birth, menstruation, and hormones are also key predictors of metabolism. We cannot make recommendations that fit all individuals' needs related to weight-based goals. We encourage you to work with a registered dietitian to discuss your individual goals and needs that reach beyond this book.

BECOMING A SPORTS NUTRITION SUPERSTAR

We've outlined the nuances of eating as an athlete. But going back to basics isn't just *basic*—general good nutrition strategies should further amp up your athleticism. Your eating patterns as a whole—your consistency in eating healthfully and in good amounts—plays the largest role in your performance. Be sure to incorporate these everyday healthy tips.

1 INCLUDE CARBOHYDRATES

In addition to providing the body (and brain) with energy, a wide variety of carbohydrate-containing foods also provides an assortment of rich nutrients and antioxidants. Whole and ancient grains and seeds such as quinoa, brown rice, amaranth, farro, wheat berries, and barley are rich in protein, fiber, B vitamins, antioxidants, and many beneficial trace minerals; starchy vegetables and tubers pack a punch with fiber, protein, vitamin C, vitamin B6, potassium, and manganese. Carbs carry the plate.

2 CHOOSE LEAN PROTEINS

Protein is the building block for the cells in your body. Now that you are aware that 10 ounces of steak after exercise isn't necessary to reach your goals, we encourage you to consider the types of protein you put on your plate. We recommend incorporating lean protein sources as a way to minimize saturated fat intake (found in animal fats and tropical oils). In addition to lean meats and fish, all beans and legumes, tofu, and low-fat dairy products pack lean protein.

3 EAT THE RAINBOW

Eating a colorful variety of plant-based foods provides your body with the greatest access to fiber and a wide array of vitamins and minerals, all with potential anti-oxidant and anti-inflammatory effects. Every plant pigment is associated with some stellar nutritional benefits thanks to its phytonutrients. Pack post-workout meals with colorful, fiber-rich foods for a healthy heart, regulation of hunger and fullness, and proper digestion.

4 ENJOY HEART-HEALTHY FATS AND OILS

Unsaturated fats, or "good fats," not only enhance the eating experience and satiation, they provide numerous health benefits, including improved cholesterol levels and heart health and absorption of fat soluble vitamins (A, D, E, and K). Foods rich in omega-3 fatty acids are well known to extend anti-inflammatory benefits throughout the body. Good fats include olive oil, safflower and sunflower oil (and other plant-based, non-tropical oils), canola oil, nuts and seeds, avocados, olives, and fatty fish.

5 MEET MICRONUTRIENTS

Micronutrients (vitamins and minerals) are involved in a wide variety of important body processes like maintaining energy and bone metabolism, and they play a role in immune and antioxidant function, oxygen transport, red blood cell production, and the repair of skeletal muscle. Eating a varied, balanced diet will often be sufficient to meet your micronutrient needs. In some cases, higher levels of activity can increase micronutrient use, which means your requirements may be higher. Particular micronutrients of interest for the everyday athlete include:

Vitamin D builds and maintains bones and teeth alongside calcium, magnesium, and phosphorus. Research studies have linked adequate vitamin D status with musculoskeletal benefits such as increased muscle protein synthesis. Vitamin D is obtained by direct sun exposure and is found in a limited number of foods like fatty fish (salmon, mackerel) and fortified items like milks, bread, and some ready-to-eat cereals.

Calcium works in close conjunction with vitamin D to build and maintaining bones and teeth, and also plays a number of key roles related to activity, including muscle contraction. Calcium-rich foods include dairy products, some green vegetables (broccoli, kale, spinach), almonds, and fortified foods.

Iron plays an important role in bringing oxygen to muscle cells in order to maintain the function of your muscles. If you follow a vegetarian or vegan diet or are underfueling your body, you may be at risk of inadequate iron intake. Some rich sources of iron include red meat, dark poultry, whole eggs, fish, dark green leafy vegetables, legumes, nuts, seeds, whole grains, and fortified cereals. Iron that comes from plant-based foods is better absorbed when eaten in combination with a vitamin C–rich food.

B vitamins are needed to convert food energy into ATP. As your activity levels increase, so does your energy demand, and thus the more B vitamins will be recruited to convert food energy to ATP. Rich sources of B vitamins include poultry, meat, whole grains, cereals, dark leafy greens, tuna, and beans.

6 TRY ELECTROLYTES

Water is typically sufficient for hydration; however, in hot weather or during prolonged exercise (more than 60 minutes), your body may lose more electrolytes (such as sodium and potassium) that need to be replaced. Electrolytes play a role in balancing water inside and outside of the cells. When you sweat more and potentially lose more electrolytes, you're losing mainly sodium. Sodium is necessary for maintaining fluid balance and muscle contraction. Salty snacks before or after exercise as well as electrolyte beverages containing sodium and glucose (see page 239) do the trick. Potassium works with sodium in the body to maintain fluid balance and muscle contractions; unlike sodium, potassium losses are not nearly as high. Consuming potassium-rich foods like bananas, potatoes, oranges, dried fruits, legumes, and whole grains before and after workouts is usually sufficient.

BONUS INGREDIENTS

You may want to consider adding these to your grocery lists to give you a leg up.

Tart Cherry Juice
Drinking tart cherry juice (rich in antioxidant and anti-inflammatory compounds) both before and after activity has been shown to lessen pain and accelerate recovery.

Beet Root
This vibrant root vegetable is rich in nitrates, which may improve blood flow, improve lung function, and strengthen muscle contractions.

SCIENCE-BACKED ›› TEST KITCHEN–APPROVED

Now that you've learned what fuel your body needs to exercise best, you're probably wondering if it will taste any good. As always, we wouldn't settle for anything less than delicious.

Eating for exercise isn't meant to be restrictive, hard, or bland (even if you find that elsewhere). When we selected the recipes for this book, we eschewed cliché steamed broccoli, unseasoned chicken, and chalky protein shakes. However, we understand the nutritional benefits of broccoli so we pack it into Frittata Bites with Broccoli, Sun-Dried Tomatoes, and Mozzarella (page 44) for a post-workout protein and nutrient punch, and sauté it to a verdant tender-crisp in Stir-Fried Chicken and Broccoli (page 124). Shred chicken into Chicken and Rice Salad with Turmeric and Herbs (page 102) for a flavorful, fueling meal before heading to the gym. And we developed drinks—balanced concoctions of beneficial carbohydrates and protein (like our Spiced Coffee Protein Drink, page 241) are ultradelicious.

Our recipe selection came down to two basic concepts: **moderation and calibration.** Dietitian-backed nutrition guidelines guarantee that all the recipes contain moderate amounts of sodium, low saturated fat, and minimal added sugars. We developed dishes for flavor, without excluding any delicious ingredients. (You'll find cheese and steak, and beloved dishes such as pancakes and calzones—all to be consumed, of course, in moderation.) Then, we calibrated those dishes to meet nutritional benchmarks for workouts and time frames (e.g., a lower-fat cheese before a workout, a smaller portion of steak paired with an abundant carbohydrate to support training). All of our recipes, from meals to drinks, were made to fit within the previously mentioned 3:1, 2:1, and 4:1 ratios, depending on timing and your workout that day.

HOW TO MAKE THESE RECIPES WORK FOR YOU

Every recipe in this book is designed with you in mind, no matter your schedule or athletic pursuits. We created a dashboard at the top of each recipe to show all the different ways it can work for you. The directives are simple: When to eat it, how to eat it depending on your associated activity, and, in some cases, how you can make the meal a convenient snack-size portion. Flexibility in eating is the key to long-term success and we want you to be able to tailor our recipes to your lifestyle—which might change from day to day. Here's a breakdown of the recipe dashboard:

When to Eat It
A recipe's nutritional profile will suit certain mealtimes. These wraps (on page 160) are a stand-out meal as they're not limited to one time frame. They can be eaten *before* a workout or *after* a workout. Furthermore, this recipe is super nutritious, so you can enjoy a wrap (or half) at any other non-workout-associated time.

Workouts
Recipes can be modified for when you're doing a workout that's out of the everyday definition. An endurance workout requires a higher carb-to-protein ratio (4:1), while a strength or interval workout needs a lower ratio (2:1). This wrap can be optimized for any activity with simple pantry-friendly adjustments.

Make It a Snack
Some recipes are ideal for portioning into helpful snacks or smaller meals. Here, you have the option to eat half a wrap and store the rest for later.

SALMON NIÇOISE SALAD WRAPS

Serves 2   Total Time: 35 minutes

WHEN TO EAT
> **Pre-Workout** 3 to 4 hours before
> **Post-Workout** Within 2 hours
> **Maintenance**

WORKOUTS
> **Everyday**
> **Endurance** Serve with grapes or baked snack chips (see page 274).
> **Strength or Interval** Increase salmon to 2 cans.

MAKE IT A SNACK
Eat half a wrap.

12 ounces Yukon Gold potatoes, peeled and cut into 1-inch pieces

¼ teaspoon table salt, plus salt for cooking vegetables

4 ounces green beans, trimmed and cut into 1-inch lengths

¼ cup plain low-fat Greek yogurt

4 teaspoons extra-virgin olive oil, divided

4 teaspoons lemon juice,

WHY THIS RECIPE WORKS >> Salmon niçoise is a nice change of pace from the classic tuna; an even more exciting shift is enclosing it in a portable, bready wrap for a perfectly calibrated meal for an athlete. For the potato component, we mash creamy Yukon Golds into a hummus-like spread that holds the wrap together. Canned salmon should be in your pantry; it's widely available and has a long shelf life. This recipe can easily be doubled.

1 Place potatoes and ½ teaspoon salt in large saucepan, add cold water to cover by 2 inches, and bring to boil over high heat. Reduce heat to medium and cook until potatoes are just tender, 6 to 8 minutes. Add green beans and cook until vegetables are fully tender, 3 to 5 minutes.

MEALS ON THE RUN

Planning ahead and taking healthful food that fuels or replenishes you on the go, regardless of time and place, make eating for activities a sustainable lifestyle.

If you work out first thing in the morning and don't go back home before heading to work, it's easy to bring a pre-packed post-workout breakfast with you instead of relying on fast-food orders that don't fit your nutritional needs. Or, say you don't have the option to cook lunch after your midday workout: Pack a leftover dish that's just as delicious served at room temperature (we indicate this in the recipes). Handle anything life throws at you with some helpful tips to get ahead of your meal planning. Future You will thank you.

SCORING STORAGE CONTAINERS

Storing your food is an important part of make-ahead life, so you'll want airtight, leakproof containers to ensure ultimate freshness and to prevent spills in your bag. Our winners come in a variety of sizes, so pick one that works for you.

Plastic
Rubbermaid Brilliance Food Storage Container
This durable container has a flat shape for compact stacking and a shallow profile that helps heat up food evenly. Plus, its built-in rubber gasket gives it a tight seal while being easy to clean.

Glass
OXO Good Grips Smart Seal Container
The base of this container can go in the oven and its plastic lid resists warping in the dishwasher.

Bento-Style Lunchbox
Monbento MB Square—Litchi
Two 4-ounce containers that can be used together or separately let you pack different components or prep two meals at once.

Reusable Storage Bags
BlueAvocado (re)zip
Plastic sandwich bags are one-time use. These bags are environmentally friendly alternatives. Their zipper allows you to seal the bag securely.

7 WAYS TO BECOME A MEAL-PLANNING STAR

1 Store Smart

To keep leftovers at their best with textures intact, store garnishes (nuts, herbs, croutons, pickled vegetables, etc.) separately. For a second serving of salad, avoid pretossing with dressings or vinaigrettes as it might become soggy in the fridge overnight. That said, ingredients like proteins, cooked vegetables, and grains can be tossed together, refrigerated, and enjoyed as a composed dish for a ready-to-eat serving.

2 Make the Freezer Your Friend

Everyone loves grab-and-go premade foods, but you can skip the frozen aisle at the grocery and still pull a nutritious homemade meal out of your freezer weeks after preparing it. In the recipes, we indicate dishes that can be frozen and how to wrap them to keep out freezer burn and keep in freshness, and how best to reheat the food later when you need it.

3 Reuse, Recycle

Smartly plan your eating to use the remaining ingredients from one recipe to jump-start another later on. Freeze the remaining half can of coconut milk from a recipe in cubes to use in a measured amount in another. Use half an avocado in a recipe like our shrimp salad (page 185) and the other half in the morning for loaded avocado toast (page 39).

4 Reheat Right

Certain dishes need help on the second heating. If you're hesitant to overcook something, try warming it over a lower heat. Wrapping your frozen burrito in a damp paper towel before microwaving helps bring moisture back. Soups and stews often benefit from a little water (or broth) to return them to the right consistency. For leftovers with raw produce, eat at room temperature or cold so the fresh ingredients don't get mushy in the microwave.

5 Have Staple Foods on Hand

When you don't have time to cook a full meal, having plain proteins like a chicken breast, bases like a small pot of farro, and vegetables in the fridge is the simplest way to put together a nutritionally balanced plate or bowl. They can also be used to bolster an existing dish with more carbohydrates or protein when you need them. We've provided supplemental recipes to help you have these items ready to go (see pages 282–299).

6 Revitalize

Some flavors can meld nicely in the fridge when storing for later, but others can turn dull. To refresh your leftovers and keep them from tasting bland the second time around, season with more than salt and pepper: Enliven your meal with a spritz of lemon juice or a splash of vinegar, or add a condiment like hot sauce or garlic oil to bring welcome new flavor.

7 Give It a New Look

Some things just aren't the same reheated. Instead of reheating leftover salmon fillet that will never be the same, try flaking it over greens or grains and giving it a drizzle of vinaigrette for a new dish to eat at room temperature. Some dishes like Chicken and Rice Salad with Turmeric and Herbs (page 102) don't take well to reheating but can be scooped on a salad or served in a wrap with some sprouts and the yogurt sauce as a spread. Or, tuck Quinoa Taco Salad (page 204) into an actual taco on its second life.

BREAKING DOWN A RECIPE

Eating in accordance with the workout-calibrated ratio of carbohydrates to protein, with the right amounts of fat and fiber, might be a new concept to you. It can be daunting to start a new way of eating, but we've done the work for you—so you can focus on the workout. Using our Garlicky Chicken and Rice Soup (page 67), let's take a look at what our recipes have to offer.

Flexible Serving Sizes
Most of our recipes here make one or two servings so you can tailor your eating to *your* specific routine. Soup stores great, so two servings gives you a portion of leftover soup, or one to eat and one to share if needed. When applicable, like with this recipe, we indicate if the recipe can be easily doubled if you're feeding a group. (If a master recipe is one that serves more than two, that means it's great made in bulk and kept on hand, like snacks and some breakfast items.)

Timing in Mind
The total cook time for most of our recipes is under an hour to accommodate busy schedules and fast fueling necessities. Forty minutes is all it takes to bring this comforting soup to life.

Know Your Nutritionals
Displayed at the bottom of each page is the nutritional data for that recipe, per serving. For this soup, you'll see that fiber amounts are kept intentionally low (white rice, a moderate amount of vegetables), so the meal doesn't upset digestion when eaten before working out.

Carefully Calibrated Ingredients
You may notice this recipe flips the script on the average chicken soup a bit, with a visibly more generous amount of comforting rice and a smaller amount of chicken. It's delicious, almost creamy, this way, but it also provides the 3:1 ratio of carbohydrates to protein for eating in conjunction with a workout.

Make-Ahead Capabilities
After most recipes, you'll find meal prep options, from freezing portions to storing them in the fridge for a few days. Leftovers for tomorrow? Easy. Frozen pancakes to quickly get you out the door a month later? Even better. This soup can be safely stored in the fridge for up to 3 days.

GARLICKY CHICKEN AND RICE SOUP
(PAGE 67)

Serves 2   Total Time: 40 minutes

—

Cal 450; Total Fat 10g; Sat Fat 1.5g; Chol 55mg; Sodium 820mg;
Total Carb 67g; Dietary Fiber 5g; Total Sugars 8g; Protein 21g

A WEEK IN AN ACTIVE LIFE

Look forward to your week with meal planning that is simple to achieve and meals that are satisfying to eat. We don't propose a rigid approach to eating and menus in this book because we understand life is usually not so structured. You might have varied fitness goals and activity interests that you cycle through each week. Your schedule might vary, fitting in with one of the suggested scenarios on pages 12–15—or not. Here is a sample week of menus to inspire you in these cases. (If your activities look the same every day, that's great and with our principles, they should be simple to plan around.) Take advantage of make-ahead options such as freezing and preparing multiple portions to help your week run smoothly. And remember, food is fuel so be sure to implement snacking when needed.

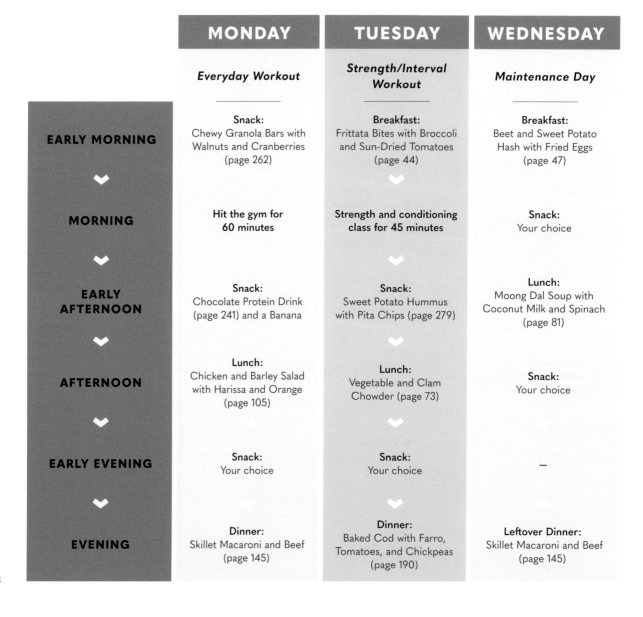

	MONDAY	TUESDAY	WEDNESDAY
	Everyday Workout	*Strength/Interval Workout*	*Maintenance Day*
EARLY MORNING	Snack: Chewy Granola Bars with Walnuts and Cranberries (page 262)	Breakfast: Frittata Bites with Broccoli and Sun-Dried Tomatoes (page 44)	Breakfast: Beet and Sweet Potato Hash with Fried Eggs (page 47)
MORNING	Hit the gym for 60 minutes	Strength and conditioning class for 45 minutes	Snack: Your choice
EARLY AFTERNOON	Snack: Chocolate Protein Drink (page 241) and a Banana	Snack: Sweet Potato Hummus with Pita Chips (page 279)	Lunch: Moong Dal Soup with Coconut Milk and Spinach (page 81)
AFTERNOON	Lunch: Chicken and Barley Salad with Harissa and Orange (page 105)	Lunch: Vegetable and Clam Chowder (page 73)	Snack: Your choice
EARLY EVENING	Snack: Your choice	Snack: Your choice	—
EVENING	Dinner: Skillet Macaroni and Beef (page 145)	Dinner: Baked Cod with Farro, Tomatoes, and Chickpeas (page 190)	Leftover Dinner: Skillet Macaroni and Beef (page 145)

THURSDAY	FRIDAY	SATURDAY	SUNDAY
Everyday Workout	*Endurance Workout*	*Maintenance Day*	*Everyday Workout*
Leftover Breakfast: Frittata Bites with Broccoli and Sun-Dried Tomatoes (page 44)	**Breakfast:** Pumpkin Spice Waffles with Yogurt and Blueberries (page 62)	**Breakfast:** Mangú (page 51)	**Leftover Breakfast:** Pumpkin Spice Waffles with Yogurt and Blueberries (page 62)
Snack: Zucchini Bread (page 260)	**Snack:** Half portion of Red Lentil Kibbeh (page 202)	**Snack:** Your choice	**Snack:** Honey-Nut Crispy Rice Cereal Bar (page 265)
Use the elliptical after a yoga class	**Lunch:** Orzo Salad with Cucumber, Feta, and Mint (page 214)	**Leftover Lunch:** Creamy Butternut Squash Orzo with Chicken (page 112)	**Go for a leisurely bike ride**
Lunch: Couscous with Smoked Trout, Apricots, and Pickled Peppers (page 166)	**Go for a long run**	**Snack:** Your choice	**Leftover Lunch:** Lemongrass Beef and Rice Noodle Bowl (page 139)
Snack: Your choice	**Snack:** Toasted Corn and Bean Salsa with Tortilla Chips (page 280)	—	**Snack:** Your choice
Dinner: Creamy Butternut Squash Orzo with Chicken (page 112)	**Dinner:** Spiced Cauliflower Burgers (page 197)	**Dinner:** Lemongrass Beef and Rice Noodle Bowl (page 139)	**Dinner:** Salmon Tacos with Cabbage Slaw and Lime Crema (page 165) with some rice

EAT RIGHT FOR YOUR TYPE

Some athletes might have a food allergy, a dietary restriction, or are just looking to eat more plant-based meals. Look to these lists for the recipes in the book that are best for your lifestyle. Recipes included here may contain an option in the ingredient list to make the recipe work for you. For example, many soups call for "2 cups chicken or vegetable broth" and so can be made vegetarian or plant based when other ingredients otherwise are as such.

PLANT-BASED

DAIRY-FREE

GLUTEN-FREE

BREAKFAST

SAUTÉED GRAPE AND ALMOND BUTTER TOAST

Serves 1   Total Time: 15 minutes

WHEN TO EAT
> **Post-Workout** Within 2 hours
> **Maintenance**

WORKOUTS
> **Everyday**
> **Endurance** Increase grapes to 6 ounces (or banana to 2).
> **Strength or Interval** Serve with an egg cooked to your liking (see pages 292–295).

MAKE IT A SNACK
Eat half a toast.

½ teaspoon extra-virgin olive oil

3 ounces seedless red or green grapes, halved (¾ cup)

½ teaspoon honey

½ teaspoon minced fresh thyme or ⅛ teaspoon dried

Pinch table salt

¼ teaspoon grated lemon zest plus ½ teaspoon juice

2 tablespoons natural almond butter

1 (2-ounce) slice rustic whole-grain bread, about ½ inch thick, toasted

---

Cal 430; Total Fat 22g;
Sat Fat 3g; Chol 0mg;
Sodium 430mg; Total Carb 49g;
Dietary Fiber 8g;
Total Sugars 21g; Protein 15g

WHY THIS RECIPE WORKS ›› PB&J fans: This upgrade from soggy white bread and a sugary filling replenishes the everyday athlete while keeping that classic flavor combination. The topped toast features hearty whole-grain bread to keep you sustained, a slick of almond butter, plus a sautéed grape topping enhanced with lemon and thyme that takes just a few minutes to prepare but tastes like a luxurious reward. Nut butters have a healthy amount of (good) fats and so they aren't always ideal in large quantities before a workout when they might aggravate digestion; but their protein is a boon afterwards. We prefer unsweetened natural almond butter in this recipe, but any style of nut butter can be used. This recipe serves one but can easily be scaled to serve up to four.

1 Heat oil in 8- or 10-inch nonstick skillet over medium-high heat until shimmering. Add grapes, honey, thyme, and salt and cook, stirring occasionally, until grapes begin to soften and juices thicken, 3 to 5 minutes. Off heat, stir in lemon zest and juice.

2 Spread almond butter evenly over toasted bread and arrange on serving plate. Top with grape mixture and serve.

SAUTÉED BANANA AND PEANUT BUTTER TOAST
Omit honey. Substitute 1 thinly sliced peeled small banana for grapes, ⅛ teaspoon vanilla extract for thyme, and peanut butter for almond butter. Cook banana until softened at edges, 2 to 3 minutes.

MEAL PREP Grape topping can be refrigerated for up to 3 days. (Banana topping cannot be made ahead.)

LOADED AVOCADO TOAST WITH PINEAPPLE-BASIL SALSA

Serves 1   **Total Time: 15 minutes**

WHEN TO EAT
› **Post-Workout** Within 2 hours
› **Maintenance**

WORKOUTS
› **Endurance**
› **Everyday** Serve with an
  egg cooked to your liking
  (see pages 292–295).

MAKE IT A SNACK
Eat half a toast.

- ½ cup fresh or thawed
  frozen pineapple chunks,
  chopped
- 1 tomato, cored and
  chopped
- 1 small shallot, minced
- 1 tablespoon shredded fresh
  basil, plus extra for serving
- ¼ teaspoon grated lime zest
  plus 2 teaspoons juice,
  divided
- ½ ripe avocado, cut into
  ½-inch pieces
- ⅛ teaspoon table salt
- ⅛ teaspoon pepper
- 1 (2-ounce) slice rustic
  whole-grain bread, about
  ½ inch thick, toasted
- 1 tablespoon crumbled
  cotija cheese

WHY THIS RECIPE WORKS ›› Avocados are a top-tier food, chock-full of filling, heart-healthy fats and fiber that help you stay full for longer. Avocado toast is one of our favorite healthful snacks, but we wanted a topped toast that was a bit more substantial and could stand alone as breakfast. We really dress ours up by mashing the avocado with a citrusy vinaigrette and topping it with a robust pineapple salsa, plus some tangy cotija cheese. This recipe serves one but can easily be scaled to serve up to four.

1 Stir pineapple, tomato, shallot, basil, and 1 teaspoon lime juice together in bowl. Using fork, coarsely mash avocado, salt, pepper, lime zest, and remaining 1 teaspoon juice in second bowl.

2 Spread avocado mixture evenly over toasted bread and arrange on serving plate. Toss pineapple mixture to recombine and season with salt and pepper to taste. Top toast with pineapple mixture and cotija and sprinkle with extra basil. Serve.

MEAL PREP Pineapple salsa can be refrigerated for up to 1 day.

Cal 420; Total Fat 20g;
Sat Fat 4g; Chol 10mg;
Sodium 630mg; Total Carb 53g;
Dietary Fiber 14g;
Total Sugars 11g; Protein 13g

POACHED EGG WITH GOAT CHEESE, SPINACH, AND TOMATO TOASTS

Serves 1   Total Time: 30 minutes

WHEN TO EAT
› **Pre-Workout** 3 to 4 hours before
› **Post-Workout** Within 2 hours

WORKOUTS
› **Everyday**
› **Endurance** Serve with extra bread.
› **Strength or Interval** Increase poached eggs to 2.

---

2 tablespoons goat cheese, softened

½ teaspoon lemon juice

⅛ teaspoon table salt, divided

⅛ teaspoon pepper

1 (5-inch) piece baguette, cut on bias into 3 slices, toasted (3 ounces)

1 tomato, cored and sliced thin

½ teaspoon extra-virgin olive oil

1 small garlic clove, minced

2 ounces (2 cups) baby spinach

1 tablespoon distilled white vinegar

1 large egg

WHY THIS RECIPE WORKS ›› It may be hard to believe that this eggs Florentine–inspired dish can be made on a busy morning, but we achieve easy, creamy richness by spreading goat cheese on crusty baguette pieces and perfectly poaching an egg with a simple method. These are multipurpose toasts: Add a second egg when eating in conjunction with a strength workout, or omit it for endurance days. This recipe serves one but can easily be scaled to serve up to four. You can substitute 2 ounces frozen chopped spinach, thawed and squeezed dry, for the baby spinach.

1 Stir goat cheese, lemon juice, pinch salt, and pepper in bowl until well combined. Spread goat cheese mixture evenly over baguette slices and arrange in even layer on serving plate. Shingle tomato slices over goat cheese and sprinkle with remaining pinch salt.

2 Heat oil in 8- or 10-inch nonstick skillet over medium heat until shimmering. Add garlic and cook until fragrant, about 20 seconds. Stir in spinach and cook until wilted, about 1 minute. Arrange spinach over tomato slices. Wipe skillet clean with paper towels.

3 Fill now-empty skillet nearly to rim with water, add vinegar, and bring to boil over high heat. Remove skillet from heat. Crack egg into small bowl. Gently tip bowl so egg slides into skillet, cover, and let sit for 4 minutes for medium-cooked yolk. (For firmer yolk, let egg stand in water, checking every 30 seconds, until egg reaches desired doneness.) Using slotted spoon, gently lift egg from water and let drain over skillet. Season with salt and pepper to taste and serve with toasts.

MEAL PREP Wilted spinach mixture can be refrigerated for up to 2 days. Poached eggs can be refrigerated in bowl of cold water for up to 2 days. To reheat, transfer eggs to small pot of water heated to 150 degrees. Cover for 3 minutes so they reach serving temperature.

Cal 410; Total Fat 12g;
Sat Fat 4g; Chol 195mg;
Sodium 760mg; Total Carb 56g;
Dietary Fiber 5g;
Total Sugars 4g; Protein 20g

SHIITAKE MUSHROOM AND SCALLION SCRAMBLE POCKET

Serves 1   Total Time: 25 minutes

WHEN TO EAT
› **Post-Workout** Within 2 hours
› **Maintenance**

WORKOUTS
› **Strength or Interval**
› **Everyday** Serve with grapes.

MAKE IT A SNACK
Eat half a scramble-packed pita.

---

2 large eggs

⅛ teaspoon table salt

⅛ teaspoon pepper

1 teaspoon extra-virgin olive oil, divided

4 ounces shiitake mushrooms, stemmed and sliced thin

1 scallion, sliced thin

2 tablespoons shredded cheddar cheese

1 (6½-inch) whole-wheat pita bread, halved

WHY THIS RECIPE WORKS ›› A pocket pita makes a scrambled egg breakfast conveniently portable. Even better, you can prepare them the day before. To make our filling cohesive (for travel and reheating), we folded in the mushrooms when the egg curds were still a bit wet so the egg could set up around the mushrooms. Cheese provided further cohesion. Oyster or cremini mushrooms can be substituted for the shiitakes; trim the stems but do not remove them. This recipe serves one but can easily be scaled to serve up to four.

1 Beat eggs, salt, and pepper with fork in bowl until well combined and uniform yellow color (do not overbeat).

2 Heat ½ teaspoon oil in 8- or 10-inch nonstick skillet over medium heat until shimmering. Stir in mushrooms and 2 tablespoons water, cover, and cook until mushrooms are softened, 4 to 6 minutes. Uncover and continue to cook, stirring occasionally, until liquid has evaporated and mushrooms are lightly browned, 2 to 3 minutes. Transfer mushrooms to bowl. Wipe skillet clean with paper towels.

3 Heat remaining ½ teaspoon oil in now-empty skillet over medium-high heat until shimmering. Add egg mixture and, using rubber spatula, constantly and firmly scrape along bottom and sides of skillet until eggs begin to clump and spatula just leaves trail on bottom of skillet, 30 to 60 seconds. Reduce heat to low and gently but constantly fold eggs until clumped and just slightly wet, 30 to 60 seconds.

4 Off heat, fold in mushroom mixture, scallion, and cheddar. Season with salt and pepper to taste. Serve scrambled egg mixture in pita.

MEAL PREP Packed pitas can be refrigerated for up to 1 day. Serve at room temperature or reheated in microwave.

Cal 450; Total Fat 20g;
Sat Fat 7g; Chol 385mg;
Sodium 870mg; Total Carb 46g;
Dietary Fiber 7g;
Total Sugars 5g; Protein 25g

FRITTATA BITES WITH BROCCOLI AND SUN-DRIED TOMATOES

Serves 4 (makes 12 frittatas)   **Total Time: 1 hour**

WHEN TO EAT
› **Post-Workout** Within 2 hours
› **Maintenance**

WORKOUTS
› **Strength or Interval**
› **Everyday** Serve with extra toast.

MAKE IT A SNACK
Eat 2 frittata bites and 1 slice toast.

- 8 ounces Yukon Gold potatoes, peeled and cut into ½-inch pieces
- 1 onion, chopped fine
- 1 tablespoon extra-virgin olive oil
- ¼ teaspoon table salt, divided
- ⅛ teaspoon pepper
- 8 ounces frozen broccoli florets, thawed, patted dry, and cut into ½-inch pieces
- 1½ ounces shredded part-skim mozzarella cheese (⅓ cup)
- ¼ cup oil-packed sun-dried tomatoes, patted dry and chopped fine
- 8 large eggs
- ¼ cup 1 percent low-fat milk
- 8 (2-ounce) slices rustic whole-grain bread, about ½ inch thick, toasted

Cal 610; Total Fat 21g;
Sat Fat 6g; Chol 380mg;
Sodium 840mg; Total Carb 68g;
Dietary Fiber 11g;
Total Sugars 11g; Protein 34g

WHY THIS RECIPE WORKS ›› These vegetable-packed grab-and-go frittatas blow coffeehouse egg bites out of the water. By making a muffin tin's worth, you can prepare multiple breakfasts at once. Eggs are an excellent source of protein because they are rich in beneficial vitamins and minerals and have anti-inflammatory properties. We supplement potatoes with convenient frozen veggies.

1 Adjust oven rack to lower-middle position and heat oven to 425 degrees. Toss potatoes and onion with oil, ⅛ teaspoon salt, and pepper and microwave in covered bowl until potatoes are tender and translucent around edges, 5 to 8 minutes, stirring halfway through microwaving. Remove bowl from microwave and let cool slightly, about 2 minutes. Stir in broccoli, cheese, and tomatoes.

2 Generously spray 12-cup nonstick muffin tin with canola oil spray, then divide potato mixture evenly among cups. Whisk eggs and remaining ⅛ teaspoon salt together in large bowl until well combined and uniform yellow color; do not overbeat. Using ladle, evenly distribute egg mixture over filling in muffin cups.

3 Bake until frittatas are lightly puffed and just set in center, 15 to 20 minutes. Transfer muffin tin to wire rack and let cool slightly, about 10 minutes. Run butter knife around edges of frittatas to loosen, then gently remove from muffin tin. Serve 3 frittata bites with 2 slices toasted bread.

FRITTATA BITES WITH PEAS, GOAT CHEESE, AND BASIL
Substitute 8 ounces thawed frozen peas for broccoli, ⅓ cup crumbled goat cheese for mozzarella, and 2 tablespoons chopped fresh basil for sun-dried tomatoes.

MEAL PREP Frittatas can be refrigerated for up to 2 days. Eat with freshly toasted bread.

BEET AND SWEET POTATO HASH WITH FRIED EGGS

Serves 1   Total Time: 40 minutes

WHEN TO EAT
> **Post-Workout** Within 2 hours
> **Maintenance**

WORKOUTS
> **Everyday**
> **Endurance** Increase sweet potatoes to 12 ounces.

MAKE IT A SNACK
Eat half serving of hash with 1 egg.

---

8 ounces sweet potatoes, peeled and cut into ½-inch pieces

2 teaspoons canola oil, divided

⅛ teaspoon table salt

⅛ teaspoon pepper

1 small onion, chopped

1 garlic clove, minced

½ teaspoon minced fresh thyme or ¼ teaspoon dried

¼ teaspoon smoked paprika

1 (8.25-ounce) can diced beets, rinsed and patted dry

1 teaspoon lemon juice, plus lemon wedges for serving

2 large eggs

Cal 480; Total Fat 19g;
Sat Fat 4g; Chol 370mg;
Sodium 880mg; Total Carb 60g;
Dietary Fiber 11g;
Total Sugars 25g; Protein 19g

WHY THIS RECIPE WORKS >> Athletes can eat comfort food like anyone, and a beet and sweet potato hash fills the bill. Making traditional hash can slow down your morning, so we use canned beets and parcook the sweet potatoes in the microwave. This recipe serves one but can easily be scaled to serve up to four; use 1 (14.5-ounce) can of beets for every two servings.

1 Toss sweet potatoes with 1 teaspoon oil, salt, and pepper and microwave in covered bowl until tender, 5 to 8 minutes, stirring halfway through microwaving.

2 Heat ½ teaspoon oil in 10-inch nonstick skillet over medium-high heat until shimmering. Add onion and cook until softened, about 3 minutes. Stir in garlic, thyme, and paprika and cook until fragrant, about 30 seconds.

3 Stir in sweet potatoes, beets, and lemon juice. Using back of spatula, gently pack sweet potato–beet mixture into skillet and cook, undisturbed, for 2 minutes. Flip hash, 1 portion at a time, and lightly repack into skillet. Repeat flipping process every few minutes until mixture is well browned, 6 to 8 minutes. Season with salt and pepper to taste. Transfer hash to serving plate. Wipe skillet clean with paper towels.

4 Crack eggs into bowl. Heat remaining ½ teaspoon oil in now-empty skillet over medium-high heat until shimmering. Pour eggs into skillet, cover, and cook for 1 minute. Remove skillet from heat and let sit, covered, 15 to 45 seconds for runny yolks, 45 to 60 seconds for soft but set yolks, and about 2 minutes for medium-set yolks. Slide eggs onto plate with hash. Serve with lemon wedges.

MEAL PREP Hash (without eggs) can be refrigerated for up to 3 days.

BLACK BEAN BREAKFAST BURRITOS

Makes 6 burritos   **Total Time: 50 minutes**

WHEN TO EAT
› **Pre-Workout** 3 to 4 hours before
› **Post-Workout** Within 2 hours
› **Maintenance**

WORKOUTS
› **Everyday**
› **Endurance** Serve with grapes or baked snack chips (see page 274).

MAKE IT A SNACK
Eat half a burrito.

1½ cups long-grain white rice, rinsed

2¼ cups plus 1 tablespoon water, divided

¼ teaspoon table salt, divided

8 large eggs

3 scallions, sliced thin

1½ teaspoons ground cumin

½ teaspoon chili powder

1 teaspoon extra-virgin olive oil

8 ounces frozen chopped kale or spinach, thawed and squeezed dry

1 (15-ounce) can black beans, rinsed

¼ cup chopped fresh cilantro

2 tablespoons lime juice

6 (10-inch) whole-wheat flour tortillas

—

Cal 520; Total Fat 12g;
Sat Fat 3g; Chol 250mg;
Sodium 890mg; Total Carb 79g;
Dietary Fiber 5g; Total Sugars 1g;
Protein 24g

**WHY THIS RECIPE WORKS ›› ** Ditch the freezer-section burrito; you can make a warm, portable breakfast burrito to either fuel your workout or sink your teeth into when you're done. Eat one right away and freeze extras for later; reheat them at home or toss one in your bag and microwave it at your destination.

1 Bring rice, 2¼ cups water, and ⅛ teaspoon salt to simmer in large saucepan over medium heat. Reduce heat to low, cover, and simmer until rice is tender and liquid is absorbed, 16 to 18 minutes. Remove pot from heat, lay clean folded dish towel underneath lid, and let rest for 10 minutes. Fluff rice with fork and season with salt and pepper to taste; set aside.

2 Whisk eggs, scallions, cumin, chili powder, remaining ⅛ teaspoon salt, and remaining 1 tablespoon water together in large bowl until well combined and uniform yellow color; do not overbeat. Heat oil in 12-inch nonstick skillet over medium-high heat until shimmering. Add egg mixture and, using rubber spatula, constantly and firmly scrape along bottom and sides of skillet until eggs begin to clump and spatula just leaves trail on bottom of skillet, 30 to 60 seconds. Reduce heat to low and gently but constantly fold eggs until clumped and just slightly wet, 30 to 60 seconds. Off heat, fold in kale, beans, cilantro, and lime juice. Season with salt and pepper to taste.

3 Wrap tortillas in damp dish towel and microwave until warm and pliable, about 1 minute. Lay tortillas on counter and spread ½ cup rice evenly across center of each tortilla, close to bottom edge. Top with ½ cup egg mixture. Working with 1 tortilla at a time, fold sides, then bottom of tortilla over filling, then continue to roll tightly into wrap. Serve.

MEAL PREP Burritos can be wrapped in lightly greased aluminum foil, sealed in zipper-lock bags, and frozen for up to 2 months. To reheat, thaw frozen burritos in refrigerator for 8 hours and heat in 400-degree oven for 20 to 30 minutes. Or, remove foil, wrap frozen or thawed burrito in damp paper towel, and microwave for 2 to 4 minutes.

MANGÚ

Serves 2   Total Time: 40 minutes

WHEN TO EAT
› **Pre-Workout** 3 to 4 hours before
› **Post-Workout** Within 2 hours
› **Maintenance**

WORKOUTS
› **Everyday**
› **Endurance** Increase plantains to 1 pound.
› **Strength or Interval** Increase egg whites to 6.

---

12 ounces unripe plantains, peeled and sliced ½ inch thick (1½ cups)

⅛ teaspoon table salt, divided, plus salt for cooking plantains

1½ teaspoons extra-virgin olive oil, divided

½ small red onion, sliced ½ inch thick

2 tablespoons red wine vinegar

2 tablespoons grated Parmesan cheese

4 large egg whites, lightly beaten

WHY THIS RECIPE WORKS ›› Mangú is a Dominican breakfast of mashed plantains, rich in complex carbohydrates, fiber, and vitamins. It's often served with a hearty trio known as "tres golpes," or "three hits" of flavor—salami, cheese, and eggs. This workout-friendly version comes with crispy Parmesan egg whites and traditional pickled onions. Look for unripe plantains that are green and firm. To peel plantains, cut off both ends. Slice skin lengthwise from end to end. Pull skin apart and remove fruit. This recipe can easily be doubled using a 10-inch nonstick skillet.

1 Place plantains and ½ teaspoon salt in large saucepan, add cold water to cover by 2 inches, and bring to boil over high heat. Reduce heat to medium-high and cook until plantains are very tender, 15 to 20 minutes. Reserve 1 cup cooking water. Drain plantains and return to now-empty saucepan. Add 1 teaspoon oil and ½ cup reserved cooking water and mash with potato masher until mostly smooth. Season with salt and pepper to taste. Cover to keep warm.

2 Heat remaining ½ teaspoon oil in 8-inch nonstick skillet over medium heat until shimmering. Add onion and pinch salt and cook until softened, 3 to 5 minutes. Stir in vinegar and cook until evaporated, about 1 minute. Transfer onion to small bowl; set aside. Wipe skillet clean with paper towels.

3 Sprinkle Parmesan evenly over now-empty skillet. Cook over medium heat until golden, 2 to 3 minutes. Pour eggs over Parmesan, tilting skillet to fill bare spots, and sprinkle with remaining pinch salt. Cook until bottom of eggs is just set and top is still slightly wet, 2 to 4 minutes. Cover and let sit, off heat, until top of eggs is set, 2 to 4 minutes. Run spatula under perimeter of eggs to loosen, then fold in half. Cut into 4 wedges. Serve each portion of plantains with 2 egg wedges and onions.

MEAL PREP Cooked plantains and onions can be refrigerated for up to 2 days.

Cal 480; Total Fat 12g;
Sat Fat 3.5g; Chol 10mg;
Sodium 770mg; Total Carb 75g;
Dietary Fiber 6g;
Total Sugars 36g; Protein 24g

BREAKFAST

SAVORY BREAKFAST GRITS WITH PEPPERS AND JACK CHEESE

Serves 1   Total Time: 35 minutes

WHEN TO EAT
> **Pre-Workout** 3 to 4 hours before
> **Post-Workout** Within 2 hours

WORKOUTS
> **Everyday**
> **Endurance** Serve with bread.
> **Strength or Interval** Serve with Scrambled Egg Whites (page 293).

---

1 teaspoon extra-virgin olive oil

¼ cup finely chopped red bell pepper

1 shallot, chopped fine

¼ cup old-fashioned grits

⅛ teaspoon chili powder

1 cup 1 percent low-fat milk

¼ teaspoon table salt

2 tablespoons shredded Monterey Jack cheese

1 tablespoon chopped fresh cilantro

Lime wedges

WHY THIS RECIPE WORKS ›› Breakfast porridges are simple to make and eat, so we set out to create one that was suitable for either end of your workout. And we took things to the savory side: Grits were the best choice because they are easier to digest than the steel-cut oats we like for oatmeal, so you can get up and hit a spin class right away or eat first and wait a few hours before getting your exercise on. Boiling the grits in milk provides richness while also supplying our porridge with extra protein. This recipe can easily be scaled to serve up to four; use a larger saucepan as needed.

1 Heat oil in small saucepan over medium heat until shimmering. Add bell pepper and shallot and cook until softened and lightly browned, 5 to 7 minutes. Stir in grits and chili powder and cook, stirring often, until fragrant, about 3 minutes.

2 Whisk in milk and salt and bring to boil. Reduce heat to low, cover, and simmer, whisking often, until thick and creamy, 10 to 15 minutes. Off heat, stir in cheese. Season with salt and pepper to taste, and adjust consistency as needed with extra milk or water.

3 Transfer grits to serving bowl and top with cilantro. Serve with lime wedges.

MEAL PREP Grits can be refrigerated for up to 3 days. To reheat, warm 1 cup cooked grits and ¼ cup water on stovetop or in microwave, stirring frequently.

Cal 380; Total Fat 12g;
Sat Fat 5g; Chol 25mg;
Sodium 790mg; Total Carb 51g;
Dietary Fiber 3g;
Total Sugars 16g; Protein 17g

BREAKFAST

CONGEE WITH JAMMY EGG, PEANUTS, AND SCALLIONS

Serves 2   Total Time: 1 hour

WHEN TO EAT
› **Pre-Workout** 3 to 4 hours before
› **Post-Workout** Within 2 hours

WORKOUTS
› **Endurance**
› **Everyday** Serve with tofu (see page 291), shredded chicken (see page 289), or extra Easy-Peel Jammy Eggs.

4 cups water

¾ cup long-grain white rice, rinsed

½ cup chicken or vegetable broth

¼ teaspoon table salt

2 Easy-Peel Jammy Eggs (page 295), halved

2 tablespoons dry-roasted unsalted peanuts, chopped coarse

2 scallions, sliced thin

2 teaspoons rice vinegar

1 teaspoon soy sauce

1 teaspoon chili oil (optional)

WHY THIS RECIPE WORKS ›› Congee, the comforting rice porridge that is eaten in Asian countries (under different names), is perfect to accompany an exercise routine thanks to its starchy nature. Topping options are numerous: For congee that's ideal before or after working out, we went with toppings that pack protein: Salty, tangy, and savory additions such as scallions, rice vinegar, and soy sauce enhance the richness of the jammy eggs and unsalted peanuts. Congee consistencies vary across versions; this thicker congee is filling and fueling. Jasmine rice can be substituted for conventional long-grain white rice; do not use basmati.

1 Combine water, rice, broth, and salt in large saucepan and bring to boil over high heat. Reduce heat to maintain vigorous simmer. Cover pot, tucking wooden spoon horizontally between pot and lid to hold lid ajar. Cook, stirring occasionally, until mixture is thickened, glossy, and reduced to about 3 cups, 35 to 40 minutes.

2 Top each 1½-cup portion with 1 jammy egg, 1 tablespoon peanuts, half the scallions, 1 teaspoon vinegar, ½ teaspoon soy sauce, and ½ teaspoon chili oil, if using.

MEAL PREP Rice porridge can be refrigerated for up to 3 days. To reheat, warm 1½ cups cooked porridge and 3 tablespoons water on stovetop or in microwave, stirring frequently.

Cal 400; Total Fat 12g;
Sat Fat 2.5g; Chol 185mg;
Sodium 820mg; Total Carb 58g;
Dietary Fiber 1g; Total Sugars 1g;
Protein 15g

CHERRY-ALMOND MUESLI

Serves 4   Total Time: 10 minutes, plus 12 hours soaking

WHEN TO EAT
> **Post-Workout** Within 2 hours
> **Maintenance**

WORKOUTS
> **Endurance**
> **Everyday** Increase milk to 1 cup per serving.

MAKE IT A SNACK
Eat half a serving.

Dry Mix

   2 cups old-fashioned rolled oats

  ½ cup dried unsweetened cherries

  ⅓ cup whole almonds, toasted and chopped coarse

  ⅓ cup roasted unsalted pepitas

  ½ teaspoon ground cinnamon (optional)

Muesli

  1 percent low-fat milk

    Blackberries, blueberries, or raspberries

WHY THIS RECIPE WORKS ›› This chewy, crunchy overnight muesli is full of dried cherries, toasted almonds, and roasted pepitas—making it an easy breakfast, perfect for replenishing after a long run or maintaining consistent energy throughout the morning. Prepare each portion of muesli in its own container and a sustaining breakfast becomes as simple as taking it with you wherever you go and throwing your favorite berries on top. Muesli can also be served like cereal (without soaking overnight) with milk or yogurt.

1 For the dry mix Combine oats, cherries, almonds, pepitas, and cinnamon, if using, in large bowl. Transfer to storage container with tight-fitting lid.

2 For each serving of muesli Combine ¾ cup dry mix and ½ cup milk in bowl or container. Cover and refrigerate for at least 12 or up to 24 hours. Top with ¼ cup berries.

MEAL PREP Dry muesli mixture can be stored at room temperature for up to 2 weeks.

Cal 410; Total Fat 14g;
Sat Fat 2.5g; Chol 5mg;
Sodium 60mg; Total Carb 60g;
Dietary Fiber 8g;
Total Sugars 25g; Protein 15g

HONEYED STRAWBERRY YOGURT BOWL WITH MUESLI

Serves 1   **Total Time: 20 minutes**

WHEN TO EAT
› **Pre-Workout** 3 to 4 hours before
› **Post-Workout** Within 2 hours
› **Maintenance**

WORKOUTS
› **Everyday**
› **Endurance** Increase muesli to ⅔ cup.
› **Strength or Interval** Increase yogurt to 1 cup.

MAKE IT A SNACK
Eat half a serving.

---

1 tablespoon honey

2 teaspoons lemon juice

½ cup strawberries, hulled and sliced thin

¾ cup plain low-fat Greek yogurt

⅓ cup muesli

WHY THIS RECIPE WORKS ›› A yogurt bowl is a quick breakfast standard, but with the proper calibration of its three components—here creamy protein-rich Greek yogurt, fresh macerated strawberries, and crunchy muesli—the quick dish can also be a flavor and nutritional standout. You can pack the components separately and combine them when you're at your desk for the perfect parfait. We prefer our homemade Cherry-Almond Muesli (page 56) in this recipe; if using store-bought muesli, look for brands that contain no more than 7 grams of fat per ⅓-cup serving. This recipe serves one but can easily be scaled to serve up to four.

1 Whisk honey and lemon juice together in small bowl until honey has dissolved. Add strawberries and toss to combine; let sit until strawberries have released some of their juice, about 10 minutes.

2 Top yogurt with muesli and strawberry mixture. Serve.

MEAL PREP Strawberry mixture can be refrigerated for up to 1 day.

Cal 400; Total Fat 11g;
Sat Fat 3.5g; Chol 10mg;
Sodium 85mg; Total Carb 60g;
Dietary Fiber 5g;
Total Sugars 39g; Protein 22g

BREAKFAST

BANANA-OAT PANCAKES WITH VANILLA-MAPLE YOGURT

Serves 5 (makes 15 pancakes)   Total Time: 45 minutes

WHEN TO EAT
› **Post-Workout** Within 2 hours

WORKOUTS
› **Everyday**
› **Endurance** Serve 4 pancakes with 2 tablespoons yogurt sauce.
› **Strength or Interval** Serve with an egg cooked to your liking (see pages 292–295).

MAKE IT A SNACK
Eat 2 pancakes with ¼ cup yogurt sauce.

2½ cups plain low-fat Greek yogurt

5 teaspoons maple syrup

1 teaspoon vanilla extract

2 very ripe large bananas, peeled and mashed (1 cup)

1½ cups 1 percent low-fat milk

1 cup (3 ounces) old-fashioned rolled oats

1¼ cups (6¼ ounces) all-purpose flour

2½ teaspoons baking powder

¼ teaspoon table salt

2 large eggs

2 tablespoons canola oil

2 tablespoons sugar

WHY THIS RECIPE WORKS ›› A modestly sweet pancake filled with oats and bananas is not only delicious but more beneficial than you might think. The pancakes are low on the glycemic index so they satisfy and maintain energy long after a workout. And they reach beyond breakfast: A small serving is an easy snack to fit into your day because the make-ahead pancakes can be frozen.

1 Whisk yogurt, maple syrup, and vanilla together in small bowl; refrigerate until ready to serve.

2 Whisk bananas, milk, and oats together in large bowl and let sit until oats are softened, about 5 minutes. Whisk flour, baking powder, and salt together in second large bowl. Add eggs, oil, and sugar to banana mixture and whisk until smooth. Add banana mixture to flour mixture and whisk until just combined.

3 Spray 12-inch nonstick skillet with canola oil spray and heat over medium heat until hot, about 1 minute. Using ¼-cup measure, scoop three ¼-cup portions batter into skillet. Cook until edges are set, first side is golden, and bubbles on surface are just beginning to break, 2 to 3 minutes. Flip pancakes and cook until second side is golden, 1 to 3 minutes; transfer to serving plate or wire rack. Repeat with remaining batter, spraying skillet with canola oil spray as needed. Top each 3-pancake portion with ½ cup yogurt sauce before serving.

MEAL PREP Refrigerate yogurt sauce for up to 3 days. Freeze pancakes in plastic wrap in bundles of 2 or 3, sealed in zipper-lock bags, for up to 1 month. To reheat, microwave frozen pancakes in single layer until hot, about 2 minutes, flipping halfway through.

—

Cal 450; Total Fat 12g;
Sat Fat 3.5g; Chol 85mg;
Sodium 430mg; Total Carb 67g;
Dietary Fiber 3g;
Total Sugars 23g; Protein 20g

PUMPKIN SPICE WAFFLES WITH YOGURT AND BLUEBERRIES

Serves 8 (makes four 7-inch waffles)   **Total Time: 45 minutes**

WHEN TO EAT

› **Pre-Workout** 3 to 4 hours before
› **Post-Workout** Within 2 hours
› **Maintenance**

WORKOUTS

› **Everyday**
› **Endurance** Serve 1 waffle with ¼ cup yogurt and ½ cup blueberries.
› **Strength or Interval** Serve with Scrambled Egg Whites (page 293).

MAKE IT A SNACK

Eat ¼ waffle with 2 tablespoons of yogurt and ¼ cup blueberries.

2½ cups (7½ ounces) oat flour

½ cup (2½ ounces) all-purpose flour

1 teaspoon ground cinnamon

1 teaspoon baking powder

½ teaspoon baking soda

½ teaspoon table salt

¼ teaspoon ground nutmeg

¼ teaspoon ground cardamom

1 (15-ounce) can unsweetened pumpkin puree

1¼ cups plain low-fat yogurt, plus extra for serving

2 large eggs

2 tablespoons canola oil

¼ cup (1¾ ounces) sugar

1 teaspoon grated fresh ginger

Blueberries

Cal 340; Total Fat 9g;
Sat Fat 2.5g; Chol 50mg;
Sodium 420mg; Total Carb 51g;
Dietary Fiber 5g;
Total Sugars 21g; Protein 16g

WHY THIS RECIPE WORKS ›› The pumpkin puree in this recipe doesn't just satisfy pumpkin spice fans, it helps deliver potassium that facilitates muscle contractions. To rid the puree of excess moisture, we blot it with paper towels. Do not use toasted oat flour in this recipe. If your waffle has an indicator light or alert, we suggest still following the visual cues to determine doneness.

1 Adjust oven rack to middle position and heat oven to 200 degrees. Whisk oat flour, all-purpose flour, cinnamon, baking powder, baking soda, salt, nutmeg, and cardamom together in large bowl.

2 Line rimmed baking sheet with triple layer of paper towels. Spread pumpkin on paper towels in even layer. Cover pumpkin with second triple layer of paper towels and press firmly until paper towels are saturated. Peel back top layer of towels and discard. Grasp bottom towels and fold pumpkin in half; peel back towels. Transfer pumpkin to second large bowl and discard towels. Whisk yogurt, eggs, oil, sugar, and ginger into pumpkin until combined. Whisk pumpkin mixture into flour mixture until well combined and smooth. Set wire rack in now-empty baking sheet and place in oven.

3 Heat waffle iron according to manufacturer's instructions and lightly spray with canola oil spray. Add mounded 1 cup batter to waffle iron and cook according to manufacturer's instructions until waffle is deep golden and has crisp, firm exterior. Serve immediately or transfer to wire rack in oven. Repeat with remaining batter, spraying waffle iron with additional oil. Serve each ½-waffle portion with ⅓ cup yogurt and ½ cup blueberries.

MEAL PREP Freeze waffles, separated by parchment and sealed in zipper-lock bags, for up to 1 month. To reheat, toast frozen waffles on lowest setting until warmed through and crisp on the outside.

SOUPS

GARLICKY CHICKEN AND RICE SOUP

Serves 2   Total Time: 40 minutes

WHEN TO EAT
› **Pre-Workout** 3 to 4 hours before
› **Post-Workout** Within 2 hours

WORKOUTS
› **Everyday**
› **Endurance** Serve with baked snack chips (see page 274).
› **Strength or Interval** Increase chicken to 8 ounces.

6 garlic cloves, minced

1 tablespoon extra-virgin olive oil

1 small onion, chopped fine

1 carrot, peeled, halved lengthwise, and sliced ¼ inch thick

1 celery rib, minced

⅛ teaspoon table salt

1 teaspoon minced fresh thyme or ¼ teaspoon dried

2 cups chicken or vegetable broth

2 cups water

4 ounces boneless, skinless chicken thighs, trimmed and cut into ½-inch pieces

⅔ cup long-grain white rice, rinsed

½ cup frozen peas

Lemon wedges

WHY THIS RECIPE WORKS ›› If you find yourself seeking comfort after your circuit training session, or just craving something warming and filling, few things nourish like a well-rounded chicken and rice soup enriched with a hefty dose of garlic. This soup increases the comfort with its more generous portion of white rice—it's there to fuel and replenish, but the other upshot is a soup with more texture and body. This recipe can easily be doubled in a Dutch oven.

1 Heat garlic and oil in large saucepan over medium-low heat, stirring often, until garlic is fragrant and beginning to brown, about 3 minutes. Increase heat to medium and add onion, carrot, celery, and salt. Cook until softened and lightly browned, 5 to 7 minutes. Stir in thyme and cook until fragrant, about 30 seconds.

2 Stir in broth, water, chicken, and rice, scraping up any browned bits. Bring to simmer and cook until rice is tender and chicken is cooked through, 12 to 15 minutes.

3 Stir in peas and cook until heated through, about 1 minute. Season with salt and pepper to taste. Serve with lemon wedges.

MEAL PREP Soup can be refrigerated for up to 3 days.

Cal 450; Total Fat 10g;
Sat Fat 1.5g; Chol 55mg;
Sodium 820mg; Total Carb 67g;
Dietary Fiber 5g;
Total Sugars 8g; Protein 21g

CHICKEN TORTILLA SOUP WITH POBLANOS AND HOMINY

Serves 2   Total Time: 30 minutes

WHEN TO EAT
> **Pre-Workout** 3 to 4 hours before
> **Post-Workout** Within 2 hours

WORKOUTS
> **Everyday**
> **Endurance** Serve with extra tortilla chips.
> **Strength or Interval** Increase chicken to 8 ounces.

1 tablespoon canola oil

1 small onion, chopped fine

2 poblano chiles, stemmed, seeded, and chopped

1–2 teaspoons chili powder

1½ cups chicken broth

1 cup water

1 (15-ounce) can white or yellow hominy, rinsed

4 ounces boneless, skinless chicken breast or tenderloins, trimmed

2 cups (2 ounces) baked corn tortilla chips, broken into 1-inch pieces

2 tablespoons chopped fresh cilantro

Lime wedges

WHY THIS RECIPE WORKS ›› This sustaining soup is packed with flavor. Hominy (dried maize kernels) is the major source of carbohydrates, and it lends the soup a fitting earthy and nutty corn flavor. The requisite broken-up tortilla chips are the second booster of corn and carbs. When buying tortilla chips, look for brands that contain no more than 3 grams of fat per 1-cup serving. Or, you can use our homemade Baked Corn Tortilla Chips (page 274). This recipe can easily be doubled in a Dutch oven.

1 Heat oil in large saucepan over medium heat until shimmering. Add onion and poblanos and cook until softened and lightly browned, 5 to 7 minutes. Stir in chili powder and cook until fragrant, about 30 seconds.

2 Stir in broth, water, hominy, and chicken, bring to simmer, and cook until chicken registers 160 degrees, 5 to 10 minutes. Transfer chicken to cutting board, let cool slightly, then shred into bite-size pieces using 2 forks.

3 Return soup to simmer, stir in shredded chicken, and cook until heated through, about 1 minute. Season with salt and pepper to taste. Top each portion with 1 cup tortilla chips and 1 tablespoon cilantro. Serve with lime wedges.

MEAL PREP Soup can be refrigerated for up to 3 days.

Cal 430; Total Fat 12g;
Sat Fat 1g; Chol 40mg;
Sodium 870mg; Total Carb 61g;
Dietary Fiber 2g;
Total Sugars 4g; Protein 20g

BEEF AND BARLEY SOUP

Serves 2   Total Time: 1 hour

WHEN TO EAT
› **Post-Workout** Within 2 hours
› **Maintenance**

WORKOUTS
› **Everyday**
› **Endurance** Serve with bread.
› **Strength or Interval** Increase beef to 8 ounces.

---

4 ounces beef blade steak, trimmed and cut into ½-inch pieces

2 teaspoons canola oil

4 ounces cremini or white mushrooms, trimmed and sliced thin

2 carrots, peeled and chopped

1 small onion, chopped fine

1 tablespoon tomato paste

2 garlic cloves, minced

1 teaspoon minced fresh thyme or ¼ teaspoon dried

2 cups beef or chicken broth

1 cup water

⅛ teaspoon table salt

⅛ teaspoon pepper

⅔ cup quick-cooking barley, rinsed

2 tablespoons chopped fresh parsley or chives

WHY THIS RECIPE WORKS ›› Hearty and umami-packed, this beef and barley soup is good for your soul and your active body. We chose blade steak because the inexpensive cut is easy to purchase in appropriately modest quantities. And with this amount, browning can happen in one batch rather than multiple. A generous amount of chewy, nutty barley, with its high fiber content, satisfies and fills you, especially after a workout. With one hour and one saucepan, you are on your way to a nourishing and delectable meal. This recipe can easily be doubled in a Dutch oven.

1 Pat beef dry with paper towels. Heat oil in large saucepan over medium heat until just smoking. Add beef and cook until well browned on all sides, 2 to 4 minutes; transfer to bowl.

2 Add mushrooms, carrots, and onion to fat left in saucepan and cook until softened and lightly browned, 5 to 7 minutes. Stir in tomato paste, garlic, and thyme and cook until fragrant and tomato paste begins to brown, about 1 minute.

3 Stir in broth, water, salt, pepper, and browned beef and any accumulated juices, scraping up any browned bits. Bring to simmer and cook for 15 minutes. Stir in barley and simmer until barley and beef are tender, 10 to 15 minutes. Stir in parsley and season with salt and pepper to taste. Serve.

MEAL PREP Soup can be refrigerated for up to 3 days.

Cal 460; Total Fat 12g;
Sat Fat 2.5g; Chol 40mg;
Sodium 780mg; Total Carb 67g;
Dietary Fiber 14g;
Total Sugars 7g; Protein 24g

VEGETABLE AND CLAM CHOWDER

Serves 2   Total Time: 30 minutes

WHEN TO EAT
› **Pre-Workout** 3 to 4 hours before
› **Post-Workout** Within 2 hours

WORKOUTS
› **Everyday**
› **Endurance** Serve with extra oyster crackers.
› **Strength or Interval** Increase clams to 2 cans.

---

2 teaspoons canola oil

1 small onion, chopped fine

1 teaspoon minced fresh thyme or ¼ teaspoon dried

2 (8-ounce) bottles clam juice, divided

12 ounces russet potatoes, peeled and cut into ½-inch pieces

¼ teaspoon pepper

2 ounces frozen chopped spinach, thawed and squeezed dry

½ cup frozen corn

1 (6.5-ounce) can minced clams, drained

4 teaspoons heavy cream or half-and-half (optional)

1 teaspoon lemon juice

⅔ cup oyster crackers

2 tablespoons minced fresh parsley

WHY THIS RECIPE WORKS ›› Chowder might sound like a once-in-a-while treat, but you can enjoy it in conjunction with any workout when the creaminess comes from starchy, power-packed potatoes rather than a glut of cream. For body, we pull out a portion of potatoes during cooking and mash them by hand before adding them back to the soup. The canned clams are accessible, low in fat, and high in protein. To give the chowder one thing it typically lacks—vegetables and vitamins—we add chopped frozen spinach and corn. If you prefer, skip the oyster crackers and serve each portion with a slice of bread. This recipe can easily be doubled in a Dutch oven.

1 Heat oil in large saucepan over medium heat until shimmering. Add onion and cook until softened, 3 to 5 minutes. Stir in thyme and cook until fragrant, about 30 seconds.

2 Stir in clam juice, potatoes, and pepper and bring to simmer. Cover and cook until potatoes are tender, 10 to 12 minutes. Using slotted spoon, transfer ½ cup potatoes to bowl and mash with potato masher until mostly smooth; return mashed potatoes to saucepan. Stir in spinach, corn, and clams, return to simmer, and cook until vegetables are heated through, about 2 minutes. Off heat, stir in cream, if using, and lemon juice, and season with salt and pepper to taste. Top each portion with ⅓ cup oyster crackers and 1 tablespoon parsley. Serve.

MEAL PREP Soup can be refrigerated for up to 3 days.

Cal 410; Total Fat 11g;
Sat Fat 3g; Chol 45mg;
Sodium 750mg; Total Carb 58g;
Dietary Fiber 5g;
Total Sugars 5g; Protein 21g

POTATO-LEEK SOUP WITH CRISPY HAM

Serves 2   **Total Time: 45 minutes**

WHEN TO EAT
› **Pre-Workout** 3 to 4 hours before
› **Post-Workout** Within 2 hours

WORKOUTS
› **Everyday**
› **Endurance** Serve with bread.
› **Strength or Interval** Serve with shredded chicken (see page 289), tofu (see page 291), or extra Easy-Peel Jammy Eggs.

- 2 teaspoons extra-virgin olive oil
- 3 ounces thinly sliced low-sodium deli ham, chopped
- 1 pound leeks, white and light green parts only, halved lengthwise, sliced thin, and washed thoroughly
- 1 teaspoon minced fresh thyme or ¼ teaspoon dried
- 1½ cups chicken broth
- 1¼ cups water
- 1 pound russet potatoes, peeled and cut into 1-inch pieces
- 2 Easy-Peel Jammy Eggs (page 295), halved lengthwise
- 1 tablespoon minced fresh parsley, tarragon, dill, or chives

---

Cal 410; Total Fat 11g;
Sat Fat 2.5g; Chol 205mg;
Sodium 880mg; Total Carb 58g;
Dietary Fiber 5g;
Total Sugars 8g; Protein 21g

WHY THIS RECIPE WORKS ›› This classic hearty soup should automatically be filling and fueling with its 2 pounds of leeks and potatoes, but the frequent addition of rich bacon or pancetta, while delicious, can slow you down before a workout. For race-ready soup with smoky, savory flavor without all the fat, we incorporated low-sodium deli ham. We crisped the ham in a pan for garnishing, which also infused the oil with a delicious flavor for sautéing the hefty pound of leeks. The leeks gave this dish its foremost flavor while also providing antioxidants and a dose of vitamin C, both of which can help reduce damage to muscles from exercising. To fine-tune our balance of carbs and protein, we added jammy eggs—the yolks melted into the already creamy soup. This recipe can easily be doubled in a Dutch oven.

1 Heat oil in large saucepan over medium heat until shimmering. Add ham and cook, stirring often, until lightly browned and beginning to crisp, 3 to 5 minutes; using slotted spoon, transfer ham to paper towel–lined plate.

2 Add leeks to oil left in saucepan and cook until softened and lightly browned, 6 to 8 minutes. Stir in thyme and cook until fragrant, about 30 seconds. Stir in broth, water, and potatoes and bring to simmer. Cover and cook until vegetables are tender, 15 to 18 minutes.

3 Using potato masher, mash soup in saucepan until potatoes are mostly broken down and soup is thickened. Season with salt and pepper to taste. Top each portion with half of crispy ham, 1 jammy egg, and 1½ teaspoons parsley. Serve.

MEAL PREP Soup can be refrigerated for up to 3 days.

MISO-GINGER UDON SOUP

Serves 2   **Total Time: 35 minutes**

WHEN TO EAT
› **Pre-Workout** 3 to 4 hours before
› **Post-Workout** Within 2 hours

WORKOUTS
› **Everyday**
› **Strength or Interval** Top with tofu (see page 291) or shredded chicken (see page 289).

---

6 ounces dried udon noodles

4 teaspoons grated fresh ginger

2 teaspoons canola oil

1 carrot, peeled, halved lengthwise, and sliced ¼ inch thick

½ cup frozen shelled edamame beans

1 teaspoon soy sauce, plus extra for seasoning

2 tablespoons white or red miso

2 scallions, sliced thin

1 teaspoon sesame seeds, toasted

1 teaspoon toasted sesame oil (optional)

WHY THIS RECIPE WORKS ›› For this umami extravaganza, we took inspiration from the numerous miso-ginger soups out there that are bolstered with carbohydrates from thick udon noodles. For a vegetable element to balance out the noodles, we added nutritious (and convenient) frozen edamame which need only a few minutes in the simmering water to become tender. We flavored the delicate broth with grated fresh ginger, soy sauce, and perfectly salty miso, then topped it with sesame seeds, sesame oil, and scallions. This recipe can easily be doubled in a Dutch oven.

1 Bring 2 quarts water to boil in large pot. Add noodles and cook, stirring often, until tender. Drain noodles, rinse well, and drain again; set aside.

2 Heat ginger and canola oil in large saucepan over medium-low heat, stirring often, until ginger is fragrant and beginning to brown, about 2 minutes. Stir in 3¾ cups water, carrot, edamame, and soy sauce, scraping up any browned bits. Increase heat to medium, bring to simmer, and cook until vegetables are tender, 3 to 5 minutes.

3 Transfer ½ cup hot broth to small bowl or measuring cup and whisk in miso. Stir noodles and miso mixture into soup and return to brief simmer. Off heat, season with extra soy sauce to taste. Top each portion with half of scallions, ½ teaspoon sesame seeds, and ½ teaspoon sesame oil, if using. Serve.

MEAL PREP Noodles (tossed with 1 teaspoon oil) and soup can be refrigerated separately for up to 3 days.

Cal 460; Total Fat 12g;
Sat Fat 0.5g; Chol 0mg;
Sodium 850mg; Total Carb 69g;
Dietary Fiber 3g;
Total Sugars 6g; Protein 21g

HOT-AND-SOUR RICE NOODLE SOUP WITH SHRIMP

Serves 2   Total Time: 30 minutes

WHEN TO EAT
› **Pre-Workout** 3 to 4 hours before
› **Post-Workout** Within 2 hours

WORKOUTS
› **Everyday**
› **Endurance** Increase noodles to 6 ounces.
› **Strength or Interval** Increase shrimp to 1 pound.

---

4 ounces rice
vermicelli noodles

1 cup chicken or
vegetable broth

2½ cups water

2½ tablespoons Thai green or
red curry paste

6 ounces cremini or white
mushrooms, trimmed and
sliced thin

1 jalapeño chile, stemmed,
and sliced into thin rings

8 ounces large shrimp
(26 to 30 per pound),
peeled, deveined, and
tails removed, halved
lengthwise

1 tomato, cored, seeded,
and chopped

1 tablespoon lime juice

2 tablespoons chopped fresh
cilantro, Thai basil, or mint

2 teaspoons chili oil
(optional)

WHY THIS RECIPE WORKS ›› Thai curry paste flavors this colorful, super-quick—30 minutes quick—soup so you can exercise and then eat (or eat then exercise). Sliced jalapeño and mushrooms add vitamins, varied textures, and depth to the already-complex combo of shrimp, lime juice, and chopped fresh herbs. This recipe can easily be doubled in a Dutch oven.

1 Bring 2 quarts water to boil in large pot. Off heat, add noodles and let sit, stirring occasionally, until tender, about 5 minutes. Drain noodles, rinse well, and drain again; set aside.

2 Bring broth and water to simmer in large saucepan over medium heat, then whisk in curry paste until dissolved. Add mushrooms and jalapeño, return to simmer, and cook until vegetables are crisp-tender, about 1 minute. Stir in shrimp and simmer until opaque throughout, about 1 minute.

3 Stir noodles, tomato, and lime juice into soup and return to brief simmer. Off heat, season with salt and pepper to taste. Top each portion with 1 tablespoon cilantro and 1 teaspoon chili oil, if using. Serve.

MEAL PREP Noodles (tossed with 1 teaspoon oil) and soup can be refrigerated separately for up to 3 days.

Cal 370; Total Fat 7g;
Sat Fat 0.5g; Chol 105mg;
Sodium 890mg; Total Carb 58g;
Dietary Fiber 2g;
Total Sugars 7g; Protein 18g

SOUPS

79

MOONG DAL SOUP WITH COCONUT MILK AND SPINACH

Serves 2   **Total Time: 45 minutes**

WHEN TO EAT
> **Post-Workout** Within 2 hours
> **Maintenance**

WORKOUTS
> **Strength or Interval**
> **Everyday** Serve with bread or a simple grain (see pages 284–287).

---

1 tomato, cored and chopped

2 tablespoons chopped fresh cilantro

1 tablespoon lime juice, plus lime wedges for serving

1 jalapeño chile, stemmed, seeded, and minced

2 tablespoons canola oil

1 small onion, chopped fine

1 tablespoon grated fresh ginger

2 garlic cloves, minced

1 teaspoon ground cumin

½ teaspoon turmeric

2½ cups chicken or vegetable broth

1 cup water

¾ cup split mung beans, picked over and rinsed

⅓ cup canned coconut milk

2 ounces frozen chopped spinach, thawed and squeezed dry

—

Cal 490; Total Fat 19g;
Sat Fat 11g; Chol 0mg;
Sodium 750mg; Total Carb 58g;
Dietary Fiber 11g;
Total Sugars 5g; Protein 26g

WHY THIS RECIPE WORKS ›› This aromatic, creamy soup made from moong dal (buttery split mung beans) is ready in no time, and is perfect after hitting the weights. Split mung beans are ideal for athletes because they contain protein, carbs, and fiber—and they cook down more quickly than other legumes. Coconut milk combines with warm spices and punchy fresh ingredients for creamy matrimony. If you can't find split mung beans, you can substitute split red lentils; do not use yellow lentils or split pigeon peas (toor dal). The remaining coconut milk can be frozen into cubes in an ice tray for use in other recipes. This recipe can easily be doubled in a Dutch oven.

1 Combine tomato, cilantro, lime juice, and half of jalapeño in small bowl. Season with salt and pepper to taste; set aside.

2 Heat oil in large saucepan over medium heat until shimmering. Add onion and cook until softened and lightly browned, 5 to 7 minutes. Stir in ginger, garlic, cumin, turmeric, and remaining jalapeño and cook until fragrant, about 1 minute

3 Stir in broth, water, and beans and bring to simmer. Reduce heat to low and cook, partially covered, until beans are beginning to break down, 10 to 12 minutes.

4 Whisk soup vigorously until beans are completely broken down and soup is thickened, about 30 seconds. Stir in coconut milk and spinach, return to simmer, and cook until spinach is heated through, about 2 minutes. Season with salt and pepper to taste. Top each portion with half of tomato mixture. Serve.

MEAL PREP Soup can be refrigerated for up to 3 days.

SOUPS

CHIPOTLE–BLACK BEAN SOUP WITH CORN AND TOMATOES

Serves 2   Total Time: 30 minutes

WHEN TO EAT
› **Post-Workout** Within 2 hours
› **Maintenance**

WORKOUTS
› **Everyday**
› **Endurance** Serve with baked tortilla chips (see page 274).
› **Strength or Interval** Serve with tofu (see page 291), tempeh (see page 291), or shredded chicken (page see 289).

---

1 tablespoon canola oil

1 onion, chopped fine

2 (15-ounce) cans black beans, rinsed

2 cups water

2–3 teaspoons minced canned chipotle chiles in adobo sauce

½ cup frozen corn

½ teaspoon grated lime zest, plus lime wedges for serving

2 ounces cherry or grape tomatoes, quartered

2 tablespoons plain low-fat Greek yogurt

2 tablespoons chopped fresh cilantro

WHY THIS RECIPE WORKS ›› When you don't have time to plan a meal for after a workout, pull out this recipe. The ingredient list is short—but the soup is long on flavor. Smoky chipotle chiles in adobo sauce give the hearty bean soup character and depth with the crack of a can. We coarsely mash the beans after they cook, which helps to thicken the soup before we stir in colorful corn that delivers more carbs. The soup is finished with some lime zest and a dollop of Greek yogurt. Throw the leftover serving in a thermos the next day for a take-along lunch. This recipe can easily be doubled in a Dutch oven.

1 Heat oil in large saucepan over medium heat until shimmering. Add onion and cook until softened, 3 to 5 minutes. Stir in beans, water, and chipotle, bring to simmer, and cook, stirring occasionally, until beans begin to break down, 5 to 7 minutes.

2 Using potato masher, coarsely mash beans in saucepan until beans are mostly broken down and soup is thickened. Stir in corn and return to brief simmer.

3 Off heat, stir in lime zest and season with salt and pepper to taste. Top each portion with half of tomatoes, 1 tablespoon yogurt, and 1 tablespoon cilantro. Serve with lime wedges.

MEAL PREP Soup can be refrigerated for up to 3 days.

Cal 380; Total Fat 9g;
Sat Fat 1g; Chol 0mg;
Sodium 760mg; Total Carb 63g;
Dietary Fiber 21g;
Total Sugars 6g; Protein 19g

SOUPS

83

CREAMY SUN-DRIED TOMATO SOUP

Serves 2   Total Time: 20 minutes

WHEN TO EAT

› **Post-Workout** Within 2 hours
› **Maintenance**

WORKOUTS

› **Everyday**
› **Endurance** Serve with extra oyster crackers.
› **Strength or Interval** Serve with tofu (see page 291), tempeh (see page 291), or shredded chicken (see page 289).

---

2 (15-ounce) cans cannellini beans, drained

2 cups water

¼ cup oil-packed sun-dried tomatoes, patted dry and chopped coarse

2 tablespoons grated Parmesan cheese, divided

⅔ cup oyster crackers

2 tablespoons shredded fresh basil

WHY THIS RECIPE WORKS ›› Omit the cream from creamy tomato soup and replace it with fiber- and protein-rich cannellini beans and you have something just as smooth, but even more satisfying. Processing oil-packed sun-dried tomatoes with the beans ensures deep summer-ripe tomato flavor—no summer tomatoes needed. If you prefer, skip the oyster crackers and serve each portion with a (1-ounce) slice of bread. This recipe can easily be doubled in a Dutch oven.

1 Bring beans, water, and tomatoes to simmer in large saucepan over medium heat and cook, stirring occasionally, until beans begin to break down, 5 to 7 minutes.

2 Process soup and 4 teaspoons Parmesan in blender until smooth, about 2 minutes. Return soup to now-empty saucepan and return to simmer, adjusting consistency with hot water as needed. Season with salt and pepper to taste. Top each portion with ⅓ cup oyster crackers, 1 tablespoon basil, and 1 teaspoon Parmesan.

MEAL PREP Soup can be refrigerated for up to 3 days.

Cal 360; Total Fat 5g;
Sat Fat 1.5g; Chol 5mg;
Sodium 830mg; Total Carb 60g;
Dietary Fiber 18g;
Total Sugars 2g; Protein 18g

CREAMY CHESTNUT SOUP WITH MUSHROOMS

Serves 2   Total Time: 1¼ hours

WHEN TO EAT

› **Post-Workout** Within 2 hours

WORKOUTS

› **Endurance**
› **Everyday** Serve with tofu (see page 291) or shredded chicken (see page 289).

---

1 cup water, divided

⅛ ounce dried porcini mushrooms, rinsed

2 teaspoons extra-virgin olive oil, divided, plus extra for drizzling

8 ounces white, cremini, or shiitake mushrooms, trimmed and sliced thin

¼ teaspoon table salt, divided

1 small onion, chopped

¼ teaspoon pepper

¼ teaspoon ground cumin

¼ teaspoon ground cardamom

Pinch cinnamon

1½ cups (7 ounces) peeled and cooked chestnuts, chopped

1 cup chicken or vegetable broth

¾ cup plain low-fat Greek yogurt

2 tablespoons minced fresh parsley

—

Cal 380; Total Fat 10g;
Sat Fat 2g; Chol 5mg;
Sodium 620mg; Total Carb 61g;
Dietary Fiber 5g;
Total Sugars 18g; Protein 14g

WHY THIS RECIPE WORKS ›› Buttery chestnuts are used in myriad ways, including in soup. Their benefit for athletes: They're lower in fat than most nuts and are a great source of carbohydrates (plus, they are often sold already cooked). The sweet chestnuts get depth from mushrooms and warmth from spices, inspired by Turkish kestane çorbasi. Processing the soup with yogurt gives it more creaminess (and protein). Boiled or roasted chestnuts can be used in this recipe. This recipe can easily be doubled in a Dutch oven.

1 Microwave ¼ cup water and porcini mushrooms in covered bowl until steaming, about 1 minute. Let sit until softened, about 5 minutes. Drain mushrooms in fine-mesh strainer lined with coffee filter, reserving soaking liquid, and chop mushrooms fine. Heat 1 teaspoon oil in large saucepan over medium heat until shimmering. Add fresh mushrooms and ⅛ teaspoon salt, cover, and cook until softened, about 3 minutes. Uncover and continue to cook, stirring occasionally, until liquid has evaporated and mushrooms begin to brown, 5 to 7 minutes; transfer to bowl and set aside.

2 Heat remaining 1 teaspoon oil in now-empty saucepan over medium heat until shimmering. Add onion and cook until softened and lightly browned, 5 to 7 minutes. Stir in porcini mushrooms, pepper, cumin, cardamom, and cinnamon and cook until fragrant, about 30 seconds. Stir in chestnuts, broth, reserved porcini soaking liquid, remaining ¾ cups water, and remaining ⅛ teaspoon salt and bring to simmer. Cover and cook until chestnuts are very tender, about 20 minutes.

3 Process soup and yogurt in blender until smooth, about 2 minutes. Return soup to again-empty saucepan and return to simmer, adjusting consistency with hot water as needed. Season with salt and pepper to taste. Top each portion with half of mushrooms and 1 tablespoon parsley, and drizzle with ½ teaspoon extra oil. Serve.

MEAL PREP Soup can be refrigerated for up to 3 days.

SWEET POTATO AND PEANUT SOUP

Serves 2   Total Time: 40 minutes

WHEN TO EAT
› **Post-Workout** Within 2 hours
› **Maintenance**

WORKOUTS
› **Endurance**
› **Everyday** Serve with tofu (see page 291), tempeh (see page 291), or shredded chicken (see page 289).

- ½ teaspoon canola oil
- 1 small onion, chopped fine
- ½ cup finely chopped red bell pepper
- 2 garlic cloves, minced
- ½ teaspoon ground coriander
- ⅛ teaspoon cayenne pepper (optional)
- 2 cups chicken or vegetable broth
- 1 pound sweet potatoes, peeled and cut into ½-inch pieces
- ½ cup dry-roasted unsalted peanuts, chopped coarse, divided
- ⅛ teaspoon table salt
- 2 tablespoons chopped fresh cilantro

WHY THIS RECIPE WORKS ›› The combination of peanuts and sweet potatoes—inspired by sweet, earthy, nutty West African soups—is loaded with lots of carbohydrates, potassium, magnesium and plenty of protein for refueling after an endurance workout. Maafe, also known as groundnut soup, is an all-time favorite African dish, common in West and Central Africa but with wide variation in its preparation due to its popularity and regional differences. The soup is naturally creamy without cream and boasts lots of body from the sweet potato puree. It can easily be vegan by choosing vegetable broth. The rich soup is finished with chopped peanuts for contrasting crunch and a refreshing sprinkle of fresh cilantro. This recipe can easily be doubled in a Dutch oven.

1 Heat oil in large saucepan over medium heat until shimmering. Add onion and bell pepper and cook until softened, 3 to 5 minutes. Stir in garlic, coriander, and cayenne, if using, and cook until fragrant, about 30 seconds.

2 Stir in broth, potatoes, ¼ cup peanuts, and salt and bring to simmer. Cook, partially covered, until sweet potatoes are tender, 10 to 15 minutes.

3 Process soup in blender until smooth, about 2 minutes. Return soup to now-empty saucepan and return to simmer, adjusting consistency with hot water as needed. Season with salt and pepper to taste.

4 Top each portion with 2 tablespoons peanuts and 1 tablespoon cilantro. Serve.

MEAL PREP Soup can be refrigerated for up to 3 days.

Cal 440; Total Fat 20g;
Sat Fat 3g; Chol 0mg;
Sodium 840mg; Total Carb 55g;
Dietary Fiber 12g;
Total Sugars 18g; Protein 14g

POULTRY

CURRIED CHICKEN SALAD SANDWICHES WITH APRICOTS

Serves 2   Total Time: 45 minutes

WHEN TO EAT

> **Pre-Workout** 3 to 4 hours before
> **Post-Workout** Within 2 hours
> **Maintenance**

WORKOUTS

> **Strength or Interval**
> **Everyday** Serve with grapes or baked snack chips (see page 274).

MAKE IT A SNACK

Eat half a sandwich.

1 (6-ounce) boneless, skinless chicken breast, trimmed

1 teaspoon curry powder, divided

⅛ teaspoon table salt, divided

1½ teaspoons extra-virgin olive oil, divided

Pinch ground cinnamon

3 tablespoons plain low-fat yogurt

1 teaspoon lemon juice

2 tablespoons finely chopped dried apricots

2 tablespoons slivered almonds, toasted

2 tablespoons minced celery

2 scallions, sliced thin

2 large leaves Bibb, Boston, or iceberg lettuce

4 (2-ounce) slices whole-grain sandwich bread, toasted if desired

---

Cal 450; Total Fat 13g;
Sat Fat 1.5g; Chol 65mg;
Sodium 810mg; Total Carb 58g;
Dietary Fiber 8g;
Total Sugars 15g; Protein 31g

WHY THIS RECIPE WORKS ›› With the right modifications, chicken salad can be optimized to satisfy your goals and appetite, and feel just as creamy and delicious as any version of the beloved deli salad. We replaced the traditional mayonnaise with low-fat yogurt in this protein-packed sandwich filling—the yogurt keeps the fat amount in check while also providing great tang. We bloomed curry powder and cinnamon with oil in the microwave for extra flavor, then whisked them into the creamy dressing; their warm notes pair nicely with the nutty and fiberful whole-grain bread. This recipe can easily be doubled using a 10- or 12-inch skillet.

1 Pat chicken dry with paper towels and sprinkle with ½ teaspoon curry powder and pinch salt. Heat ½ teaspoon oil in 8- or 10-inch skillet over medium heat until just smoking. Add chicken and cook until well browned on first side, about 3 minutes. Flip chicken, add 2 tablespoons water, and cover skillet. Reduce heat to low and cook until chicken registers 160 degrees, about 3 minutes. Transfer chicken to cutting board, let cool for 15 minutes, then cut into ½-inch pieces.

2 Microwave cinnamon, remaining ½ teaspoon curry powder, and remaining 1 teaspoon oil in large bowl until fragrant, about 10 seconds; let cool slightly. Whisk in yogurt, lemon juice, and remaining pinch salt.

3 Add chicken, apricots, almonds, celery, and scallions and toss to combine. Season with salt and pepper to taste. Divide lettuce leaves and chicken salad between 2 slices of bread, then top with remaining bread slices. Serve.

MEAL PREP Chicken salad can be refrigerated for up to 2 days.

POULTRY

93

CHIPOTLE CHICKEN TACOS WITH RADISH AND CILANTRO SALAD

Serves 2   **Total Time: 45 minutes**

WHEN TO EAT
› **Pre-Workout** 3 to 4 hours before
› **Post-Workout** Within 2 hours

WORKOUTS
› **Strength or Interval**
› **Everyday** Serve with a simple grain (see pages 284–287).

MAKE IT A SNACK
Eat 2 tacos.

---

1 teaspoon canola oil

2 garlic cloves, minced

1 teaspoon minced canned chipotle chile in adobo sauce

½ cup orange juice

¼ cup fresh cilantro leaves, plus 1 tablespoon chopped

1 tablespoon Worcestershire sauce

1 teaspoon yellow mustard

¼ teaspoon table salt

6 ounces boneless, skinless chicken thighs, trimmed

8 radishes, trimmed, halved, and sliced thin

1½ teaspoons lime juice, plus lime wedges for serving

6 (6-inch) corn tortillas, warmed

¼ cup crumbled cotija cheese

Cal 390; Total Fat 13g;
Sat Fat 3.5g; Chol 95mg;
Sodium 830mg; Total Carb 44g;
Dietary Fiber 1g; Total Sugars 7g;
Protein 24g

WHY THIS RECIPE WORKS ›› While we love slow-cooked taco fillings, sometimes we want quick chicken tacos that we can make any night of the week around working out. We poach moist boneless, skinless thighs for just 10 minutes in a liquid of orange juice, garlic, and canned chipotle chiles that imbues the chicken with fruity heat. The poaching liquid thickens to a flavorful sauce for the chicken that we then brighten by topping with a radish salad. To warm tortillas, wrap them in a damp dish towel and microwave until warm and pliable, about 30 seconds. Alternatively, heat individual tortillas in dry skillet or over gas flame. This recipe can easily be doubled using a large saucepan.

1 Heat oil in small saucepan over medium heat until shimmering. Add garlic and chipotle and cook until fragrant, about 30 seconds. Stir in orange juice, chopped cilantro, Worcestershire, mustard, and salt and bring to simmer. Nestle chicken into sauce. Reduce heat to medium-low, cover, and cook until chicken registers 175 degrees, 10 to 12 minutes, flipping chicken halfway through cooking.

2 Remove saucepan from heat. Transfer chicken to cutting board, let cool slightly, then shred into bite-size pieces using 2 forks. Return chicken and any accumulated juices to saucepan and cook over low heat until sauce is slightly thickened and chicken is heated through, 2 to 4 minutes.

3 Combine radishes, lime juice, and cilantro leaves in bowl; season with salt and pepper to taste. Divide chicken among tortillas, then top with radish salad and cotija. Serve tacos with lime wedges.

MEAL PREP Chicken filling can be refrigerated for up to 2 days.

STEAMED BAO WITH HOISIN CHICKEN AND CUCUMBER

Serves 2   Total Time: 40 minutes

WHEN TO EAT
› **Pre-Workout** 3 to 4 hours before
› **Post-Workout** Within 2 hours

WORKOUTS
› **Everyday**
› **Endurance** Serve with cooked rice (see page 285).
› **Strength or Interval** Increase chicken to 8 ounces.

MAKE IT A SNACK
Eat 1 bao.

---

1 teaspoon canola oil

2 scallions, white and green parts separated and sliced thin

¼ cup hoisin sauce

2 tablespoons water

1 (6-ounce) boneless, skinless chicken breast, trimmed

2 teaspoons toasted sesame seeds

6 (1-ounce) frozen lotus leaf bao

¼ English cucumber, quartered lengthwise and sliced thin

½ cup fresh cilantro leaves and stems, trimmed

Lime wedges

Sriracha

Cal 560; Total Fat 12g;
Sat Fat 1g; Chol 65mg;
Sodium 590mg; Total Carb 86g;
Dietary Fiber 2g;
Total Sugars 17g; Protein 32g

WHY THIS RECIPE WORKS ›› A beloved street food in many parts of Asia, pleasantly sweet, pillowy stuffed bao buns (here with glazed chicken instead of the traditional pork) contain an ideal balance of carbs and protein for any everyday athlete. You can find frozen, presteamed lotus leaf bao, distinguished by their flat and folded shape, at Asian grocery stores and online. This recipe can easily be doubled using a large saucepan.

1 Heat oil in small saucepan over medium heat until shimmering. Add scallion whites and cook until softened, about 1 minute. Stir in hoisin and water and bring to simmer. Nestle chicken into sauce. Reduce heat to medium-low, cover, and cook until chicken registers 160 degrees, 10 to 12 minutes, flipping chicken halfway through cooking.

2 Remove saucepan from heat. Transfer chicken to cutting board, let cool slightly, then shred into bite-size pieces using 2 forks. Return chicken to saucepan and cook over low heat until sauce is thickened and chicken is heated through, 2 to 4 minutes. Stir in sesame seeds and scallion greens.

3 Cut piece of parchment slightly smaller than diameter of bamboo or collapsible steamer basket; place parchment in basket. Poke 20 small holes in parchment and lightly spray with canola oil spray. Place bao on parchment, making sure they are not touching. Set basket over simmering water and cook, covered, until puffed and heated through, 4 to 6 minutes. Remove basket from water and let bao cool for 5 minutes. (Or, wrap frozen bao in damp dish towel. Place on plate and microwave for about 1 minute, flipping halfway through microwaving). Divide chicken among bao, then top with cucumber and cilantro. Serve with lime wedges and sriracha.

MEAL PREP Chicken filling can be refrigerated for up to 2 days.

MANGO TURKEY SLOPPY JOES

Serves 2   **Total Time: 30 minutes**

WHEN TO EAT
› **Pre-Workout** 3 to 4 hours before
› **Post-Workout** Within 2 hours
› **Maintenance**

WORKOUTS
› **Everyday**
› **Endurance** Serve with grapes or baked snack chips (see page 274).
› **Strength or Interval** Increase turkey to 6 ounces.

½ cup coleslaw mix

2½ teaspoons cider vinegar, divided

1 tablespoon canola oil

½ red, orange, or yellow bell pepper, chopped fine

1 shallot, chopped fine

1 garlic clove, minced

½ teaspoon chili powder

4 ounces 93 percent lean ground turkey

1 (8-ounce) can tomato sauce

1 cup fresh or thawed frozen mango chunks, chopped

2 teaspoons packed brown sugar

1 teaspoon Worcestershire sauce

2 burger buns, toasted if desired

Cal 390; Total Fat 10g;
Sat Fat 2g; Chol 20mg; Sodium
840mg; Total Carb 57g;
Dietary Fiber 7g;
Total Sugars 30g; Protein 22g

WHY THIS RECIPE WORKS ›› We didn't want a classic sloppy joe again after tasting this lighter, balanced take with bright, flavorful additions. Saucing the sloppy filling with a can of tomato sauce seasoned with chili powder and garlic was an appealing alternative to the cloying ketchup found in many version. Mixing naturally sweet jewel-size bites of mango into the sauce not only bulked up our sloppy joe, it replaced some of the turkey, providing more beneficial carbs and fiber. You can substitute ½ cup shredded red or green cabbage for the coleslaw mix and lean ground chicken for the turkey. Fresh or thawed frozen mango will work in this recipe. This recipe can easily be doubled using a 12-inch skillet.

1 Toss coleslaw mix and 1½ teaspoons vinegar together in small bowl. Season with salt and pepper to taste; set aside.

2 Heat oil in 10- or 12-inch nonstick skillet over medium heat until shimmering. Add bell pepper and shallot and cook until softened and lightly browned, 4 to 6 minutes. Stir in garlic and chili powder and cook until fragrant, about 30 seconds.

3 Add turkey and cook, breaking up meat with wooden spoon, until no longer pink, about 2 minutes. Stir in tomato sauce, mango, sugar, Worcestershire, and remaining 1 teaspoon vinegar. Bring to simmer and cook until sauce is slightly thickened, 3 to 5 minutes. Season with salt and pepper to taste. Divide turkey mixture between bun bottoms, then top with coleslaw mixture and bun tops. Serve.

MEAL PREP Cabbage slaw and turkey mixture can be refrigerated separately for up to 2 days.

CHICKEN, ARTICHOKE, AND SPINACH CALZONES

Serves 2   Total Time: 50 minutes

WHEN TO EAT
› **Post-Workout** Within 2 hours
› **Maintenance**

WORKOUTS
› **Strength or Interval**
› **Everyday** Serve with grapes or baked snack chips (see page 274).

MAKE IT A SNACK
Eat half a calzone

- ½ cup shredded cooked chicken
- 4 ounces frozen artichoke hearts, thawed, patted dry, and chopped
- 4 ounces frozen chopped spinach, thawed and squeezed dry
- 1 ounce part-skim block mozzarella cheese, shredded (¼ cup)
- ¼ cup crumbled feta cheese
- 2 tablespoons chopped fresh basil
- ⅛ teaspoon table salt
- ⅛ teaspoon pepper
- 8 ounces store-bought pizza dough, room temperature, split into 2 pieces
- 2 teaspoons extra-virgin olive oil

Cal 550; Total Fat 16g;
Sat Fat 6g; Chol 70mg;
Sodium 870mg; Total Carb 61g;
Dietary Fiber 6g; Total Sugars 1g;
Protein 37g

WHY THIS RECIPE WORKS ›› Leave the heavy lifting at the gym, and use chicken you've already cooked (see page 289) or rotisserie chicken for these deceptively simple calzones. They're a convenient, portable package for a hearty filling of artichoke hearts and spinach mixed with mozzarella (for melt) and feta cheese (for flavor). Pizza dough is often sold in 1-pound packages. Leftover dough can be used to make Skillet Pizza with Broccoli and Red Onion (page 198). This recipe can easily be doubled.

1 Adjust oven rack to middle position and heat oven to 475 degrees. Line rimmed baking sheet with aluminum foil and spray with canola oil spray. Combine chicken, artichokes, spinach, mozzarella, feta, basil, salt, and pepper in bowl.

2 Press and roll 1 dough piece into 8-inch round on lightly floured counter. Spread half of chicken mixture evenly over bottom half of round, leaving 1 inch border at edge. Fold top half of dough over filling and crimp edges to seal; transfer to prepared sheet. Repeat with remaining dough and filling.

3 Using sharp knife, cut two 1-inch steam vents on top of each calzone, then brush tops evenly with oil. Bake until golden brown, 18 to 22 minutes, rotating halfway through baking. Transfer calzones to wire rack and let cool for 5 minutes before serving.

MEAL PREP Baked calzones can be refrigerated for up to 2 days. Reheat in 400-degree oven until internal temperature reaches 160 degrees, 25 to 30 minutes.

CHICKEN AND RICE SALAD WITH TURMERIC AND HERBS

Serves 2   Total Time: 1 hour

WHEN TO EAT
› **Pre-Workout** 3 to 4 hours before
› **Post-Workout** Within 2 hours

WORKOUTS
› **Strength or Interval**
› **Everyday** Increase rice to 1 cup and water (for cooking rice) to 1⅔ cups.

¾ cup long-grain white rice, rinsed

½ teaspoon table salt, divided

3½ teaspoons extra-virgin olive oil, divided

1 garlic clove, minced

¾ teaspoon ground turmeric, divided

½ teaspoon ground cumin

½ teaspoon paprika

1 tablespoon lemon juice

1 (6-ounce) boneless, skinless chicken breast, trimmed

4 ounces cherry or grape tomatoes, halved

⅓ English cucumber, quartered lengthwise and sliced thin

2 radishes, trimmed, halved, and sliced thin

¼ cup torn fresh cilantro, dill, parsley, or mint

¼ cup Herb Yogurt Sauce (page 303)

Cal 460; Total Fat 11g;
Sat Fat 2g; Chol 65mg;
Sodium 650mg; Total Carb 62g;
Dietary Fiber 2g; Total Sugars 5g;
Protein 28g

WHY THIS RECIPE WORKS ›› Look further than lettuce: An easily transportable rice salad with ample carbohydrates can fuel or replenish much better. We combine turmeric, garlic, paprika, and cumin in a fragrant dressing for warm rice, tasty bites of chicken, and crunchy, refreshing vegetables. This recipe can easily be doubled using a large pot and a 10- to 12-inch skillet.

1 Bring rice, 1¼ cups water, and ⅛ teaspoon salt to simmer in large saucepan over medium heat. Reduce heat to low, cover, and simmer until rice is tender and liquid is absorbed, 16 to 18 minutes. Remove pot from heat, lay clean folded dish towel underneath lid, and let sit for 10 minutes. Fluff rice with fork and season with salt and pepper to taste; set aside.

2 Microwave 1 tablespoon oil, garlic, ½ teaspoon turmeric, cumin, and paprika in large bowl until fragrant, about 10 seconds; let cool slightly. Whisk in lemon juice, 1 tablespoon water, and ⅛ teaspoon salt; set aside.

3 Pat chicken dry with paper towels and sprinkle with remaining ¼ teaspoon salt and remaining ¼ teaspoon turmeric. Heat remaining ½ teaspoon oil in 8- or 10-inch skillet over medium heat until just smoking. Add chicken and cook until well browned on first side, about 3 minutes. Flip chicken, add 2 tablespoons water, and cover skillet. Reduce heat to low and cook until chicken registers 160 degrees, about 3 minutes. Transfer chicken to cutting board, let cool slightly, then cut into ½-inch pieces.

4 To bowl with oil-spice mixture, add rice, chicken and any accumulated juices, tomatoes, cucumber, radishes, and cilantro and toss to combine. Season with salt and pepper to taste. Drizzle each portion with 2 tablespoons yogurt sauce. Serve warm or at room temperature.

MEAL PREP Rice salad and yogurt sauce can be refrigerated separately for up to 2 days.

CHICKEN AND BARLEY SALAD WITH HARISSA AND ORANGE

Serves 2   Total Time: 1 hour

WHEN TO EAT
› **Post-Workout** Within 2 hours
› **Maintenance**

WORKOUTS
› **Everyday**
› **Strength or Interval** Increase chicken to 8 ounces.

MAKE IT A SNACK
Eat half a portion.

¾ cup pearl barley

½ teaspoon table salt, plus salt for cooking barley

1 (6-ounce) boneless, skinless chicken breast, trimmed

2 tablespoons harissa, divided

½ teaspoon extra-virgin olive oil

1 orange

1 tablespoon lemon juice

2 carrots, peeled and shredded

2 tablespoons raisins

2 tablespoons chopped fresh mint, cilantro, or parsley

Cal 580; Total Fat 16g;
Sat Fat 2.5g; Chol 60mg;
Sodium 900mg; Total Carb 84g;
Dietary Fiber 17g;
Total Sugars 18g; Protein 29g

WHY THIS RECIPE WORKS ›› Good-for-you grains and lean, satisfying chicken are coated in a harissa dressing in this salad—the heat brightened with fresh orange and sweetened with carrots and raisins. Plus, it makes perfect leftovers because you can enjoy the salad at any temperature. Do not substitute hulled or hull-less barley in this recipe. If using quick-cooking or presteamed barley, decrease the cooking time in step 1. We prefer to use our homemade Harissa (page 302) but you can substitute store-bought. This recipe can easily be doubled using a large pot and a 10- or 12-inch skillet.

1 Bring 2 quarts water to boil in large saucepan. Add barley and ½ teaspoon salt, return to boil, and cook until grains are tender with slight chew, 20 to 40 minutes. Drain barley, spread onto plate or rimmed baking sheet, and let cool completely, 10 to 15 minutes.

2 Pat chicken dry with paper towels and rub with 1 teaspoon harissa. Heat oil in 8- or 10-inch skillet over medium heat until just smoking. Add chicken and cook until well browned on first side, about 3 minutes. Flip chicken, add 2 tablespoons water, and cover skillet. Reduce heat to low and cook until chicken registers 160 degrees, about 3 minutes. Transfer chicken to cutting board, let cool slightly, then shred into bite-size pieces using 2 forks.

3 Cut away peel and pith from orange. Quarter orange, then slice crosswise into ¼-inch-thick pieces. Whisk remaining 5 teaspoons harissa, lemon juice, and ½ teaspoon salt together in large bowl. Add barley, chicken, orange, carrots, raisins, and mint and toss to combine. Season with salt and pepper to taste. Serve warm or at room temperature.

MEAL PREP Salad can be refrigerated for up to 2 days.

LEMON-HERB COUSCOUS WITH CHICKEN AND DRIED CHERRIES

Serves 2   Total Time: 40 minutes

WHEN TO EAT
› **Pre-Workout** 3 to 4 hours before
› **Post-Workout** Within 2 hours

WORKOUTS
› **Everyday**
› **Endurance** Increase couscous and boiling water to 1 cup each.
› **Strength or Interval** Increase chicken to 8 ounces.

---

1 tablespoon extra-virgin olive oil, divided

1 tablespoon lemon juice

1 small shallot, minced

1 garlic clove, minced

¾ cup boiling water

¾ cup couscous

½ teaspoon table salt, divided

1 (6-ounce) boneless, skinless chicken breast, trimmed and cut into ¾-inch pieces

⅛ teaspoon pepper

2 tablespoons chopped dried tart cherries

¼ cup chopped fresh dill, parsley, mint, and/or tarragon

—

Cal 540; Total Fat 13g;
Sat Fat 2g; Chol 60mg;
Sodium 770mg; Total Carb 75g;
Dietary Fiber 4g;
Total Sugars 7g; Protein 32g

WHY THIS RECIPE WORKS ›› For an easy, flavor-studded couscous to satisfy the busy athlete, there's no need to settle for flimsy box instructions—and forget that dusty spice packet. You'll toss this loaded, herbaceous couscous dish together in no time, and you won't need to reheat it when you take leftovers to the gym or work. Cutting chicken into small pieces and incorporating them into the dish gives it on-the-go capabilities—no knife and folk needed. The combination of bright lemon juice, shallot, and garlic contrasted against recovery-promoting dried tart cherries and fresh herbs means you'll want to double the recipe for easy meals all week long. For an accurate measurement of boiling water, bring a kettle of water to a boil and then measure out the desired amount. This recipe can easily be doubled using a 10- or 12-inch skillet.

1 Whisk 2 teaspoons oil, lemon juice, shallot, and garlic together in small bowl; set aside. Combine boiling water, couscous, and ¼ teaspoon salt in large bowl. Cover and let sit for 10 minutes. Fluff couscous with fork; set aside.

2 Pat chicken dry with paper towels and sprinkle with remaining ¼ teaspoon salt and pepper. Heat remaining 1 teaspoon oil in 8- or 10-inch skillet over medium-high heat until shimmering. Add chicken and cook until lightly browned on all sides and cooked through, 3 to 5 minutes.

3 Transfer chicken to bowl with couscous. Add oil-shallot mixture, cherries, and dill and gently toss to combine. Season with salt and pepper to taste. Serve warm or at room temperature.

MEAL PREP Couscous with chicken can be refrigerated for up to 3 days.

CHICKEN AND WHITE BEAN PANZANELLA

Serves 2   **Total Time: 30 minutes**

WHEN TO EAT
› **Post-Workout** Within 2 hours
› **Maintenance**

WORKOUTS
› **Strength or Interval**
› **Everyday** Serve with grapes.

---

5 teaspoons extra-virgin olive oil, divided

1 tablespoon red wine vinegar

⅛ teaspoon table salt, divided

⅛ teaspoon pepper, divided

8 ounces tomatoes, cored and chopped, seeds and juice reserved

1 (15-ounce) can cannellini beans, rinsed

1 shallot, sliced thin

2 tablespoons chopped fresh basil

3 (2-ounce) slices whole-grain sandwich bread, cut or torn into ½- to ¾-inch pieces

1 (6-ounce) boneless, skinless chicken breast, trimmed and cut into ¾-inch pieces

1 ounce (about 1 cup) baby arugula

½ ounce Parmesan cheese, shaved with vegetable peeler

Cal 610; Total Fat 20g;
Sat Fat 4g; Chol 65mg;
Sodium 900mg; Total Carb 66g;
Dietary Fiber 11g;
Total Sugars 11g; Protein 42g

WHY THIS RECIPE WORKS ›› With its base of bread, panzanella is a treat for the recovering athlete. And incorporating chicken (and beans) into the bread salad is surprisingly streamlined when you take your toasting to a skillet: We skip the oven and baking sheet and crisp the bread cubes on the stove before cooking the chicken. Then we add a quick shallot-basil vinaigrette to marinate the tomatoes and beans as well as permeate the toasted bread. It might come as a pleasant surprise that the salad can be ready whenever you are: With the toasted bread it is flavorful—but not soggy—the next day. This recipe can easily be doubled using a 12-inch skillet.

1 Whisk 2 teaspoons oil, vinegar, pinch salt, and pinch pepper together in large bowl. Add tomatoes with their seeds and juice, beans, shallot, and basil and toss to coat; set aside.

2 Heat 2 teaspoons oil in 10- or 12-inch skillet over medium heat until shimmering. Add bread and cook, stirring frequently, until browned and crisp, 6 to 8 minutes. Transfer bread to bowl with tomato mixture and gently toss to combine. Wipe skillet clean with paper towels.

3 Pat chicken dry with paper towels and sprinkle with remaining pinch salt and remaining pinch pepper. Heat remaining 1 teaspoon oil in now-empty skillet over medium-high heat until shimmering. Add chicken and cook until lightly browned on all sides and cooked through, 3 to 5 minutes.

4 Transfer chicken to bowl with bread mixture, add arugula, and gently toss to combine. Season with salt and pepper to taste. Top each portion with Parmesan. Serve warm or at room temperature.

MEAL PREP Panzanella can be refrigerated for up to 1 day.

CHICKEN BUN CHA BOWLS

Serves 2   Total Time: 40 minutes

WHEN TO EAT
› **Pre-Workout** 3 to 4 hours before
› **Post-Workout** Within 2 hours

WORKOUTS
› **Everyday**
› **Endurance** Increase noodles to 6 ounces.
› **Strength or Interval** Increase chicken to 8 ounces.

¼ cup hot water

5 teaspoons fish sauce, divided

¾ teaspoon grated lime zest plus 4 teaspoons lime juice, plus lime wedges for serving

1 tablespoon plus ½ teaspoon sugar, divided

½ Thai chile, stemmed and minced

1 garlic clove, minced

4 ounces rice vermicelli noodles

½ teaspoon canola oil

1 small shallot, minced

¼ teaspoon pepper

¼ teaspoon baking soda

6 ounces ground chicken

1 carrot, peeled and shaved into ribbons with vegetable peeler

¼ English cucumber, quartered lengthwise and sliced thin

¼ cup torn fresh mint leaves

—

Cal 410; Total Fat 9g; Sat Fat 2g;
Chol 75mg; Sodium 830mg;
Total Carb 62g; Dietary Fiber 3g;
Total Sugars 10g; Protein 21g

WHY THIS RECIPE WORKS ›› In this exceptionally storage-friendly take on Vietnamese bun cha, lean ground chicken stands in for the usual pork. The protein-packed chicken patties are flavored with fish sauce, shallot, lime zest, and black pepper and sit atop a bed of rice noodles that provide ample carbs to fuel and support. Bonus: The dressed rice noodles don't clump so you can eat one bowl and completely assemble the second one for lunch tomorrow. For a milder dish, omit the Thai chile. Do not substitute other types of noodles here. This recipe can easily be doubled using a large pot and cooking chicken patties in 2 batches.

1 Whisk hot water, 1 tablespoon fish sauce, lime juice, 1 tablespoon sugar, Thai chile, and garlic together in small bowl until sugar dissolves; set sauce aside. Bring 2 quarts water to boil in large saucepan. Off heat, add noodles and let sit, stirring occasionally, until tender, about 5 minutes. Drain noodles, rinse well, and drain again. Toss noodles with oil; set aside.

2 Spray 10- or 12-inch nonstick skillet evenly with canola oil spray. Combine lime zest, shallot, pepper, baking soda, remaining 2 teaspoons fish sauce, and remaining ½ teaspoon sugar in medium bowl. Add chicken and gently knead with hands until well combined. Using your moistened hands, form chicken mixture into six 2-inch-wide patties and place in prepared skillet. Cook patties over medium-high heat until well browned and meat registers 160 degrees, 2 to 4 minutes per side. Transfer patties to bowl with sauce and gently toss to coat. Let sit for 5 minutes.

3 Divide noodles between serving bowls, then top each portion with carrot, cucumber, and chicken patties. Drizzle remaining sauce over noodles and vegetables and sprinkle with mint. Serve with lime wedges.

MEAL PREP Fully assembled bowl can be refrigerated for up to 2 days.

CREAMY BUTTERNUT SQUASH ORZO WITH CHICKEN

Serves 2   **Total Time: 50 minutes**

WHEN TO EAT
› **Pre-Workout** 3 to 4 hours before
› **Post-Workout** Within 2 hours
› **Maintenance**

WORKOUTS
› **Everyday**
› **Endurance** Increase orzo to ¾ cup and broth to 2⅔ cups.
› **Strength or Interval** Increase chicken to 8 ounces.

- ⅓ cup panko bread crumbs
- 1 tablespoon extra-virgin olive oil, divided
- 2 tablespoons minced fresh chives
- 1 teaspoon lemon zest plus 1 teaspoon juice, plus lemon wedges for serving
- 1 (6-ounce) boneless, skinless chicken breast, trimmed and cut into ¾-inch pieces
- Pinch table salt
- ⅛ teaspoon pepper
- ⅔ cup orzo
- 2 garlic cloves, minced
- 12 ounces butternut squash, peeled, seeded, and cut into ½-inch pieces (2 cups)
- 2 cups chicken broth, plus extra as needed
- 2 ounces (2 cups) baby spinach
- 1 tablespoon grated Parmesan cheese

Cal 530; Total Fat 12g;
Sat Fat 2g; Chol 65mg;
Sodium 870mg; Total Carb 72g;
Dietary Fiber 6g;
Total Sugars 7g; Protein 33g

WHY THIS RECIPE WORKS ›› This comforting, risotto-like dish is as satisfying and familiar as creamy casseroles, but with lighter ingredients and less dairy. Cutting the chicken into small morsels means that everything—orzo, squash, spinach, Parmesan cheese, and chicken—can be stirred together and eaten at once. A lemon-chive panko topping is the perfect contrast to the creamy orzo for extra crunch (and exercise-necessary carbs). This recipe can easily be doubled using a Dutch oven.

1 Microwave panko and 1 teaspoon oil in bowl, stirring occasionally, until golden, 2 to 4 minutes; let cool completely. Stir in chives and lemon zest and season with salt and pepper to taste; set aside.

2 Pat chicken dry with paper towels and sprinkle with salt and pepper. Heat 1 teaspoon oil in large saucepan over medium-high heat until shimmering. Add chicken and cook until lightly browned on all sides, 3 to 5 minutes; transfer to plate.

3 Heat remaining 1 teaspoon oil in now-empty saucepan over medium heat. Add orzo and garlic and cook until fragrant, about 1 minute. Stir in squash and broth, bring to simmer, and cook, stirring often, until orzo and squash are tender, about 15 minutes.

4 Off heat, stir in spinach, chicken and any accumulated juices, and lemon juice. Let sit until spinach is wilted and sauce is thickened, about 5 minutes. Stir in Parmesan until creamy; adjust consistency with extra hot broth as needed. Season with salt and pepper to taste. Top each portion with panko mixture. Serve with lemon wedges.

MEAL PREP Cooked chicken and orzo mixture can be refrigerated for up to 3 days. Top with panko mixture before serving.

PENNE WITH CHICKEN CACCIATORE SAUCE

Serves 2   Total Time: 40 minutes

WHEN TO EAT
› **Pre-Workout** 3 to 4 hours before
› **Post-Workout** Within 2 hours

WORKOUTS
› **Strength or Interval**
› **Everyday** Serve with bread.

---

1 (6-ounce) boneless, skinless chicken breast, trimmed and cut into ¾-inch pieces

¼ teaspoon table salt, plus salt for cooking pasta

⅛ teaspoon pepper

1 tablespoon extra-virgin olive oil, divided

4 ounces white mushrooms, trimmed and quartered

1 small onion, chopped fine

2 garlic cloves, minced

1 teaspoon minced fresh thyme or ¼ teaspoon dried

¼ teaspoon red pepper flakes

¼ cup dry red wine

1 (14.5-ounce) can diced tomatoes

6 ounces (2 cups) penne, ziti, or fusilli pasta

2 tablespoons chopped fresh parsley

—

Cal 560; Total Fat 11g;
Sat Fat 1.5g; Chol 60mg;
Sodium 860mg; Total Carb 79g;
Dietary Fiber 6g;
Total Sugars 10g; Protein 33g

WHY THIS RECIPE WORKS ›› Chicken cacciatore is a beloved braise; we pack all its flavor into a tomatoey, herby sauce with savory bite-size pieces of chicken to surround sport-supporting pasta. And if you haven't planned dinner ahead of your workout, this creative dish can be ready in under 45 minutes. For a milder dish, omit the pepper flakes. This recipe can easily be doubled using a 12-inch skillet and a large pot.

1 Pat chicken dry with paper towels and sprinkle with ¼ teaspoon salt and pepper. Heat 1 teaspoon oil in 10- or 12-inch skillet over medium-high heat until shimmering. Add chicken and cook until lightly browned on all sides, 3 to 5 minutes; transfer to plate.

2 Heat remaining 2 teaspoons oil in now-empty skillet over medium-high heat until shimmering. Add mushrooms and onion and cook until softened and lightly browned, 6 to 8 minutes. Stir in garlic, thyme, and pepper flakes and cook until fragrant, about 30 seconds.

3 Stir in wine, scraping up any browned bits, and cook until nearly evaporated, about 1 minute. Stir in tomatoes and their juice and simmer until sauce is slightly thickened, about 5 minutes. Stir in chicken and any accumulated juices and simmer until heated through, about 2 minutes. Season with salt and pepper to taste.

4 Meanwhile, bring 2 quarts water to boil in large saucepan. Add pasta and 1½ teaspoons salt and cook, stirring often, until al dente. Reserve ¼ cup cooking water, then drain pasta and return it to saucepan.

5 Add sauce to pasta and cook over medium heat until heated through, about 1 minute; adjust consistency with reserved pasta water as needed. Stir in parsley and season with salt and pepper to taste. Serve.

MEAL PREP Pasta can be refrigerated for up to 2 days.

FARFALLE AND CHICKEN WITH KALE PESTO AND CHERRY TOMATOES

Serves 2   **Total Time: 25 minutes**

WHEN TO EAT
› **Pre-Workout** 3 to 4 hours before
› **Post-Workout** Within 2 hours

WORKOUTS
› **Strength or Interval**
› **Everyday** Serve with bread.

- 6 ounces (2½ cups) farfalle pasta
- ½ teaspoon table salt, divided, plus salt for cooking pasta
- 1 (6-ounce) boneless, skinless chicken breast, trimmed and cut into ¾-inch pieces
- ⅛ teaspoon pepper
- ½ teaspoon extra-virgin olive oil
- 6 ounces cherry or grape tomatoes, halved
- 3 tablespoons Kale and Sunflower Seed Pesto (page 303)
- 2 tablespoons chopped fresh basil leaves
- 1 tablespoon grated Parmesan cheese

WHY THIS RECIPE WORKS ›› Herby, verdant, and aromatic, pesto gets even better—and better for you—when bolstered with kale and featuring complementary earthy sunflower seeds rather than pine nuts. Low in fat and sodium, the pesto is perfect for coating pasta before or after exercising. Sautéed chicken breast bulks up the dish with some protein, and cherry tomatoes offer welcome pops of sweetness. Farfalle is our pasta of choice in this dish; you can substitute 6 ounces of campanelle or medium shells, but the cup amounts will differ. This recipe can easily be doubled using a 12-inch skillet and a large pot.

1 Bring 2 quarts water to boil in large saucepan. Add pasta and 1½ teaspoons salt and cook, stirring often, until tender. Reserve ¼ cup cooking water, then drain pasta and return it to saucepan.

2 Meanwhile, pat chicken dry with paper towels and sprinkle with ¼ teaspoon salt and pepper. Heat oil in 10- or 12-inch skillet over medium-high heat until shimmering. Add chicken and cook until lightly browned on all sides, 3 to 5 minutes. Stir in cherry tomatoes and remaining ¼ teaspoon salt and cook until tomatoes are softened slightly, about 2 minutes.

3 Off heat, add chicken mixture and pesto to pasta and toss to combine; adjust consistency with reserved pasta water as needed. Season with salt and pepper to taste, and sprinkle with basil and Parmesan. Serve.

MEAL PREP Pasta can be refrigerated for up to 2 days.

Cal 510; Total Fat 13g;
Sat Fat 2g; Chol 65mg;
Sodium 900mg; Total Carb 70g;
Dietary Fiber 5g; Total Sugars 3g;
Protein 34g

POULTRY

117

POMEGRANATE CHICKEN WITH FARRO AND CUCUMBER SALAD

Serves 2   **Total Time: 1 hour**

WHEN TO EAT
> **Post-Workout** Within 2 hours
> **Maintenance**

WORKOUTS
> **Everyday**
> **Endurance** Increase farro to 1 cup and orange juice to 3 tablespoons.
> **Strength or Interval** Increase bone-in chicken to 12 ounces.

¾ cup whole farro

½ teaspoon table salt, divided, plus salt for cooking farro

1 (10-ounce) bone-in split chicken breast, trimmed and pounded to even thickness

⅛ teaspoon pepper

2 tablespoons extra-virgin olive oil

5 teaspoons pomegranate molasses, divided

1 small shallot, minced

1 teaspoon grated orange zest plus 1 tablespoon juice

⅛ teaspoon ground cinnamon

⅓ English cucumber, quartered lengthwise and sliced thin

¼ cup pomegranate seeds

2 tablespoons chopped fresh mint, parsley, cilantro, or basil

1 tablespoon chopped toasted walnuts, pecans, almonds, or pistachios

—

Cal 540; Total Fat 20g;
Sat Fat 2.5g; Chol 40mg;
Sodium 750mg; Total Carb 71g;
Dietary Fiber 8g;
Total Sugars 15g; Protein 23g

WHY THIS RECIPE WORKS ›› In this pan-roasted method, we take advantage of a shortcut for roasting chicken breasts by utilizing the pan's lid to create a stovetop oven. The chicken is enveloped in heat that creates satisfying juiciness reminiscent of a whole bird. We serve the chicken with a farro and cucumber salad with pomegranate vinaigrette. Do not use quick-cooking or presteamed farro. The cooking time for farro can vary across brands, so check for doneness after 15 minutes. This recipe can easily be doubled using a large pot and a 10- or 12-inch nonstick skillet.

1 Bring 2 quarts water to boil in large saucepan. Add farro and ½ teaspoon salt, return to boil, and cook until grains are tender with slight chew, 15 to 30 minutes. Drain farro, spread onto plate or rimmed baking sheet, and let cool completely, 10 to 15 minutes.

2 Pat chicken dry with paper towels and sprinkle with ¼ teaspoon salt and pepper. Place chicken, skin side down, in cold 8- or 10-inch nonstick skillet. Cover skillet, place over medium-low heat, and cook chicken, without moving, until skin is deep golden brown, 12 to 18 minutes. Flip chicken and continue to cook, uncovered, until chicken registers 160 degrees, 5 to 10 minutes. Transfer chicken, skin side up, to cutting board and let rest for 5 minutes.

3 Whisk oil, 4 teaspoons pomegranate molasses, shallot, orange zest and juice, 1 teaspoon water, cinnamon, and remaining ¼ teaspoon salt together in large bowl. Add farro, cucumber, pomegranate seeds, mint, and walnuts and toss to combine. Season with salt and pepper to taste. Carve chicken from bones, slice ½ inch thick, and drizzle with remaining 1 teaspoon pomegranate molasses. Serve chicken with salad.

MEAL PREP Salad and cooked chicken can be refrigerated for up to 2 days.

POULTRY

CRISPY CHICKEN WITH CABBAGE SLAW AND TONKATSU SAUCE

Serves 2   Total Time: 30 minutes

WHEN TO EAT
› **Post-Workout** Within 2 hours

WORKOUTS
› **Everyday**
› **Endurance** Increase cooked rice to 3 cups.
› **Strength or Interval** Increase chicken to 8 ounces.

2 teaspoons lemon juice

2 teaspoons soy sauce, divided

½ teaspoon toasted sesame oil

1½ cups coleslaw mix

2 scallions, sliced thin

1 tablespoon ketchup

1 tablespoon water

1½ teaspoons Worcestershire sauce

½ teaspoon Dijon mustard

¾ cup panko bread crumbs, lightly crushed

1 large egg

1 (6-ounce) boneless, skinless chicken breast, trimmed, halved horizontally, and pounded ¼ inch thick

3 tablespoons canola oil

2 cups cooked rice (page 285), warmed

WHY THIS RECIPE WORKS ›› This simple pan-fried Japanese chicken dish with a quick, homemade barbecue sauce, crunchy cabbage salad, and rice is surprisingly apt for a post-workout refuel. We were able to achieve a craveable, crispy chicken with a fraction of the oil by using a 10-inch skillet and needed only 3 tablespoons to create an even fry. And the panko coating gives the chicken a carb boost. You can substitute 1½ cups shredded red or green cabbage for the coleslaw mix. To lightly crush panko, place in a zipper-lock bag and use a rolling pin. Be sure to remove any tenderloin from the breast before halving it; reserve for another use. This recipe can easily be doubled using a 12-inch skillet.

1 Whisk lemon juice, 1 teaspoon soy sauce, and sesame oil together in medium bowl. Add coleslaw mix and scallions and toss to combine. Season with salt and pepper to taste; set aside for serving.

2 Whisk ketchup, water, Worcestershire, mustard, and remaining 1 teaspoon soy sauce together in small bowl; set aside. Spread panko in shallow dish. Beat egg in second shallow dish. Working with 1 chicken cutlet at a time, dredge cutlets in egg, allowing excess to drip off, then coat both sides with panko, pressing gently to adhere.

3 Heat oil in 10-inch skillet over medium-high heat until shimmering. Add cutlets and cook until deep golden brown, 2 to 3 minutes per side. Serve cutlets with rice, coleslaw, and tonkatsu sauce.

MEAL PREP Slaw, sauce, cooked chicken, and rice can be refrigerated separately for up to 2 days.

Cal 650; Total Fat 19g;
Sat Fat 2g; Chol 110mg;
Sodium 730mg; Total Carb 86g;
Dietary Fiber 2g;
Total Sugars 5g; Protein 30g

RED CURRY CHICKEN AND SWEET POTATOES

Serves 2   **Total Time: 35 minutes**

WHEN TO EAT
› **Post-Workout** Within 2 hours
› **Maintenance**

WORKOUTS
› **Everyday**
› **Endurance** Increase cooked rice to 3 cups.
› **Strength or Interval** Increase chicken to 8 ounces.

---

6 ounces boneless, skinless chicken thighs, trimmed and cut into ¾-inch pieces

1 tablespoon Thai red curry paste

1 teaspoon canola oil

8 ounces sweet potatoes, peeled and cut into ½-inch pieces

½ cup canned coconut milk

¼ cup water

2 tablespoons chopped fresh cilantro

2 cups cooked rice (see page 285), warmed

2 scallions, sliced thin

Lime wedges

WHY THIS RECIPE WORKS ›› These tender cubes of sweet potato—simmered in coconut milk with chunks of browned chicken—are a creamy and satisfying starch source. Seasoning with Thai red curry paste makes for a savory-sweet curry that is tasty and exercise-friendly when served over a bed of rice. The remaining coconut milk can be frozen into cubes in an ice tray for use in other recipes. This recipe can easily be doubled in a 12-inch skillet.

1 Pat chicken dry with paper towels and toss with curry paste. Heat oil in 10- or 12-inch skillet over medium-high heat until shimmering. Add chicken and cook until lightly browned on all sides, 3 to 5 minutes.

2 Stir in sweet potatoes, coconut milk, and water, scraping up any browned bits, and bring to simmer. Reduce heat to medium-low, cover, and cook until potatoes are just tender, about 10 minutes.

3 Uncover and continue to simmer until sweet potatoes are fully tender, 6 to 8 minutes. Off heat, stir in cilantro and season with salt and pepper to taste. Top rice with chicken and sweet potatoes and sprinkle with scallions. Serve with lime wedges.

MEAL PREP Curry and rice can be refrigerated seperately for up to 2 days.

Cal 590; Total Fat 18g;
Sat Fat 12g; Chol 80mg;
Sodium 860mg; Total Carb 80g;
Dietary Fiber 6g;
Total Sugars 7g; Protein 25g

STIR-FRIED CHICKEN AND BROCCOLI

Serves 2   Total Time: 45 minutes

WHEN TO EAT
› **Pre-Workout** 3 to 4 hours before
› **Post-Workout** Within 2 hours
› **Maintenance**

WORKOUTS
› **Everyday**
› **Endurance** Increase cooked rice to 3 cups.
› **Strength or Interval** Increase chicken to 8 ounces.

---

2 tablespoons oyster sauce, divided

2 teaspoons packed brown sugar

2 teaspoons rice vinegar

1 teaspoon Asian chili-garlic sauce

1 teaspoon cornstarch, divided

1 (6-ounce) boneless, skinless chicken breast, trimmed and sliced crosswise ¼ inch thick

1 tablespoon canola oil, divided

8 ounces broccoli florets, cut into 1-inch pieces

1 red, orange, or yellow bell pepper, stemmed, seeded, and sliced thin

1 red onion, halved and sliced thin

1½ teaspoons grated fresh ginger

¼ cup chopped fresh basil and/or mint

2 cups cooked rice (see page 285), warmed

Cal 560; Total Fat 10g;
Sat Fat 1g; Chol 60mg;
Sodium 830mg; Total Carb 85g;
Dietary Fiber 7g; Total Sugars 12g;
Protein 31g

WHY THIS RECIPE WORKS ›› Satisfying vegetables (sweet bell pepper, onion, and earthy broccoli) are the stars of this stir-fry—they're enveloped in a gingery sauce that's pleasantly light but packed with flavor. A convenient boneless, skinless chicken breast contributes just the right amount of protein. Steaming and then stir-frying broccoli helps maintain its color and tender-crisp texture. This recipe can easily be doubled using a 12-inch skillet.

1 Whisk 5 teaspoons oyster sauce, 2 tablespoons water, sugar, vinegar, chili-garlic sauce, and ½ teaspoon cornstarch together in small bowl; set aside. Toss chicken with remaining 1 teaspoon oyster sauce, remaining ½ teaspoon cornstarch, and 1 teaspoon water; let sit for 5 minutes.

2 Heat 1 teaspoon oil in 10- or 12-inch nonstick skillet over medium-high heat until shimmering. Add chicken and cook until no longer pink, 1 to 2 minutes per side. Transfer to plate.

3 Add 1 teaspoon oil to now-empty skillet and increase heat to high. Add broccoli and cook for 30 seconds. Add ¼ cup water, cover, and reduce heat to medium. Steam broccoli until just tender, about 2 minutes.

4 Uncover broccoli, stir in bell pepper and onion, and cook until vegetables are tender and water is evaporated, about 3 minutes. Push vegetables to sides of skillet. Add remaining 1 teaspoon oil and ginger to center and cook, mashing mixture into skillet, until fragrant, about 30 seconds.

5 Return chicken and any accumulated juices to skillet and toss to combine. Stir in oyster sauce mixture and cook until sauce is slightly thickened, about 1 minute. Off heat, stir in basil. Serve with rice.

MEAL PREP Cooked chicken, vegetables, and rice can be refrigerated for up to 2 days.

ONE-POT CHICKEN AND RICE

Serves 2   Total Time: 1 hour

WHEN TO EAT
› **Pre-Workout** 3 to 4 hours before
› **Post-Workout** Within 2 hours

WORKOUTS
› **Everyday**
› **Endurance** Serve with baked tortilla chips (see page 274).
› **Strength or Interval** Increase chicken to 10 ounces.

4 garlic cloves, minced, divided

1 teaspoon minced fresh oregano or ¼ teaspoon dried

½ teaspoon paprika, divided

½ teaspoon ground coriander, divided

¼ teaspoon ground cumin, divided

¼ teaspoon table salt, divided

6 ounces boneless, skinless chicken thighs, trimmed and cut into 1-inch pieces

1 tablespoon canola oil

1 onion, chopped fine

1 green bell pepper, stemmed, seeded, and chopped fine

¾ cup long-grain white rice, rinsed

1¼ cups chicken broth

2 tomatoes, cored and chopped

2 tablespoons minced fresh cilantro

Lime wedges

—

Cal 490; Total Fat 11g;
Sat Fat 1.5g; Chol 80mg;
Sodium 740mg; Total Carb 71g;
Dietary Fiber 4g;
Total Sugars 8g; Protein 26g

**WHY THIS RECIPE WORKS ›› ** Inspired by arroz con pollo, we wanted to create a quick, pantry-friendly dish starring the failproof, fuel-boosting combination of rice and chicken. Cutting flavorful boneless, skinless chicken thighs into small pieces ensures that the chicken and rice cook at the same rate when covered. We spice our chicken, rice, and vegetables with a complementary mix of oregano, paprika, coriander, and cumin, bloomed and then simmered with chopped fresh tomatoes. This recipe can easily be doubled using a Dutch oven; increase broth to 2¼ cups.

1 Combine half of garlic, oregano, ¼ teaspoon paprika, ¼ teaspoon coriander, ⅛ teaspoon cumin, and ⅛ teaspoon salt in medium bowl. Add chicken and toss to coat.

2 Heat oil in large saucepan over medium heat until shimmering. Add onion, bell pepper, and remaining ⅛ teaspoon salt and cook until softened and lightly browned, 6 to 8 minutes. Stir in rice, remaining garlic, remaining ¼ teaspoon paprika, remaining ¼ teaspoon coriander, and remaining ⅛ teaspoon cumin and cook until fragrant, about 30 seconds. Stir in broth and tomatoes, scraping up any browned bits, and bring to boil.

3 Nestle chicken into rice mixture and reduce heat to low. Cover and simmer until rice is tender and liquid is absorbed, 16 to 18 minutes. Remove saucepan from heat, lay clean folded dish towel underneath lid, and let rest for 10 minutes. Fluff rice with fork and season with salt and pepper to taste. Sprinkle each portion with cilantro and serve with lime wedges.

MEAL PREP Cooked chicken and rice can be refrigerated for up to 3 days.

POULTRY

127

BEEF, PORK & LAMB

STEAK TACOS WITH NECTARINE SALSA

Serves 2   Total Time: 35 minutes

WHEN TO EAT
› **Pre-Workout** 3 to 4 hours before
› **Post-Workout** Within 2 hours
› **Maintenance**

WORKOUTS
› **Strength or Interval**
› **Everyday** Serve with a simple grain (see pages 284–287).

MAKE IT A SNACK
Eat 1 taco.

---

1 nectarine or peach, halved, pitted, and cut into ¼-inch pieces

½ red, orange, or yellow bell pepper, chopped fine

2 tablespoons chopped fresh cilantro

1 small shallot, minced

½ jalapeño pepper, seeded and minced

1 tablespoon lime juice, plus lime wedges for serving

½ teaspoon table salt, divided

⅛ teaspoon pepper

½ teaspoon ground cumin

½ teaspoon ground paprika

6 ounces flank steak, trimmed

1 teaspoon canola oil

6 (6-inch) corn tortillas, warmed

—

Cal 400; Total Fat 11g;
Sat Fat 2.5g; Chol 60mg;
Sodium 800mg; Total Carb 53g;
Dietary Fiber 3g;
Total Sugars 14g; Protein 24g

WHY THIS RECIPE WORKS ›› Lean flank steak is tucked into corn tortillas, along with an at-home nectarine salsa, for an excellent red-meat workout-boosting meal. The nectarines add pleasant sweetness and a lively tang while providing refueling carbs (in addition to the tortillas). To warm the tortillas, wrap them in a damp dish towel and microwave until warm and pliable, about 30 seconds. Alternatively, heat individual tortillas in a dry skillet or over a gas flame. This recipe can easily be doubled using a 12-inch skillet.

1 Combine nectarine, bell pepper, cilantro, shallot, jalapeño, lime juice, ¼ teaspoon salt, and pepper in bowl and toss to combine; set salsa aside.

2 Combine cumin, paprika, and remaining ¼ teaspoon salt in small bowl. Pat steak dry with paper towels and rub with spice mixture.

3 Heat oil in 10- or 12-inch skillet over medium-high heat until just smoking. Add steak and cook until well browned and meat registers 120 to 125 degrees (for medium-rare) or 130 to 135 degrees (for medium), 3 to 6 minutes per side. Transfer steak to cutting board, tent loosely with aluminum foil, and let rest for 5 minutes.

4 Slice steak thin against grain. Toss salsa to recombine and season with salt and pepper to taste. Divide steak among tortillas, then top with salsa. Serve tacos with lime wedges.

MEAL PREP Sliced steak and salsa can be refrigerated separately for up to 1 day.

SPICED LAMB FLATBREADS WITH CUCUMBER AND TOMATO SALAD

Serves 2 (makes 2 flatbreads)   **Total Time: 40 minutes**

WHEN TO EAT
› **Post-Workout** Within 2 hours
› **Maintenance**

WORKOUTS
› **Everyday**
› **Endurance** Serve with a simple grain (see pages 284–287).
› **Strength or Interval** Increase lamb to 6 ounces.

MAKE IT A SNACK
Eat half a flatbread plus 1 cup of salad.

½ English cucumber, quartered lengthwise and sliced thin

1 large tomato, cored and chopped

½ teaspoon table salt, divided

1 small red onion, sliced thin, divided

¼ cup chopped fresh parsley, divided

2½ teaspoons extra-virgin olive oil

2½ teaspoons lemon juice, plus lemon wedges for serving

1 red, orange, or yellow bell pepper, stemmed, seeded, and chopped

2 tablespoons tomato paste

4 teaspoons paprika

1 garlic clove, peeled

½ teaspoon ground allspice

½ teaspoon ground cumin

4 ounces ground lamb

2 (12 by 9-inch) lavash breads

Cal 500; Total Fat 19g;
Sat Fat 7g; Chol 40mg;
Sodium 770mg; Total Carb 60g;
Dietary Fiber 8g;
Total Sugars 10g; Protein 22g

WHY THIS RECIPE WORKS ›› Inspired by Armenian lahmajun, this delicate, meaty flatbread works with a busy athlete's schedule. Ground lamb processed to a paste with pantry spices tops store-bought lavash, with a refreshing salad on the side. If two flatbreads do not fit on your baking sheet, bake them in batches. This recipe can also easily be doubled by baking in batches.

1 Adjust oven rack to upper-middle position and heat oven to 500 degrees. Toss cucumber, tomato, and ¼ teaspoon salt in colander set over bowl and let drain for 15 minutes. Transfer drained vegetables to medium bowl; discard liquid. Add half of onion, 1 tablespoon parsley, oil, and lemon juice and toss to combine; set salad aside.

2 Process bell pepper, tomato paste, paprika, garlic, allspice, cumin, remaining onion, remaining 3 tablespoons parsley, and remaining ¼ teaspoon salt in food processor until finely chopped, about 15 seconds, scraping down sides of bowl as needed. Break lamb into small pieces and add to food processor; pulse to combine, 8 to 10 pulses.

3 Using back of spoon or rubber spatula, spread half of lamb mixture evenly over each lavash, leaving ⅛-inch border. Arrange lavash on greased baking sheet and bake until bottom is well browned and edges are lightly browned, 3 to 6 minutes. Transfer flatbreads to cutting board. Toss salad to recombine and season with salt and pepper to taste. Slice each flatbread into 6 pieces. Serve with salad and lemon wedges.

MEAL PREP Salad and lamb mixture can be refrigerated separately for up to 1 day. Baked flatbreads can be refrigerated for up to 1 day; reheat in 400-degree oven or eat at room temperature.

GRIDDLED PORK SANDWICHES

Serves 2   Total Time: 40 minutes

WHEN TO EAT
› **Post-Workout** Within 2 hours

WORKOUTS
› **Strength or Interval**
› **Everyday** Serve with grapes or baked snack chips (see page 274).

MAKE IT A SNACK
Eat half a sandwich.

1 (4-ounce) boneless pork chop, ½ to ¾ inch thick, trimmed

Pinch table salt

⅛ teaspoon pepper

1 teaspoon vegetable oil

2 tablespoons chopped dill pickles

2 tablespoons chopped jarred banana peppers

2 (6-inch) whole-grain sub rolls, split lengthwise

2 teaspoons mayonnaise

2 teaspoons yellow mustard

2 (½-ounce) slices Swiss cheese

1 teaspoon extra-virgin olive oil

WHY THIS RECIPE WORKS ›› This sandwich is a nod to the Cubano, but a little leaner and easier to put together on a workout day. Instead of slow-roasting pork shoulder and layering on salty ham, we simply sear lean pork chops and slice them thin. Sandwiching the chops in whole-grain rolls provides good fiber, and griddling the sandwiches melts the cheese and melds the flavors to make the sandwich taste rich. You can substitute white rolls for the whole-grain. This recipe can easily be doubled with two 4-ounce chops or one 8-ounce chop, using a 12-inch skillet.

1 Pat pork dry with paper towels and sprinkle with salt and pepper. Heat vegetable oil in 10-inch nonstick skillet over medium heat until just smoking. Add pork and cook until well browned and meat registers 140 degrees, 2 to 4 minutes per side. Transfer pork to cutting board, tent loosely with aluminum foil, and let rest for 5 minutes. Wipe skillet clean with paper towels.

2 Slice pork thin. Combine pickles and banana peppers in small bowl. Spread rolls with mayonnaise and mustard. Layer pork, pickle mixture, and cheese onto roll bottoms (finishing with cheese on top). Fold roll tops over filling and press down to flatten sandwiches.

3 Spray now-empty skillet evenly with olive oil spray. Place sandwiches in skillet and use large pot or Dutch oven to compress sandwiches for 15 to 20 seconds. Cook (keeping pot on sandwiches but not pressing down) over medium-low heat until first side is golden brown, 5 to 7 minutes. Remove pot and brush top of each sandwich with ½ teaspoon olive oil. Flip sandwiches, replace pot on top of sandwiches, and cook until second side is golden brown, 3 to 4 minutes. Serve.

MEAL PREP Griddled sandwiches can be refrigerated for up to 1 day. Eat cold, at room temperature, or reheated in skillet.

Cal 450; Total Fat 19g;
Sat Fat 5g; Chol 50mg;
Sodium 860mg; Total Carb 49g;
Dietary Fiber 7g; Total Sugars 9g;
Protein 25g

MARINATED PORK SANDWICHES WITH PICKLED VEGETABLES

Serves 2   **Total Time: 50 minutes**

WHEN TO EAT
› **Post-Workout** Within 2 hours
› **Maintenance**

WORKOUTS
› **Everyday**
› **Endurance** Serve with grapes or baked snack chips (see page 274).
› **Strength or Interval** Increase pork to 6 ounces.

MAKE IT A SNACK
Eat half a sandwich.

¾ teaspoon grated lime zest, divided, plus 3 tablespoons juice, divided (2 limes)

1 tablespoon packed dark brown sugar, divided

1 teaspoon fish sauce, divided

2½ teaspoons sriracha, divided

1 carrot, peeled and cut into 2-inch-long matchsticks

4 radishes, trimmed and cut into matchsticks

⅛ teaspoon red pepper flakes

1 (4-ounce) boneless pork chop, ½ to ¾ inch thick, trimmed

1 teaspoon canola oil

2 tablespoons mayonnaise

2 (6-inch) whole-grain sub rolls, split lengthwise and toasted

¼ English cucumber, halved lengthwise and sliced thin

½ cup fresh cilantro leaves

½ jalapeño chile, seeded and sliced thin

—

Cal 500; Total Fat 19g; Sat Fat 3g; Chol 40mg; Sodium 890mg; Total Carb 63g; Dietary Fiber 9g; Total Sugars 19g; Protein 22g

WHY THIS RECIPE WORKS ›› Quick-seasoned pickles, which are typical of banh mi–inspired sandwiches, give these layered (in ingredients and flavor) make-ahead marinated pork sandwiches crunch and bite. A savory sriracha-lime mayo glues things together. Prepare all the components ahead of time and place them on the bun when you're back from the gym. You can substitute white rolls for the whole-grain ones. This recipe can easily be doubled with two 4-ounce chops or one 8-ounce chop, using a 12-inch skillet.

1 Whisk ½ teaspoon lime zest and 2 tablespoons juice, 1½ teaspoons sugar, ½ teaspoon fish sauce, and ½ teaspoon sriracha together in bowl until sugar has dissolved. Stir in carrot and radishes; refrigerate for at least 15 minutes or up to 1 day. Drain vegetables and discard liquid; set aside.

2 Whisk pepper flakes, remaining 1 tablespoon lime juice, remaining 1½ teaspoons sugar, and remaining ½ teaspoon fish sauce in second bowl until sugar has dissolved. Add pork chop and toss to coat. Cover and refrigerate for at least 15 minutes or up to 1 hour.

3 Lift pork from marinade and pat dry with paper towels; discard marinade. Heat oil in 10-inch nonstick skillet over medium heat until just smoking. Add pork and cook until well browned and meat registers 140 degrees, 2 to 4 minutes per side. Transfer pork to cutting board, tent with aluminum foil, and let rest for 5 minutes. Slice pork thin. Whisk mayonnaise, remaining ¼ teaspoon lime zest, remaining 2 teaspoons sriracha, and any accumulated pork juices together in bowl. Spread rolls with mayonnaise mixture. Layer pork, pickled vegetables, cucumber, cilantro, and jalapeño into rolls. Serve.

MEAL PREP Sandwiches can be refrigerated for up to 1 day. Eat cold or at room temperature.

LEMONGRASS BEEF AND RICE NOODLE BOWL

Serves 2   **Total Time: 45 minutes**

WHEN TO EAT
› **Pre-Workout** 3 to 4 hours before
› **Post-Workout** Within 2 hours
› **Maintenance**

WORKOUTS
› **Everyday**
› **Strength or Interval** Increase beef to 8 ounces.

MAKE IT A SNACK
Eat half a portion.

---

6 ounces rice vermicelli

1½ teaspoons canola oil, divided

2 tablespoons lime juice, plus lime wedges for serving

2 tablespoons fish sauce, divided

1 tablespoon minced lemongrass, divided

1½ teaspoons sugar, divided

1 teaspoon Asian chili-garlic sauce, divided

6 ounces flank steak, trimmed

1 carrot, peeled and shredded

¼ English cucumber, cut into 2-inch-long matchsticks

1 ounce (½ cup) bean sprouts

2 tablespoons Thai basil and/or mint leaves

1 tablespoon dry-roasted peanuts, chopped

—

Cal 550; Total Fat 13g;
Sat Fat 3g; Chol 60mg;
Sodium 840mg; Total Carb 82g;
Dietary Fiber 4g;
Total Sugars 7g; Protein 27g

WHY THIS RECIPE WORKS ›› Inspired by Vietnamese bun bo xao, this dish consists of dressed rice noodles topped with beef, crunchy vegetables, herbs, and peanuts. It is served at room temperature, so it's forgiving for toting around. To prepare lemongrass, trim stalk to bottom 6 inches, trim root end, and remove any dried outer layers; mince. We prefer Thai basil, but you can substitute Italian basil. This recipe can easily be doubled using a 12-inch skillet and a large pot.

1 Bring 2 quarts water to boil in large saucepan. Off heat, add noodles and let sit, stirring occasionally, until tender, about 5 minutes. Drain noodles, rinse well, and drain again. Toss noodles with ½ teaspoon oil; set aside. Whisk lime juice, 5 teaspoons fish sauce, 1½ teaspoons lemongrass, 1 teaspoon sugar, and ½ teaspoon chili-garlic sauce together in small bowl until sugar is dissolved; set sauce aside.

2 Whisk remaining 1 teaspoon fish sauce, remaining 1½ teaspoons lemongrass, remaining ½ teaspoon sugar, and remaining ½ teaspoon chili-garlic sauce together in bowl. Add steak and toss to coat. Heat remaining 1 teaspoon oil in 10- or 12-inch skillet over medium-high heat until just smoking. Add steak and cook until well browned and meat registers 120 to 125 degrees (for medium-rare) or 130 to 135 degrees (for medium), 3 to 6 minutes per side. Transfer steak to cutting board, tent loosely with aluminum foil, and let rest for 5 minutes.

3 Slice steak thin against grain. Divide noodles between serving bowls, then top each portion with steak, carrot, cucumber, and sprouts. Whisk any accumulated juices from steak into reserved sauce and drizzle evenly over each portion. Sprinkle with basil and peanuts. Serve with lime wedges.

MEAL PREP Fully assembled bowls can be refrigerated for up to 1 day.

SOPA SECA WITH CHIPOTLE PORK, BLACK BEANS, AND TOMATOES

Serves 2   Total Time: 45 minutes

WHEN TO EAT
› **Post-Workout** Within 2 hours
› **Maintenance**

WORKOUTS
› **Everyday**
› **Endurance** Serve with baked tortilla chips (see page 274).
› **Strength or Interval** Increase pork to 6 ounces.

MAKE IT A SNACK
Eat half a portion.

---

4 ounces 100 percent whole-wheat thin spaghetti

2 teaspoons canola oil, divided

4 ounces ground pork

1 small onion, chopped fine

½ green bell pepper, chopped fine

1 tablespoon tomato paste

1 tablespoon minced canned chipotle chile in adobo sauce

1 teaspoon ground cumin

1 garlic clove, minced

1½ cups water

1 (15-ounce) can black beans, rinsed

6 ounces cherry or grape tomatoes, halved

2 tablespoons fresh cilantro leaves

1 tablespoon crumbled cotija cheese

—

Cal 550; Total Fat 20g;
Sat Fat 6g; Chol 45mg;
Sodium 530mg; Total Carb 70g;
Dietary Fiber 18g;
Total Sugars 8g; Protein 27g

WHY THIS RECIPE WORKS ›› Sopa seca is a vibrant one-pot pasta meal popular in Central Mexico. Thin strands of fideos pasta are cooked in a flavorful broth until it is reduced to a thick, rich sauce. This pasta dish fits well in an athlete's diet because it is loaded with beneficial ingredients to replenish the body. We use ground pork flavored with chipotle chile in adobo sauce in lieu of fattier chorizo, and opt for nutty whole-wheat pasta (which gets even nuttier from toasting) for extra fiber. A can of black beans also ups the fiber and filling factors. Crumbled fresh cotija and cilantro complement the vegetables, pork, pasta, and beans. You can substitute traditional spaghetti for the whole-wheat. This recipe can easily be doubled using a 12-inch skillet.

1 Loosely wrap spaghetti in dish towel, then press bundle against corner of counter to break into 1- to 2-inch lengths. In 10- or 12-inch nonstick skillet, toast pasta in 1 teaspoon oil over medium-high heat, tossing frequently with tongs, until golden, about 4 minutes; transfer to bowl.

2 Heat remaining 1 teaspoon oil in now-empty skillet over medium heat until shimmering. Add pork, onion, and bell pepper and cook until vegetables are softened and lightly browned, 4 to 6 minutes. Stir in tomato paste, chipotle, cumin, and garlic and cook until fragrant, about 30 seconds. Stir in toasted pasta, water, and beans and bring to simmer. Cover and cook, stirring often, until pasta is tender, about 10 minutes.

3 Off heat, stir in tomatoes and season with salt and pepper to taste. Sprinkle each portion with cilantro and cotija. Serve.

MEAL PREP Pasta can be refrigerated for up to 2 days.

ONE-POT SHELLS WITH SAUSAGE, MUSHROOMS, AND PEAS

Serves 2   **Total Time: 55 minutes**

WHEN TO EAT
› **Pre-Workout** 3 to 4 hours before
› **Post-Workout** Within 2 hours
› **Maintenance**

WORKOUTS
› **Everyday**
› **Endurance** Serve with bread.
› **Strength or Interval** Increase sausage to 8 ounces.

MAKE IT A SNACK
Eat half a portion.

- 2 teaspoons extra-virgin olive oil, divided
- 6 ounces sweet or hot Italian sausage, casings removed
- 8 ounces cremini or white mushrooms, trimmed and sliced thin
- 1 small onion, chopped fine
- ¼ teaspoon table salt
- ⅛ teaspoon red pepper flakes
- ¼ cup dry white wine
- 2 cups water
- 6 ounces (2¼ cups) medium pasta shells
- ½ cup frozen peas, thawed
- ½ cup chopped fresh basil leaves, plus extra for serving
- 1 teaspoon grated lemon zest, plus lemon wedges for serving

---

Cal 550; Total Fat 12g;
Sat Fat 3g; Chol 20mg;
Sodium 710mg; Total Carb 79g;
Dietary Fiber 6g;
Total Sugars 8g; Protein 28g

WHY THIS RECIPE WORKS ›› This robust dish uses pasta shells to capture the delicious bites of sausage, sautéed mushrooms, and onions that are simmered in white wine. While the ingredients are mouthwatering, the meal is light because the sauce forms from cooking everything together until thickened from the pasta's starch. We freshen the savory dish by stirring in fresh basil and grated lemon zest. We prefer medium shells for this recipe, but you can substitute elbow macaroni. This recipe can easily be doubled using a Dutch oven.

1 Heat 1 teaspoon oil in large saucepan over medium heat until shimmering. Add sausage and cook, breaking up meat with wooden spoon, until no longer pink, about 3 minutes; transfer to bowl.

2 Heat remaining 1 teaspoon oil in now-empty saucepan over medium-high heat until shimmering. Add mushrooms, onion, and salt, cover, and cook until vegetables are softened and mushrooms begin to release their liquid, about 5 minutes. Uncover and continue to cook until liquid has evaporated and vegetables begin to brown, about 5 minutes. Stir in pepper flakes and cook until fragrant, about 30 seconds.

3 Stir in wine, scraping up any browned bits, and cook until nearly evaporated, about 2 minutes. Stir in water and pasta, bring to simmer, and cook, stirring often, until pasta is tender, 10 to 12 minutes (some liquid will remain in bottom of pot). Off heat, stir in sausage and peas and let sit until peas are heated through and sauce is thickened, about 5 minutes. Stir in basil and lemon zest and season with salt and pepper to taste. Serve with lemon wedges and extra basil.

MEAL PREP Pasta can be refrigerated for up to 3 days.

SKILLET MACARONI AND BEEF

Serves 2 **Total Time: 45 minutes**

WHEN TO EAT
› **Post-Workout** Within 2 hours
› **Maintenance**

WORKOUTS
› **Strength or Interval**
› **Everyday** Serve with bread.

MAKE IT A SNACK
Eat half a portion.

---

1 teaspoon extra-virgin olive oil

1 small onion, chopped fine

½ red, orange, or yellow bell pepper, chopped fine

⅛ teaspoon table salt

⅛ teaspoon pepper

6 ounces 90 percent lean ground beef

3 garlic cloves, minced

1 tablespoon minced fresh oregano or 1 teaspoon dried

1 (14.5-ounce) can crushed tomatoes

1 cup beef, chicken, or vegetable broth

1¼ cups (5 ounces) 100 percent whole-wheat elbow macaroni

2 tablespoons shredded cheddar cheese

WHY THIS RECIPE WORKS ›› Think outside the box with this nostalgic, very-homemade cheeseburger macaroni that is surprisingly workout-friendly. We skip the high-sodium seasoning packet and other prefab ingredients and keep the ingredient list simple, calling for plenty of sustaining lean ground beef, nutritious whole-wheat macaroni, crushed tomatoes, and some staple aromatics. Made entirely in one skillet, the final dish is as simple as any. We prefer elbow macaroni for this recipe, but you can substitute medium shells; and you can sub traditional pasta for the whole-wheat. This recipe can easily be doubled using a 12-inch skillet.

1 Heat oil in 10- or 12-inch nonstick skillet over medium heat until shimmering. Add onion, bell pepper, salt, and pepper and cook until softened and lightly browned, 4 to 6 minutes. Stir in beef and cook, breaking up meat with wooden spoon, until no longer pink, about 3 minutes. Stir in garlic and oregano and cook until fragrant, about 30 seconds.

2 Stir in tomatoes, broth, and macaroni and bring to boil. Cover, reduce heat to low, and cook, stirring occasionally, until pasta is tender, 10 to 12 minutes. Off heat, let sit until sauce is thickened, about 5 minutes. Stir to recombine and season with salt and pepper to taste. Sprinkle each portion with 1 tablespoon cheddar. Serve.

MEAL PREP Pasta can be refrigerated for up to 2 days.

Cal 530; Total Fat 16g;
Sat Fat 5g; Chol 65mg;
Sodium 870mg; Total Carb 66g;
Dietary Fiber 13g;
Total Sugars 13g; Protein 33g

FUSILLI WITH PORK, SPINACH, AND ROSEMARY

Serves 2   Total Time: 40 minutes

WHEN TO EAT
› **Post-Workout** Within 2 hours
› **Maintenance**

WORKOUTS
› **Strength or Interval**
› **Everyday** Increase pasta to
  8 ounces.

MAKE IT A SNACK
Eat half a portion.

1 teaspoon extra-virgin
  olive oil

1 small onion, chopped fine

⅛ teaspoon table salt, plus
  salt for cooking pasta

4 ounces ground pork

1 teaspoon minced fresh
  rosemary, divided

1 garlic clove, minced

¼ teaspoon red pepper flakes

¾ cup chicken broth

6 ounces (2 cups)
  100 percent whole-wheat
  fusilli, penne, or ziti pasta

5 ounces (5 cups)
  baby spinach

2 tablespoons grated
  Parmesan cheese

1½ teaspoons red wine vinegar

Cal 510; Total Fat 19g;
Sat Fat 6g; Chol 45mg;
Sodium 860mg; Total Carb 59g;
Dietary Fiber 11g;
Total Sugars 3g; Protein 26g

WHY THIS RECIPE WORKS ›› Comfort food and workout food are not mutually exclusive—this savory, rich, earthy dish brings comfort to the table in 40 minutes. Ground pork, when combined with sautéed onion, garlic, rosemary, and red pepper flakes, has a sausage-like profile without all the extra fat and salt. Comfort food and greens also aren't incompatible, so we fortify the dish by wilting in spinach, which is fiberful and rich in beneficial B vitamins (see page 21). A finishing splash of red wine vinegar brightens all the flavors. You can substitute traditional pasta for the whole-wheat. This recipe can easily be doubled using a 12-inch skillet and a large pot.

1 Heat oil in 10- or 12-inch skillet over medium heat until shimmering. Add onion and salt and cook until softened and lightly browned, 4 to 6 minutes. Stir in pork and cook, breaking up meat with wooden spoon, until no longer pink, about 3 minutes. Stir in ½ teaspoon rosemary, garlic, and pepper flakes and cook until fragrant, about 30 seconds.

2 Stir in broth, scraping up any browned bits, and bring to simmer. Reduce heat to medium-low and simmer until sauce is slightly thickened, 6 to 8 minutes.

3 Meanwhile, bring 2 quarts water to boil in large saucepan. Add pasta and 1½ teaspoons salt and cook, stirring often, until al dente. Reserve ½ cup cooking water, then drain pasta and return it to saucepan.

4 Stir spinach into pasta, one handful at a time, then add pork mixture and ¼ cup reserved cooking water. Cook over low heat until spinach is wilted and sauce is thickened, about 2 minutes. Adjust consistency with reserved pasta water as needed. Stir in Parmesan, vinegar, and remaining ½ teaspoon rosemary. Season with salt and pepper to taste. Serve.

MEAL PREP Pasta can be refrigerated for up to 2 days.

BEEF, PORK & LAMB

SEARED FLANK STEAK WITH OAT BERRIES, ZUCCHINI, AND PEPPERS

Serves 2   Total Time: 1 hour

WHEN TO EAT
› **Post-Workout** Within 2 hours
› **Maintenance**

WORKOUTS
› **Strength or Interval**
› **Everyday** Increase oat berries to 1 cup and dried cherries to ½ cup.

¾ cup oat berries (groats), rinsed

½ teaspoon table salt, divided, plus salt for cooking oat berries

2 tablespoons minced fresh dill, tarragon, or parsley

¼ teaspoon lemon zest plus 1 tablespoon juice, plus lemon wedges for serving

1 tablespoon extra-virgin olive oil, divided

6 ounces flank steak, trimmed

¼ teaspoon pepper

1 large zucchini, halved lengthwise and cut into 1-inch pieces

1 red, orange, or yellow bell pepper, stemmed, seeded, and cut into 1-inch pieces

¼ cup dried tart cherries, chopped

Cal 570; Total Fat 18g;
Sat Fat 4g; Chol 60mg;
Sodium 790mg; Total Carb 67g;
Dietary Fiber 10g;
Total Sugars 16g; Protein 32g

WHY THIS RECIPE WORKS ›› For a base of beneficial carbs, nutty oat berries are a nice change of pace from rice, with tons of nutrients and more fiber (and they're gluten-free). They don't require hands-on cooking, giving you time to sear steak and caramelize veggies on the stovetop. The steak juices from resting mixed into the oat berries bring a savory, meaty taste to the dish. This recipe can easily be doubled, using a 12-inch skillet and a large pot.

1 Bring 2 quarts water to boil in large saucepan. Add oat berries and 1½ teaspoons salt and cook until grains are tender with slight chew, 40 to 50 minutes. Drain oat berries. Combine dill, lemon zest and juice, 2 teaspoons oil, and ¼ teaspoon salt in large bowl. Add oat berries and toss to combine; set aside.

2 Pat steak dry with paper towels and sprinkle with pepper and remaining ¼ teaspoon salt. Heat remaining 1 teaspoon oil in 10- or 12-inch nonstick skillet over medium-high heat until just smoking. Add steak and cook until well browned and meat registers 120 to 125 degrees (for medium-rare) or 130 to 135 degrees (for medium), 3 to 6 minutes per side; adjust heat as needed to prevent scorching. Transfer steak to cutting board, tent loosely with aluminum foil, and let rest while cooking vegetables.

3 Heat fat left in now-empty skillet over medium-high heat until just smoking. Add zucchini and bell pepper and cook, stirring occasionally, until just tender and deep golden brown, 6 to 10 minutes.

4 Slice steak thin against grain. Stir vegetables, cherries, and any accumulated juices from steak into oat berry mixture. Season with salt and pepper to taste. Serve steak with oat berry mixture and lemon wedges.

MEAL PREP Cooked, sliced steak and oat berry mixture can be tossed together and refrigerated for up to 2 days; eat warm or at room temperature.

ONE-PAN COFFEE-RUBBED STEAK WITH SWEET POTATOES AND APPLES

Serves 2   Total Time: 55 minutes

WHEN TO EAT
> **Post-Workout** Within 2 hours
> **Maintenance**

WORKOUTS
> **Everyday**
> **Endurance** Serve with a simple grain (see pages 284–287).
> **Strength or Interval** Increase steak to 8 ounces.

1 pound sweet potatoes, unpeeled, cut lengthwise into 1-inch wedges

4 shallots, peeled and quartered lengthwise

2 tablespoons extra-virgin olive oil, divided

½ teaspoon table salt, divided

½ teaspoon pepper, divided

1 large apple, cored, halved, and sliced thin

1 teaspoon packed dark brown sugar

1 teaspoon finely ground coffee

1 teaspoon chili powder

1 (6-ounce) boneless strip steak, 1 to 1½ inches thick, trimmed

2 tablespoons minced fresh parsley, plus extra for serving

1 tablespoon red wine vinegar

Cal 530; Total Fat 19g;
Sat Fat 3.5g; Chol 45mg;
Sodium 800mg; Total Carb 68g;
Dietary Fiber 12g;
Total Sugars 30g; Protein 25g

WHY THIS RECIPE WORKS ›› This autumnal sheet-pan meal doesn't need a grain or pasta; starchy vegetables can be a great source of nourishing carbohydrates. Here, it's sweet potatoes, with sliced apple and shallots contributing further. We love how the sweet stuff pairs with the bold coffee-coated steak. Look for shallots that weigh about 1 ounce each. This recipe can easily be doubled.

1 Adjust oven rack to lower-middle position and heat oven to 450 degrees. Toss potatoes and shallots with 2 teaspoons oil, ⅛ teaspoon salt, and ¼ teaspoon pepper in large bowl. Arrange potatoes skin side down on half of rimmed baking sheet and arrange shallots in single layer next to potatoes. Roast until vegetables are softened and lightly browned, 20 to 25 minutes.

2 Toss apple with 1 teaspoon oil and ⅛ teaspoon salt in now-empty bowl. Combine sugar, coffee, chili powder, remaining ¼ teaspoon salt, and remaining ¼ teaspoon pepper in small bowl. Pat steak dry with paper towels and rub with spice mixture.

3 Place steak on empty portion of baking sheet. Arrange apple slices on top of shallots. Roast until potatoes, shallots, and apples are fully tender and meat registers 120 to 125 degrees (for medium-rare), 10 to 15 minutes. Transfer steak, bottom side up, to cutting board, tent loosely with aluminum foil, and let rest for 5 minutes.

4 Combine parsley, vinegar, and remaining 1 tablespoon oil in large bowl. Add potatoes, shallots, and apples and toss to combine. Season with salt and pepper to taste. Slice steak thin against grain and sprinkle with extra parsley. Serve steak with sweet potato mixture.

MEAL PREP Cooked, sliced steak and chopped cooked vegetables and apple can be tossed together and refrigerated for up to 2 days; eat warm or at room temperature.

SEARED PORK CHOP WITH COUSCOUS AND CELERY SALAD

Serves 2   Total Time: 40 minutes

WHEN TO EAT
› **Post-Workout** Within 2 hours
› **Maintenance**

WORKOUTS
› **Strength or Interval**
› **Everyday** Increase couscous and boiling water to 1 cup each and increase currants to ¼ cup.

¾ cup boiling water

¾ cup couscous

½ teaspoon table salt, divided

2 tablespoons extra-virgin olive oil, divided

1 tablespoon lemon juice, plus lemon wedges for serving

2 tablespoons chopped fresh parsley, divided

1 small garlic clove, minced

¼ teaspoon pepper, divided

4 celery ribs, sliced thin on bias

2 tablespoons dried currants or raisins

1 (6-ounce) boneless pork chop, ½ to ¾ inch thick, trimmed

WHY THIS RECIPE WORKS ›› We pair a classic seared pork chop with easy-to-make couscous enhanced with bites of tart dried fruit and crunchy celery. Celery often sits forgotten in the crisper drawer, but sliced thin here, it contributes refreshing, contrasting crunch and helpful nutrients to the fluffy couscous. If available, use celery ribs with leaves and include the whole leaves in the salad. This recipe can easily be doubled using a 12-inch skillet.

1 Combine boiling water, couscous, and ¼ teaspoon salt in large bowl. Cover and let sit for 10 minutes. Fluff couscous with fork.

2 Whisk 5 teaspoons oil, lemon juice, 1 tablespoon parsley, garlic, ⅛ teaspoon salt, and ⅛ teaspoon pepper together in large bowl. Add couscous, celery, and currants and toss to combine; set salad aside.

3 Pat pork dry with paper towels and sprinkle with remaining ⅛ teaspoon salt and remaining ⅛ teaspoon pepper. Heat remaining 1 teaspoon oil in 8- or 10-inch nonstick skillet over medium heat until just smoking. Add pork and cook until well browned and meat registers 140 degrees, 3 to 5 minutes per side. Transfer pork to cutting board, tent loosely with aluminum foil, and let rest for 5 minutes.

4 Slice pork ½ inch thick, transfer to serving plates, and sprinkle with remaining 1 tablespoon parsley. Serve with couscous salad and lemon wedges.

MEAL PREP Cooked, sliced pork and couscous salad can be tossed together and refrigerated for up to 2 days; eat warm or at room temperature.

Cal 520; Total Fat 17g;
Sat Fat 3g; Chol 55mg;
Sodium 700mg; Total Carb 61g;
Dietary Fiber 5g;
Total Sugars 8g; Protein 29g

BEEF, PORK & LAMB

LAMB MEATBALLS WITH LEMONY RICE AND ARTICHOKES

Serves 2   **Total Time: 1 hour**

WHEN TO EAT
› **Post-Workout** Within 2 hours

WORKOUTS
› **Everyday**
› **Endurance** Serve with pita bread.
› **Strength or Interval** Increase panko to 3 tablespoons, milk to 2 tablespoons, and lamb to 6 ounces; shape mixture into 6 meatballs.

---

2 tablespoons panko bread crumbs

1 tablespoon 1 percent low-fat milk

2 tablespoons chopped fresh parsley, divided

2 garlic cloves, minced

1 teaspoon grated lemon zest, divided, plus 1 tablespoon lemon juice, plus lemon wedges for serving

¼ teaspoon table salt, divided

¼ teaspoon pepper

4 ounces ground lamb

2 teaspoons extra-virgin olive oil

1¼ cups chicken broth

¾ cup long-grain white rice

4 ounces frozen artichoke hearts, thawed, patted dry, and quartered

4 ounces cherry or grape tomatoes, halved

Cal 490; Total Fat 17g;
Sat Fat 6g; Chol 40mg;
Sodium 850mg; Total Carb 66g;
Dietary Fiber 2g;
Total Sugars 3g; Protein 19g

WHY THIS RECIPE WORKS ›› Platefuls of spaghetti and meatballs may be the imagery associated with certain high-octane athletic pursuits, but this more modest dish of lemony rice and rich lamb meatballs is a much better (and, arguably, more flavorful) fit for the everyday athlete. Because brown rice can take a long time to cook, we went with white and instead chose to get our fiber, nutrients, and antioxidants from convenient frozen artichoke hearts that we cook directly in the flavored rice. This recipe can easily be doubled using a Dutch oven; increase broth to 2¼ cups.

1 Combine panko, milk, 1 tablespoon parsley, garlic, ¾ teaspoon lemon zest, ⅛ teaspoon salt, and pepper in large bowl. Add lamb and gently knead with hands until well combined. Using lightly moistened hands, pinch off and roll lamb mixture into 4 meatballs.

2 Heat oil in large saucepan over medium-high heat until shimmering. Brown meatballs on all sides, 4 to 6 minutes; transfer to paper towel–lined plate. Add broth to now-empty saucepan, scraping up any browned bits, and bring to boil over medium-high heat. Stir in rice, artichokes, remaining ¼ teaspoon lemon zest and the juice, and remaining ⅛ teaspoon salt and return to boil.

3 Nestle meatballs into rice mixture. Reduce heat to low, cover, and simmer until rice is tender and liquid is absorbed, 16 to 18 minutes. Off heat, scatter tomatoes over rice. Lay clean folded dish towel underneath lid, and let rest for 10 minutes. Fluff rice with fork and season with salt and pepper to taste. Sprinkle with remaining 1 tablespoon parsley and serve with lemon wedges.

MEAL PREP Cooked meatballs and rice can be refrigerated for up to 2 days.

STIR-FRIED BEEF WITH BOK CHOY AND GREEN BEANS

Serves 2   Total Time: 40 minutes

WHEN TO EAT
› **Pre-Workout** 3 to 4 hours before
› **Post-Workout** Within 2 hours
› **Maintenance**

WORKOUTS
› **Everyday**
› **Strength or Interval** Increase steak to 6 ounces.

- 1 tablespoon fish or soy sauce, divided, plus extra for seasoning
- 3 garlic cloves, minced
- 1 teaspoon packed brown sugar
- 1 teaspoon rice vinegar
- ½ teaspoon cornstarch, divided
- ⅛ teaspoon red pepper flakes
- ⅛ teaspoon baking soda
- 4 ounces flank steak, trimmed and sliced thin against grain
- 2 teaspoons canola oil, divided
- 8 ounces bok choy, halved lengthwise and cut into ½-inch strips
- 8 ounces green beans, trimmed and halved crosswise
- 1 carrot, peeled and shredded
- 2 cups cooked white rice (see page 285), warmed

Cal 460; Total Fat 9g;
Sat Fat 2g; Chol 40mg;
Sodium 700mg; Total Carb 74g;
Dietary Fiber 5g;
Total Sugars 9g; Protein 24g

WHY THIS RECIPE WORKS ›› To boost the nutritional profile of protein-rich beef stir-fry, we use more vegetables than meat but still include enough to suit your workout. We tenderize lean flank steak by soaking it in a baking soda solution. Wash the bok choy after halving so the insides can be exposed and any dirt can be easily washed away. This recipe can easily be doubled using a 12-inch skillet.

1 Whisk 2 tablespoons water, 2 teaspoons fish sauce, garlic, sugar, vinegar, ¼ teaspoon cornstarch, and pepper flakes together in small bowl; set aside. Combine 1 teaspoon water and baking soda in medium bowl. Add beef and toss to coat; let sit for 5 minutes. Add remaining 1 teaspoon fish sauce and remaining ¼ teaspoon cornstarch and toss to coat.

2 Heat 1 teaspoon oil in 10- or 12-inch nonstick skillet over medium-high heat until just smoking. Add beef in single layer and cook without stirring for 1 minute. Continue to cook, stirring occasionally, until spotty brown on both sides, about 1 minute longer; transfer to clean bowl.

3 Heat remaining 1 teaspoon oil in now-empty skillet over medium-high heat until shimmering. Add bok choy and green beans and cook for 30 seconds. Add 2 tablespoons water, cover, and reduce heat to medium. Steam vegetables until bok choy leaves begin to wilt, about 2 minutes. Uncover skillet and cook, stirring occasionally, until vegetables are spotty brown and water is evaporated, about 3 minutes.

4 Return cooked beef and any accumulated juices to skillet and toss to combine. Stir in fish sauce mixture and shredded carrot and cook until sauce is slightly thickened, about 1 minute. Season with extra fish sauce to taste. Serve with rice.

MEAL PREP Cooked beef, vegetables, and rice can be refrigerated separately for up to 2 days.

SEAFOOD

SALMON NIÇOISE SALAD WRAPS

Serves 2   Total Time: 35 minutes

WHEN TO EAT
› **Pre-Workout** 3 to 4 hours before
› **Post-Workout** Within 2 hours
› **Maintenance**

WORKOUTS
› **Everyday**
› **Endurance** Serve with grapes or baked snack chips (see page 274).
› **Strength or Interval** Increase salmon to 2 cans.

MAKE IT A SNACK
Eat half a wrap.

12 ounces Yukon Gold potatoes, peeled and cut into 1-inch pieces

¼ teaspoon table salt, plus salt for cooking vegetables

4 ounces green beans, trimmed and cut into 1-inch lengths

¼ cup plain low-fat Greek yogurt

4 teaspoons extra-virgin olive oil, divided

4 teaspoons lemon juice, divided

1 tablespoon chopped fresh dill or parsley

1 teaspoon Dijon mustard

⅛ teaspoon pepper

2 ounces (2 cups) mesclun

2 tablespoons chopped pitted niçoise or kalamata olives

2 (12 by 9-inch) lavash breads

1 (6-ounce) can skinless boneless salmon or solid white tuna packed in water, drained and flaked

---

Cal 560; Total Fat 12g;
Sat Fat 2.5g; Chol 30mg;
Sodium 660mg; Total Carb 78g;
Dietary Fiber 6g;
Total Sugars 5g; Protein 28g

WHY THIS RECIPE WORKS ›› Salmon niçoise is a nice change of pace from the classic tuna; an even more exciting shift is enclosing it in a portable, bready wrap for a perfectly calibrated meal for an athlete. For the potato component, we mash creamy Yukon Golds into a hummus-like spread that holds the wrap together. Canned salmon should be in your pantry; it's widely available and has a long shelf life. This recipe can easily be doubled.

1 Place potatoes and ½ teaspoon salt in large saucepan, add cold water to cover by 2 inches, and bring to boil over high heat. Reduce heat to medium and cook until potatoes are just tender, 6 to 8 minutes. Add green beans and cook until vegetables are fully tender, 3 to 5 minutes.

2 Using slotted spoon, transfer green beans to bowl; set aside. Drain potatoes in colander and return to now-empty saucepan. Add yogurt, 2 tablespoons water, 1 tablespoon oil, 1 tablespoon lemon juice, dill, mustard, pepper, and salt and mash with potato masher until evenly combined and mostly smooth. Season with salt and pepper to taste.

3 Add mesclun, olives, remaining 1 teaspoon oil, and remaining 1 teaspoon lemon juice to green beans and toss to combine. Season with salt and pepper to taste.

4 Working with 1 lavash at a time, place on counter with long side parallel to edge of counter. Spread half of potato mixture in rectangle 2 inches from bottom of lavash and about 1 inch from each side. Top potato mixture with half of salmon and half of green bean mixture. Fold sides of lavash over filling, then fold up bottom of lavash and fold tightly around filling. Repeat with remaining lavash, potato mixture, salmon, and green bean mixture. Cut wraps in half and serve.

MEAL PREP Wrap can be refrigerated for up to 1 day.

WASABI TUNA SALAD SANDWICHES

Serves 2   Total Time: 15 minutes

WHEN TO EAT
› **Pre-Workout** 3 to 4 hours before
› **Post-Workout** Within 2 hours

WORKOUTS
› **Everyday**
› **Endurance** Serve with grapes or baked snack chips (see page 274).
› **Strength or Interval** Increase tuna to 2 cans.

MAKE IT A SNACK
Eat half a sandwich.

2 tablespoons plain low-fat Greek yogurt

1½ tablespoons mayonnaise

¼ teaspoon grated lime zest plus 1 teaspoon juice

½–1 teaspoon wasabi paste

½ teaspoon grated fresh ginger

¼ teaspoon soy sauce

1 (6-ounce) can solid white tuna or skinless boneless salmon packed in water, drained and flaked

½ red bell pepper, chopped fine

2 scallions, sliced thin

4 (2-ounce) slices hearty white sandwich bread, toasted if desired

¼ English cucumber, sliced thin

WHY THIS RECIPE WORKS ›› Wasabi paste is a great way to invigorate a classic tuna salad sandwich. We use a little more Greek yogurt than mayonnaise to create a light base and add fresh grated ginger with the wasabi for zing. We bulk up the filling with chopped bell pepper (we welcome its sweetness) and sliced scallions. Ready in just 15 minutes, this sandwich is the perfect meal to throw together before or after exercising, and is easy enough to warrant making for a snack. Canned tuna, like canned salmon (see page 160), is a useful ingredient for any athlete to have on hand because it can be used in a number of recipes and provides protein without preparation. This recipe can easily be doubled.

1 Whisk yogurt, mayonnaise, lime zest and juice, wasabi paste, ginger, and soy sauce together in bowl. Fold in tuna, bell pepper, and scallions.

2 Divide tuna salad between 2 slices of bread, then top with cucumber slices and remaining bread slices. Serve.

MEAL PREP Tuna salad can be refrigerated for up to 1 day; stir to recombine before serving.

Cal 400; Total Fat 12g;
Sat Fat 2.5g; Chol 30mg;
Sodium 880mg; Total Carb 57g;
Dietary Fiber 3g;
Total Sugars 11g; Protein 16g

SALMON TACOS WITH CABBAGE SLAW AND LIME CREMA

Serves 2   Total Time: 30 minutes

WHEN TO EAT

› **Post-Workout** Within 2 hours
› **Maintenance**

WORKOUTS

› **Strength or Interval**
› **Everyday** Serve with a simple grain (see pages 284–287).

MAKE IT A SNACK

Eat 1 taco.

⅓ cup plain low-fat Greek yogurt

½ teaspoon grated lime zest plus 2 tablespoons juice, divided, plus lime wedges for serving

½ teaspoon table salt, divided

1 cup (2 ounces) coleslaw mix

½ small red onion, sliced thin

2 tablespoons fresh cilantro leaves

1 (6-ounce) skin-on salmon fillet, 1 to 1½ inches thick

¼ teaspoon chipotle chile powder

½ teaspoon canola oil

6 (6-inch) corn tortillas, warmed

WHY THIS RECIPE WORKS ›› The fish in fish tacos can come in a range of styles: Breaded or fried isn't a good fit for refueling, but simply searing a fish fillet is healthful and satisfying. Salmon is a good source of healthy fats and has so much richness that it needs only a simple spice rub. And salmon is a good reheater, so you can make the slaw and salmon ahead and take them to taco in no time. If using wild salmon, decrease cook time slightly and cook fillet to 120 degrees (for medium-rare). This recipe can easily be doubled using a 10- or 12-inch skillet.

1 Whisk yogurt, ¼ teaspoon lime zest, 1 tablespoon juice, and ⅛ teaspoon salt together in small bowl; set crema aside. Whisk remaining ¼ teaspoon lime zest, remaining 1 tablespoon juice, and ⅛ teaspoon salt together in large bowl. Add coleslaw mix, onion, and cilantro and toss to combine; set slaw aside.

2 Pat salmon dry with paper towels and sprinkle with chile powder and remaining ¼ teaspoon salt. Heat oil in 8- or 10-inch nonstick skillet over medium-high heat until shimmering. Cook salmon, skin side up, until well browned, 3 to 5 minutes. Flip and continue to cook until salmon is still translucent when checked with tip of paring knife and registers 125 degrees (for medium-rare), 3 to 5 minutes.

3 Transfer salmon to plate and let cool slightly, about 2 minutes. Using 2 forks, flake salmon into rough 1-inch pieces; discard skin. Divide salmon among tortillas, then top with cabbage slaw and drizzle with crema. Serve with lime wedges.

MEAL PREP Slaw, crema, and cooked salmon can be refrigerated separately for up to 2 days.

Cal 420; Total Fat 16g;
Sat Fat 3.5g; Chol 50mg;
Sodium 830mg; Total Carb 46g;
Dietary Fiber 3g; Total Sugars 7g;
Protein 25g

SEAFOOD

COUSCOUS WITH SMOKED TROUT, APRICOTS, AND PICKLED PEPPERS

Serves 2   **Total Time: 25 minutes**

WHEN TO EAT
› **Pre-Workout** 3 to 4 hours before
› **Post-Workout** Within 2 hours
› **Maintenance**

WORKOUTS
› **Everyday**
› **Strength or Interval** Increase trout to 6 ounces.

MAKE IT A SNACK
Eat half a portion.

¾ cup boiling water

¾ cup couscous

½ teaspoon table salt, divided

1 tablespoon extra-virgin olive oil, plus extra for drizzling

½ cup jarred sliced banana peppers, plus 1 tablespoon brine

1 garlic clove, minced

1 teaspoon honey

8 ounces cherry or grape tomatoes, halved

¼ cup fresh parsley leaves

3 tablespoons chopped dried apricots

2 scallions, sliced thin

4 ounces hot-smoked trout, mackerel, or salmon, skin and pin bones removed, flaked

Lemon wedges

WHY THIS RECIPE WORKS ›› Carbohydrate-abundant couscous becomes a mild canvas for featuring bites of rich, savory smoked fish. A tangy dressing soaks into and livens up the grains, which we toss with tomatoes, parsley, and banana peppers. The brine from the banana peppers doesn't go to waste as we use it instead of vinegar in the dressing. A surprise addition, dried apricots are a great source of additional carbohydrates for this pre- or post-workout meal, and their sweetness offsets the dressed grains and smoky fish. For an accurate measurement of boiling water, bring a kettle of water to a boil and then measure out the desired amount. This recipe can easily be doubled.

1 Combine boiling water, couscous, and ¼ teaspoon salt in medium bowl. Cover and let sit for 10 minutes. Fluff couscous with fork.

2 Whisk oil, banana pepper brine, garlic, honey, and remaining ¼ teaspoon salt together in large bowl. Add couscous, peppers, tomatoes, parsley, apricots, and scallions and toss to combine. Season with salt and pepper to taste. Top each portion with smoked trout. Serve with lemon wedges.

MEAL PREP Couscous and trout can be refrigerated separately for up to 1 day; season with salt and pepper to taste and eat cold, warm, or at room temperature.

Cal 510; Total Fat 12g;
Sat Fat 2.5g; Chol 45mg;
Sodium 750mg; Total Carb 72g;
Dietary Fiber 7g;
Total Sugars 16g; Protein 26g

HOT-SMOKED SALMON KEDGEREE

Serves 2   **Total Time: 35 minutes**

WHEN TO EAT
› **Post-Workout** Within 2 hours

WORKOUTS
› **Everyday**
› **Strength or Interval** Increase salmon to 6 ounces.

---

2 tablespoons
  unsalted butter

1 small onion, chopped

½ teaspoon curry powder

¼ teaspoon table salt, divided

  Pinch cayenne pepper

3 cups cooked basmati
  rice pilaf

4 ounces hot-smoked
  salmon, mackerel, or trout

2 Hard-Cooked Eggs
  (page 294), peeled and
  grated or chopped fine

¼ cup chopped fresh parsley
  and/or chives

2 tablespoons lemon juice,
  plus lemon wedges
  for serving

⅛ teaspoon pepper

WHY THIS RECIPE WORKS ›› Kedgeree, a British derivative of the Indian dish kitchari, is a jumble of buttery rice and onions infused with curry powder and dotted with flakes of smoked fish, hard-cooked eggs, and herbs. The dish is pretty close to perfect for an athlete, so we calibrated it only slightly to have just the right balance of carbs and protein, with adjustments for if you want to enjoy it after a hard workout or intense intervals. By using precooked rice (use whatever you have prepared or leftovers from the fridge), each grain remains distinct and intact, which makes the kedgeree feel light and fluffy. Grating in hard-cooked eggs distributes richness throughout; use the large holes of a box grater to grate the eggs. We prefer to use a white rice pilaf made with basmati rice in this recipe, but any long-grain white rice pilaf will work (see page 285). This recipe can easily be doubled.

1 Melt butter in 10- or 12-inch nonstick skillet over medium-low heat. Add onion, curry powder, ⅛ teaspoon salt, and cayenne and cook until softened but not browned, 4 to 6 minutes.

2 Add rice and remaining ⅛ teaspoon salt and increase heat to medium-high. Cook, stirring frequently to break up clumps and coat rice with butter, until rice is heated through, about 5 minutes. Add salmon and cook, stirring frequently, until salmon is heated through, about 5 minutes.

3 Transfer mixture to large bowl. Add eggs, parsley, chives, lemon juice, and pepper and toss to combine. Season with salt and pepper to taste. Serve with lemon wedges.

MEAL PREP Kedgeree can be refrigerated for up to 2 days; reheat in skillet or microwave.

Cal 580; Total Fat 18g; Sat Fat 9g;
Chol 230mg; Sodium 820mg;
Total Carb 77g; Dietary Fiber 1g;
Total Sugars 2g; Protein 25g

THE EVERYDAY ATHLETE COOKBOOK

SALMON AND BLACK RICE SALAD WITH SNAP PEAS AND RADISHES

Serves 2   Total Time: 45 minutes

WHEN TO EAT
› **Post-Workout** Within 2 hours
› **Maintenance**

WORKOUTS
› **Everyday**
› **Strength or Interval** Increase salmon to 6 ounces.

MAKE IT A SNACK
Eat half a portion.

¾ cup black rice

½ teaspoon plus ⅛ teaspoon table salt, plus salt for cooking rice

1 tablespoon unseasoned rice vinegar, divided

1 (4-ounce) skin-on salmon fillet, 1 to 1½ inches thick

2 teaspoons canola oil, divided

1 teaspoon toasted sesame oil

1 teaspoon grated fresh ginger

1 teaspoon honey

4 ounces sugar snap peas, strings removed, halved crosswise

1 red bell pepper, stemmed, seeded, and chopped fine

4 radishes, trimmed, halved, and sliced thin

2 tablespoons minced fresh cilantro

—

Cal 520; Total Fat 21g;
Sat Fat 3.5g; Chol 45mg;
Sodium 860mg; Total Carb 60g;
Dietary Fiber 7g; Total Sugars 7g;
Protein 26g

WHY THIS RECIPE WORKS ›› To make this flavorful flaked salmon and crunchy snap pea salad optimal for athletes we used earthy black rice as a base. It's high in fiber and contains beneficial amino acids for after exercising, which can help you recover and build muscle. These ingredients are bolstered by a lively dressing of ginger, sesame oil, honey, and rice vinegar that is flavor packed but keeps the fat in check. If using wild salmon, decrease cook time slightly and cook fillet to 120 degrees (for medium-rare). You can substitute brown rice for the black rice; it may need a few extra minutes of cooking. This recipe can easily be doubled.

1 Bring 2 quarts water to boil in large saucepan over medium-high heat. Add rice and 1½ teaspoons salt and cook until rice is tender, 20 to 25 minutes. Drain rice, spread onto platter or rimmed baking sheet, drizzle with 1 teaspoon vinegar, and let cool completely, 10 to 15 minutes.

2 Meanwhile, pat salmon dry with paper towels and sprinkle with ⅛ teaspoon salt. Heat ½ teaspoon canola oil in 8- or 10-inch nonstick skillet over medium-high heat until shimmering. Cook salmon, skin side up, until well browned, 3 to 5 minutes. Flip and continue to cook until salmon is still translucent when checked with tip of paring knife and registers 125 degrees (for medium-rare), 3 to 5 minutes. Transfer salmon to plate and let cool slightly, about 2 minutes. Using 2 forks, flake salmon into rough 2-inch pieces; discard skin.

3 Whisk sesame oil, ginger, honey, remaining ½ teaspoon salt, remaining 2 teaspoons vinegar, and remaining 1½ teaspoons canola oil in large bowl. Add cooled rice, salmon, snap peas, bell pepper, radishes, and cilantro and toss to combine. Season with salt and pepper to taste. Serve.

MEAL PREP Salad can be refrigerated for up to 1 day.

TURMERIC SCALLOPS WITH MANGO NOODLE SALAD

Serves 2   Total Time: 35 minutes

WHEN TO EAT
› **Pre-Workout** 3 to 4 hours before
› **Post-Workout** Within 2 hours
› **Maintenance**

WORKOUTS
› **Everyday**
› **Endurance** Increase noodles to 3 ounces.
› **Strength or Interval** Increase scallops to 12 ounces.

---

2 ounces rice vermicelli noodles

2½ teaspoons canola oil, divided

8 ounces large sea scallops, tendons removed

2 teaspoons grated fresh ginger

¾ teaspoon ground turmeric, divided

¾ teaspoon ground coriander, divided

1 teaspoon grated lime zest plus 1 tablespoon juice, plus lime wedges for serving

2 teaspoons honey

1 cup ½-inch mango pieces

¼ English cucumber, halved lengthwise and sliced ¼ inch thick

¼ cup fresh cilantro leaves, plus extra for serving

1 shallot, sliced thin

2 tablespoons unsalted roasted pepitas

¼ teaspoon table salt

—

Cal 430; Total Fat 12g;
Sat Fat 1.5g; Chol 25mg;
Sodium 750mg; Total Carb 64g;
Dietary Fiber 5g;
Total Sugars 30g; Protein 20g

WHY THIS RECIPE WORKS ›› Scallops are a restaurant favorite, but they're also ideal at home for athletes as a lean, ultra-quick-cooking protein. Sitting atop a rice noodle and mango salad, the scallops bring the dish into balance while a splash of turmeric-lime dressing dials up the flavor. Fresh or thawed frozen mango will work here. We recommend using "dry" scallops, which don't have chemical additives and taste better than "wet." Dry scallops will look ivory or pinkish; wet scallops are bright white. This recipe can be easily doubled using a large pot and a 12-inch skillet.

1 Bring 2 quarts water to boil in large saucepan. Off heat, add noodles and let sit, stirring occasionally, until tender, about 5 minutes. Drain noodles, rinse well, and drain again. Toss noodles with ½ teaspoon oil; set aside. Meanwhile, place scallops on clean dish towel, then top with second clean dish towel and gently press to dry. Let scallops sit between towels at room temperature for 10 minutes.

2 Microwave 1 teaspoon oil, ginger, ½ teaspoon turmeric, and ½ teaspoon coriander together in large bowl until fragrant, about 10 seconds; let cool slightly. Whisk in lime zest and juice and honey. Add noodles, mango, cucumber, cilantro leaves, shallot, and pepitas; toss to combine. Season with salt and pepper to taste. Divide noodles between serving bowls.

3 Sprinkle scallops with salt, remaining ¼ teaspoon turmeric, and remaining ¼ teaspoon coriander. Heat remaining 1 teaspoon oil in 10- or 12-inch nonstick skillet over medium-high heat until just smoking. Add scallops and cook, without moving, until well browned, 1½ to 2 minutes. Flip scallops and continue to cook until sides of scallops are firm and centers are opaque, 30 to 90 seconds longer. As scallops finish cooking, transfer to bowls with noodles. Sprinkle with extra cilantro. Serve with lime wedges.

MEAL PREP Fully assembled dish can be refrigerated for up to 1 day.

SHRIMP PAD THAI

Serves 2   Total Time: 35 minutes

WHEN TO EAT
› **Pre-Workout** 3 to 4 hours before
› **Post-Workout** Within 2 hours

WORKOUTS
› **Endurance**
› **Everyday** Increase shrimp to 6 ounces.

---

4 ounces (⅜-inch-wide) flat rice noodles

3 tablespoons lime juice (2 limes)

2 tablespoons fish sauce

2 tablespoons packed brown sugar

4 ounces large shrimp (26 to 30 per pound), peeled, deveined, and tails removed

2 teaspoons canola oil

2 garlic cloves, minced

4 ounces (2 cups) bean sprouts

2 tablespoons chopped fresh cilantro

2 tablespoons unsalted dry-roasted peanuts, chopped

WHY THIS RECIPE WORKS ›› In the same time it takes to order delivery pad thai, you can prepare your own at home, perfectly customized to work at either end of your exercise routine. In only three steps you can get a savory-sweet-sour tangle of vitamin- packed, protein-rich shrimp and chewy rice noodles. A combo of fish sauce, lime juice, and brown sugar packs a big umami punch with just a few ingredients, while freshness is a welcome finisher with crisp-tender bean sprouts and bright cilantro. This recipe can easily be doubled using a 12-inch skillet.

1 Bring 2 quarts water to boil in large saucepan. Off heat, add noodles and let sit, stirring occasionally, until softened and pliable but not fully tender, about 15 minutes. Drain noodles, rinse well, and drain again; set aside.

2 Whisk lime juice, fish sauce, and sugar together in small bowl. Pat shrimp dry with paper towels. Heat oil in 10- or 12-inch nonstick skillet over medium heat until just smoking. Add shrimp and garlic and cook, stirring occasionally, until shrimp are just opaque, 1 to 2 minutes. Transfer to plate and tent loosely with aluminum foil.

3 Add noodles and lime juice mixture to now-empty skillet and cook over medium heat until sauce is thickened slightly, 2 to 3 minutes. Add sprouts and shrimp and cook until shrimp are opaque throughout and noodles are well coated and tender, about 1 minute. To serve, sprinkle each portion with cilantro and peanuts.

MEAL PREP Fully assembled dish can be refrigerated for up to 1 day.

Cal 430; Total Fat 11g;
Sat Fat 1g; Chol 70mg;
Sodium 810mg; Total Carb 70g;
Dietary Fiber 2g;
Total Sugars 17g; Protein 17g

SEAFOOD

SKILLET-BAKED SQUID AND ORZO WITH FETA AND TOMATOES

Serves 2   Total Time: 1 hour

WHEN TO EAT

› **Pre-Workout** 3 to 4 hours before
› **Post-Workout** Within 2 hours

WORKOUTS

› **Everyday**
› **Endurance** Serve with bread.
› **Strength or Interval** Increase squid to 12 ounces.

2½ teaspoons extra-virgin olive oil

1 small onion, chopped fine

1 red bell pepper, stemmed, seeded, and chopped fine

3 garlic cloves, minced

¼ teaspoon ground cinnamon

1 cup orzo

⅓ cup dry white wine

1 cup chicken or vegetable broth

½ cup water

6 ounces squid, bodies sliced crosswise into ¼-inch-thick rings, tentacles halved

2 tomatoes, cored and chopped

⅓ cup frozen peas

⅛ teaspoon table salt

1 ounce feta cheese, crumbled (¼ cup)

2 teaspoons chopped fresh dill

Lemon wedges

—

Cal 600; Total Fat 12g;
Sat Fat 3.5g; Chol 210mg;
Sodium 730mg; Total Carb 85g;
Dietary Fiber 5g;
Total Sugars 13g; Protein 32g

WHY THIS RECIPE WORKS ›› Squid is a lean protein and great source of omega-3 fatty acids. This one-pan squid and pasta bake is a delightful composition: creamy pasta, fresh-tasting peas and tomatoes, and tender squid. By cooking both the orzo and squid in the veggie base and broth, they absorb aromatics and flavor in the oven. You can substitute 8 ounces large shrimp (peeled, deveined, tails removed, and halved lengthwise) for the squid; stir shrimp into orzo mixture after removing the skillet from the oven and let sit until the shrimp are opaque throughout, about 5 minutes. This recipe can easily be doubled using a 12-inch skillet.

1 Adjust oven rack to middle position and heat oven to 375 degrees. Heat oil in 10- or 12-inch ovensafe skillet over medium heat until shimmering. Add onion and bell pepper and cook until softened and lightly browned, 4 to 6 minutes. Stir in garlic and cinnamon and cook until fragrant, about 30 seconds.

2 Stir in orzo and cook, stirring often, until orzo is lightly browned, about 2 minutes. Stir in wine, scraping up any browned bits, and simmer until nearly evaporated, about 1 minute. Stir in broth, water, squid, tomatoes, peas, and salt and bring to simmer. Sprinkle feta evenly over orzo mixture and transfer skillet to oven. Bake until orzo and squid are tender and liquid is mostly absorbed, 25 to 30 minutes.

3 Using pot holder, remove skillet from oven and let sit for 5 minutes. Being careful of hot skillet handle, gently stir orzo to recombine. Season with salt and pepper to taste. Sprinkle each portion with dill. Serve with lemon wedges.

MEAL PREP Fully assembled dish can be refrigerated for up to 1 day.

GARLICKY SPAGHETTI WITH CLAMS

Serves 2   Total Time: 30 minutes

WHEN TO EAT
› **Post-Workout** Within 2 hours
› **Maintenance**

WORKOUTS
› **Strength or Interval**
› **Everyday** Serve with bread.

- 6 ounces 100 percent whole-wheat spaghetti
- ¼ teaspoon table salt, plus salt for cooking pasta
- 3 garlic cloves, minced (1 tablespoon)
- 4 teaspoons extra-virgin olive oil
- ⅛ teaspoon red pepper flakes
- 1 (6½-ounce) can chopped clams
- 2 anchovy fillets, rinsed, patted dry, and minced
- 1 teaspoon lemon juice
- 2 tablespoons grated Parmesan cheese
- 2 tablespoons chopped fresh basil or parsley

WHY THIS RECIPE WORKS ›› For a busy athlete's seafood pasta that doesn't require reaching past the pantry, get the flavor of the sea (and good protein) with ease from canned clams. A judicious handful of minced anchovies added to the garlicky spaghetti provides favorable seafood brininess and accentuates the flavor of the clams. You can substitute traditional pasta for the whole-wheat. This recipe can easily be doubled.

1 Bring 2 quarts water to boil in large pot. Add pasta and 1½ teaspoons salt and cook, stirring frequently, until tender. Reserve ½ cup cooking water, then drain pasta and return it to pot.

2 Meanwhile, cook garlic and oil in 8- or 10-inch nonstick skillet over medium-low heat, stirring occasionally, until garlic is lightly browned, 6 to 8 minutes. Off heat, stir in pepper flakes.

3 Add garlic mixture, clams and their juice, anchovies, lemon juice, salt, and reserved cooking water to pasta. Stir until pasta is well coated with sauce and no water remains in bottom of pot, about 1 minute. Season with salt and pepper to taste. Sprinkle each portion with Parmesan and basil before serving.

MEAL PREP Fully assembled dish can be refrigerated for up to 1 day.

Cal 510; Total Fat 17g;
Sat Fat 3.5g; Chol 40mg;
Sodium 860mg; Total Carb 58g;
Dietary Fiber 9g;
Total Sugars 2g; Protein 32g

LINGUINE WITH SHRIMP, PEAS, AND PRESERVED LEMON

Serves 2   Total Time: 30 minutes

WHEN TO EAT
› **Pre-Workout** 3 to 4 hours before
› **Post-Workout** Within 2 hours
› **Maintenance**

WORKOUTS
› **Everyday**
› **Endurance** Serve with bread.
› **Strength or Interval** Increase shrimp to 12 ounces.

---

6 ounces linguine

¼ teaspoon table salt, plus salt for cooking pasta

8 ounces large shrimp (26 to 30 per pound), peeled, deveined, and tails removed

1 tablespoon extra-virgin olive oil

2 garlic cloves, minced

¾ teaspoon ground coriander

½ cup frozen peas

⅓ preserved lemon, pulp and white pith removed, rind rinsed and minced (1½ tablespoons)

2 tablespoons chopped fresh mint

1 ounce (1 cup) pea tendrils, arugula, or watercress

WHY THIS RECIPE WORKS ›› Shrimp pasta dishes are popular for good reason: They're super quick and provide a lot of meal for not much effort. This bright and summery dish is even better because it's perfectly customizable: dress it down with convenient substitutions if you only have a little bit of time to make it because of your gym routine, or keep it dressed up when you want a special dinner. Fragrant and floral, preserved lemon is a unique ingredient that is high in flavor but low in calories and sugar—a great condiment to have on hand to quickly infuse dishes with flavor. You can substitute 1 teaspoon grated lemon zest for the preserved lemon. This recipe can easily be doubled using a 12-inch skillet.

1 Bring 2 quarts water to boil in large pot. Add pasta and 1½ teaspoons salt and cook, stirring often, until tender. Reserve ½ cup cooking water, then drain pasta and return it to pot.

2 Meanwhile, pat shrimp dry with paper towels and sprinkle with salt. Heat oil, garlic, and coriander in 10- or 12-inch skillet over medium heat until fragrant, 1 to 2 minutes. Stir in shrimp, peas, ¼ cup cooking water, and preserved lemon. Increase heat to medium-high, cover, and cook, stirring occasionally, until shrimp are just opaque, 2 to 4 minutes.

3 Add shrimp mixture and mint to pasta and toss to combine. Adjust consistency with reserved cooking water as needed. Season with salt and pepper to taste. Top each portion with pea tendrils. Serve.

MEAL PREP Pasta can be refrigerated for up to 1 day.

Cal 470; Total Fat 10g;
Sat Fat 1g; Chol 105mg;
Sodium 780mg; Total Carb 70g;
Dietary Fiber 6g;
Total Sugars 4g; Protein 25g

PESCE ALL'ACQUA PAZZA WITH ANGEL HAIR

Serves 2   Total Time: 40 minutes

WHEN TO EAT
› **Pre-Workout** 3 to 4 hours before
› **Post-Workout** Within 2 hours

WORKOUTS
› **Everyday**
› **Endurance** Serve with a bread.
› **Strength or Interval** Increase haddock to 8 ounces.

6 ounces angel hair pasta

4 teaspoons extra-virgin olive oil

2 garlic cloves, sliced thin

⅛ teaspoon red pepper flakes

1 small onion, chopped fine

8 ounces cherry or grape tomatoes, halved

½ teaspoon table salt, divided

2½ cups water, divided

⅓ cup dry white wine

12 fresh parsley stems, plus 3 tablespoons chopped fresh parsley, divided

1 (6-ounce) skin-on haddock fillet, 1 to 1½ inches thick

⅛ teaspoon pepper

Cal 520; Total Fat 12g;
Sat Fat 1.5g; Chol 45mg;
Sodium 780mg; Total Carb 71g;
Dietary Fiber 5g;
Total Sugars 6g; Protein 26g

WHY THIS RECIPE WORKS ›› Translated as "fish in crazy water," this pasta dish's name refers to the Italian tradition of cooking fish in seawater (now a winey broth). Using skin-on fish infuses the broth with collagen to give it some body. For the haddock, you can substitute black sea bass, cod, hake, or red snapper, with or without skin. This recipe can easily be doubled using a 12-inch skillet.

1 Break pasta into 1- to 2-inch lengths; set aside. Heat oil, garlic, and pepper flakes in 10- or 12-inch skillet over medium heat, stirring constantly, until garlic begins to sizzle, 1 to 2 minutes. Add onion, tomatoes, and ¼ teaspoon salt and cook until vegetables are just softened, 2 to 3 minutes. Stir in ½ cup water, wine, parsley stems, and 1½ tablespoons chopped parsley and bring to simmer.

2 Sprinkle haddock with remaining ¼ teaspoon salt and pepper. Moving aside solids as much as possible, nestle haddock skin side down into skillet (liquid will not quite cover fillets). Spoon some liquid over haddock and return to simmer. Reduce heat to low, cover, and simmer until haddock registers 110 degrees at thickest point, 3 to 5 minutes. Off heat, let sit, covered, until haddock is opaque and registers 135 degrees, 3 to 5 minutes.

3 Using thin metal spatula, carefully transfer haddock to plate and tent loosely with aluminum foil. Discard parsley stems. Return skillet to medium-high heat, stir in remaining 2 cups water, and bring to boil. Add pasta and cook, stirring occasionally, until al dente, about 3 minutes. Off heat, let sit, covered, until pasta is tender, about 1 minute. Stir in remaining chopped parsley. Season with salt and pepper to taste. Divide pasta, broth, and vegetables between shallow soup bowls. Gently divide haddock into uniform pieces and transfer to serving bowls; discard skin. Serve.

MEAL PREP Cooked pasta, broth, and fish can be refrigerated separately for up to 1 day.

SEARED SHRIMP WITH TOMATO, AVOCADO, AND LIME QUINOA

Serves 2   Total Time: 50 minutes

WHEN TO EAT
› **Post-Workout** Within 2 hours
› **Maintenance**

WORKOUTS
› **Everyday**
› **Strength or Interval** Increase shrimp to 8 ounces.

---

1 cup prewashed white quinoa

1¼ cups water

¼ teaspoon table salt, divided

¼ teaspoon grated lime zest plus 2 tablespoons juice, divided, plus lime wedges for serving

2 tablespoons chopped fresh cilantro, divided

6 ounces large shrimp (26 to 30 per pound), peeled, deveined, and tails removed

⅛–¼ teaspoon chipotle chile powder

1 tablespoon extra-virgin olive oil

1 large tomato, cored and chopped

2 garlic cloves, minced

2 scallions, sliced thin

½ avocado, cut into ½-inch pieces

Cal 530; Total Fat 20g;
Sat Fat 3g; Chol 80mg;
Sodium 670mg; Total Carb 66g;
Dietary Fiber 11g;
Total Sugars 5g; Protein 23g

WHY THIS RECIPE WORKS ›› Quinoa has healthy hype for a reason: It has essential amino acids and its nuttiness pairs well with spiced shrimp and creamy avocado. If you buy unwashed quinoa, rinse it (to remove its bitter coating) and spread it on a clean dish towel to dry for 15 minutes. This recipe can easily be doubled using a large saucepan and a 12-inch skillet; increase water to 2⅓ cups.

1 Cook quinoa in large saucepan over medium-high heat, stirring frequently, until quinoa is very fragrant and makes continuous popping sound, 5 to 7 minutes. Stir in water and ⅛ teaspoon salt and bring to simmer. Reduce heat to low, cover, and simmer until quinoa is tender and liquid is absorbed, 18 to 22 minutes, stirring once halfway through cooking. Off heat, let sit, covered, for 10 minutes. Fluff quinoa with fork, then stir in lime zest, 1 tablespoon juice, and 1 tablespoon cilantro. Season with salt and pepper to taste; cover to keep warm.

2 Pat shrimp dry with paper towels and toss with chile powder and remaining ⅛ teaspoon salt in small bowl. Heat oil in 10- or 12-inch nonstick skillet over medium-high heat until just smoking. Add shrimp in single layer and cook, without moving, until spotty brown and edges turn pink on bottom sides, about 1 minute. Flip and cook until all but very centers of shrimp are opaque, about 30 seconds; transfer to plate.

3 Return now-empty skillet to medium-high heat. Add tomato, garlic, remaining 1 tablespoon lime juice, and remaining 1 tablespoon cilantro. Cook until tomatoes are just softened, about 1 minute. Stir in shrimp and any accumulated juices and cook until shrimp are heated through, about 1 minute. Season with salt and pepper to taste. Divide quinoa mixture between serving bowls. Top each portion with shrimp mixture, scallions, and avocado. Serve with lime wedges.

MEAL PREP Cooked quinoa and shrimp mixture can be refrigerated separately for up to 1 day; top with scallions and avocado before serving.

LEMON-POACHED HALIBUT WITH ROASTED FINGERLING POTATOES

Serves 2   Total Time: 50 minutes

WHEN TO EAT
› **Post-Workout** Within 2 hours
› **Maintenance**

WORKOUTS
› **Everyday**
› **Endurance** Increase potatoes to 2 pounds and tomatoes to 12 ounces.
› **Strength or Interval** Increase halibut to 8 ounces.

1½ pounds fingerling potatoes, halved lengthwise

2 tablespoons extra-virgin olive oil, divided

½ teaspoon plus ⅛ teaspoon table salt, divided

⅛ teaspoon pepper

6 ounces cherry or grape tomatoes, halved

1 (6-ounce) skinless halibut fillet, 1 to 1½ inches thick, halved crosswise

¼ teaspoon dried oregano, divided

1 lemon, sliced thin

1 tablespoon minced fresh parsley

—

Cal 490; Total Fat 15g;
Sat Fat 2g; Chol 40mg;
Sodium 810mg; Total Carb 66g;
Dietary Fiber 9g;
Total Sugars 5g; Protein 23g

WHY THIS RECIPE WORKS ›› Make-ahead-friendly foil packets mean you can prep most of this meal the day before. We love the one-pan roasting method because the lean, meaty halibut stays moist and absorbs flavor while the starchy potatoes get crisp on the outside and creamy on the inside. And there's only one sheet to clean. Win, win, win. Use potatoes that are approximately 1 inch in diameter. You can substitute mahi-mahi, red snapper, striped bass, or swordfish for the halibut. This recipe can easily be doubled.

1 Adjust oven rack to lower-middle position and heat oven to 450 degrees. Toss potatoes with 1 tablespoon oil, ½ teaspoon salt, and pepper on rimmed baking sheet. Arrange potatoes, cut sides down, in even layer. Roast until bottoms are lightly browned, 10 to 12 minutes.

2 Lay two 16 by 12-inch rectangles of aluminum foil on counter with short sides parallel to counter edge. Divide tomatoes evenly between foil rectangles, arranging in center of lower half of each sheet of foil. Pat halibut dry with paper towels, sprinkle with oregano, remaining ⅛ teaspoon salt, and place one piece on top of each tomato pile. Top each piece of halibut with 2 lemon slices and drizzle each with 1½ teaspoons oil. Fold top half of foil over halibut, then tightly crimp edges.

3 Remove baking sheet from oven, place packets on top of potatoes, and bake until halibut registers 130 degrees (insert thermometer through packet into thickest part of fillet) and cut sides of potatoes are crisp and skins are spotty brown, 10 to 15 minutes. Carefully open packets, allowing steam to escape away from you, and let cool slightly, about 2 minutes. Season potatoes with salt and pepper to taste and divide between serving plates. Using thin metal spatula, gently slide halibut and tomatoes onto potatoes. Top with any accumulated juices. Sprinkle with parsley. Serve.

MEAL PREP Assembled packets can be refrigerated for up to 1 day.

COCONUT-GINGER HALIBUT AND COUSCOUS PACKETS

Serves 2   Total Time: 45 minutes

WHEN TO EAT
› **Pre-Workout** 3 to 4 hours before
› **Post-Workout** Within 2 hours

WORKOUTS
› **Everyday**
› **Endurance** Increase couscous and boiling water in step 1 to 1¼ cups each.
› **Strength or Interval** Increase halibut to 8 ounces.

1¼ cups boiling water, divided

1 cup couscous

¼ teaspoon table salt, divided

⅓ cup canned coconut milk

2 tablespoons chopped fresh cilantro

1 tablespoon fish sauce

1 tablespoon packed brown sugar

2 teaspoons grated fresh ginger

1 garlic clove, minced
  Pinch red pepper flakes

1 (6-ounce) skinless halibut fillet, 1 to 1½ inches thick, halved crosswise

2 teaspoons lime juice, plus lime wedges for serving

Cal 520; Total Fat 10g;
Sat Fat 7g; Chol 40mg;
Sodium 710mg; Total Carb 78g;
Dietary Fiber 5g;
Total Sugars 7g; Protein 29g

WHY THIS RECIPE WORKS ›› Cooking juicy halibut fillets on a grain is an interesting spin on the packet technique. We chose couscous since it's super-quick-cooking and goes well with the bold, Thai-inspired sauce. You can substitute mahi-mahi, red snapper, striped bass, or swordfish for the halibut. For an accurate measurement of boiling water, bring a kettle of water to a boil and then measure out the desired amount. This recipe can easily be doubled.

1 Adjust oven rack to middle position and heat oven to 400 degrees. Combine 1 cup boiling water, couscous, and ⅛ teaspoon salt in large bowl. Cover and let sit for 10 minutes. Fluff couscous with fork.

2 Whisk remaining ¼ cup boiling water, coconut milk, cilantro, fish sauce, sugar, ginger, garlic, and pepper flakes together in bowl; set sauce aside.

3 Lay two 16 by 12-inch rectangles of aluminum foil on counter with short sides parallel to counter edge. Divide couscous evenly between foil rectangles, arranging in center of lower half of each sheet of foil. Pat halibut dry with paper towels, sprinkle with remaining ⅛ teaspoon salt, and place one piece on top of each couscous mound. Spoon 1 tablespoon coconut sauce onto each piece of halibut; set aside remaining coconut sauce. Fold top half of foil over halibut and couscous, then tightly crimp edges.

4 Place packets on rimmed baking sheet and bake until halibut registers 130 degrees, 10 to 15 minutes (insert thermometer through packet into thickest part of fillet). Carefully open packets, allowing steam to escape away from you, and let cool slightly, about 2 minutes. Microwave reserved coconut sauce until warmed through, about 1 minute, then whisk in lime juice. Using thin metal spatula, gently slide halibut and couscous onto serving plates and drizzle with sauce. Serve with lime wedges.

MEAL PREP Assembled packets can be refrigerated for up to 1 day.

BAKED COD WITH FARRO, TOMATOES, AND CHICKPEAS

Serves 2   Total Time: 50 minutes

WHEN TO EAT
› **Post-Workout** Within 2 hours
› **Maintenance**

WORKOUTS
› **Strength or Interval**
› **Everyday** Increase farro to 1 cup.

- ¾ cup whole farro
- ¼ teaspoon table salt, divided, plus salt for cooking farro
- 1 (15-ounce) can chickpeas, rinsed
- 8 ounces cherry or grape tomatoes, halved
- ¼ cup chicken or vegetable broth
- 1 shallot, minced
- 2 tablespoons extra-virgin olive oil
- 2 garlic cloves, minced
- 1 teaspoon grated lemon zest plus 1½ teaspoons juice, plus lemon wedges for serving
- 1 teaspoon ground coriander, divided
- 1 teaspoon paprika, divided
- ⅛ teaspoon pepper
- 1 (6-ounce) skinless cod fillet, 1 inch thick, halved crosswise
- 2 tablespoons chopped fresh cilantro

Cal 580; Total Fat 18g;
Sat Fat 2.5g; Chol 35mg;
Sodium 710mg; Total Carb 73g;
Dietary Fiber 14g;
Total Sugars 8g; Protein 33g

WHY THIS RECIPE WORKS ›› Chewy, nutty, and wholesome farro combines with chickpeas for a powerhouse base for lean fillets of tender cod. Tomatoes, lemon juice, and lemon zest liven up the dish, while garlic, shallots, and paprika bring warm savory flavors. You can prepare the entire dish then throw it in the oven for baking when you return from lifting weights. Do not use quick-cooking or presteamed farro. The cooking time for farro can vary greatly across brands, so we recommend checking for doneness after 15 minutes. You can substitute black sea bass, haddock, hake, or pollock for the cod. This recipe can easily be doubled using a large pot and a 13 by 9-inch baking dish.

1 Adjust oven rack to middle position and heat oven to 400 degrees. Bring 2 quarts water to boil in large saucepan. Add farro and ½ teaspoon salt, return to boil, and cook until grains are tender with slight chew, 15 to 30 minutes. Drain farro and transfer to 8-inch square baking dish.

2 Stir chickpeas, tomatoes, broth, shallot, oil, garlic, lemon zest and juice, ½ teaspoon coriander, ½ teaspoon paprika, ⅛ teaspoon salt, and pepper into farro until evenly combined.

3 Pat cod dry with paper towels and sprinkle with remaining ½ teaspoon coriander, remaining ½ teaspoon paprika, and remaining ⅛ teaspoon salt. Nestle cod into farro mixture and bake until cod flakes apart when gently prodded with paring knife and registers 135 degrees, 15 to 20 minutes. Remove baking dish from oven, tent with aluminum foil, and let rest for 5 minutes. Sprinkle each portion with cilantro before serving.

MEAL PREP Fully assembled unbaked dish can be refrigerated for up to 1 day.

VEGETABLE MAINS

LEMON-TARRAGON CHICKPEA SALAD SANDWICHES

Serves 2   Total Time: 20 minutes

WHEN TO EAT
› **Post-Workout** Within 2 hours
› **Maintenance**

WORKOUTS
› **Everyday**
› **Endurance** Serve with grapes or baked snack chips (see page 274).
› **Strength or Interval** Add a chopped hard-cooked egg (see page 294) to salad mixture.

MAKE IT A SNACK
Eat half a sandwich.

1 (15-ounce) can chickpeas, rinsed, divided

3 tablespoons plain low-fat yogurt

1 tablespoon mayonnaise

¾ teaspoon grated lemon zest plus 1½ teaspoons lemon juice

¼ teaspoon table salt

2 tablespoons minced celery

1 scallion, sliced thin

1 tablespoon minced fresh tarragon, parsley, or dill

1 tomato, sliced thin

½ avocado, sliced thin

2 tablespoons alfalfa sprouts

2 leaves Bibb, Boston, or iceberg lettuce

4 slices whole-grain sandwich bread, toasted if desired

WHY THIS RECIPE WORKS ›› Chickpeas serve as a great source of protein in this deli salad that's reminiscent of creamy egg salad without all the fat. To keep this refueling recipe healthful, we use more low-fat yogurt than mayonnaise to achieve the desired consistency, but still retain the familiar flavor. We use a potato masher (no need to break out the food processor) to mash some chickpeas into a mostly smooth paste before adding more whole ones, giving the salad interesting texture. Topping it off are classics that bring welcome freshness and nutrition: tomato, avocado, and alfalfa sprouts. This recipe can easily be doubled.

1 Using potato masher or rubber spatula, mash 6 tablespoons chickpeas with yogurt, mayonnaise, lemon zest and juice, and salt in medium bowl until mostly smooth. Add remaining chickpeas and mash to coarse paste with some larger pieces remaining.

2 Fold celery, scallion, and tarragon into chickpea mixture and season with salt and pepper to taste. Divide chickpea salad over 2 slices of bread. Top with tomato, avocado, sprouts, lettuce, and remaining bread slices. Serve.

MEAL PREP Chickpea salad can be refrigerated for up to 2 days.

Cal 420; Total Fat 18g;
Sat Fat 3g; Chol 5mg;
Sodium 840mg; Total Carb 52g;
Dietary Fiber 15g;
Total Sugars 11g; Protein 17g

VEGETABLE MAINS

SPICED CAULIFLOWER BURGERS

Serves 2   Total Time: 1 hour

WHEN TO EAT
› **Post-Workout** Within 2 hours
› **Maintenance**

WORKOUTS
› **Endurance**
› **Everyday** Increase Herb Yogurt Sauce to ½ cup.

12 ounces cauliflower florets, cut into 1-inch pieces

4 teaspoons extra-virgin olive oil, divided

¼ teaspoon cumin

¼ teaspoon coriander

¼ teaspoon plus ⅛ teaspoon table salt, divided

¼ cup panko bread crumbs

1 small carrot, peeled and shredded

3 tablespoons golden raisins

1 large egg, lightly beaten

2 whole-wheat burger buns, toasted if desired

¼ cup Herb Yogurt Sauce (page 303)

2 teaspoons sliced almonds, toasted

½ cup baby arugula

WHY THIS RECIPE WORKS ›› These burgers made from cauliflower have a lot going for them: They're nutritious and fiberful and filled with complex flavor. We love the contrast between their creamy, nutty-tasting interiors and crunchy, browned exteriors. The trick is to roast the cauliflower first; this intensifies its flavor and makes it easy to mash the florets with panko and an egg for binding. Make extra and freeze the patties so you can cook once and eat four times. Use the large holes of a box grater to shred the carrot. This recipe can easily be doubled.

1 Adjust oven rack to middle position and heat oven to 450 degrees. Toss cauliflower with 2 teaspoons oil, cumin, coriander, and ¼ teaspoon salt and arrange in even layer on rimmed baking sheet. Roast until cauliflower is well browned and tender, 15 to 20 minutes. Let cool slightly, then transfer to large bowl.

2 Using potato masher, mash cauliflower until broken into rough ½-inch pieces. Stir in panko, carrot, raisins, egg, and remaining ⅛ teaspoon salt until well combined. Divide cauliflower mixture into 2 equal portions. Using lightly moistened hands, tightly pack each portion into ¾-inch-thick patty. Transfer patties to large plate, cover with plastic wrap, and refrigerate until firm, at least 15 minutes.

3 Heat remaining 2 teaspoons oil in 10- or 12-inch nonstick skillet over medium heat until shimmering. Place patties in skillet and cook until well browned and crisp on first side, 3 to 5 minutes. Using 2 spatulas, gently flip patties and cook until well browned and crisp on second side, 3 to 5 minutes. Place each patty on bun bottom and top with yogurt sauce, almonds, and arugula. Top with bun tops and serve.

MEAL PREP Shaped patties can be refrigerated for up to 1 day or frozen (chilled, wrapped in plastic, and sealed in a zipper-lock bag) for up to 1 month. Cook frozen patties as directed; do not thaw first.

Cal 430; Total Fat 19g;
Sat Fat 3.5g; Chol 95mg;
Sodium 810mg; Total Carb 56g;
Dietary Fiber 5g;
Total Sugars 22g; Protein 14g

VEGETABLE MAINS

SKILLET PIZZA WITH BROCCOLI AND RED ONION

Serves 2   Total Time: 45 minutes

WHEN TO EAT
› **Post-Workout** Within 2 hours
› **Maintenance**

WORKOUTS
› **Everyday**
› **Endurance** Increase dough to 12 ounces.
› **Strength or Interval** Increase mozzarella cheese to 4 ounces.

MAKE IT A SNACK
Eat a quarter of the pizza.

---

6 ounces broccoli florets, cut into 1-inch pieces

½ red onion, sliced thin

1 garlic clove, minced

1 tablespoon extra-virgin olive oil

8 ounces store-bought pizza dough, room temperature

¼ cup jarred tomato sauce

2 ounces part-skim block mozzarella cheese, shredded (½ cup)

1 tablespoon grated Parmesan cheese

2 tablespoons shredded fresh basil

Cal 460; Total Fat 16g;
Sat Fat 5g; Chol 25mg;
Sodium 850mg; Total Carb 59g;
Dietary Fiber 4g; Total Sugars 7g;
Protein 19g

WHY THIS RECIPE WORKS ›› Pizza can be an asset to the athlete with vegetables (fiberful broccoli carries a lot of flavor after cooking) and low-fat cheese, and this one is conveniently cooked in a skillet. Pizza dough is often sold in 1-pound packages. Leftover dough can be used to make Chicken, Artichoke, and Spinach Calzones (page 101). If you're using an electric stove, heat the burner for 3 minutes on medium heat before starting to cook the pizza.

1 Adjust oven rack 6 inches from broiler element and heat broiler. Combine broccoli, onion, and 2 tablespoons water in large bowl and microwave, covered, until broccoli is tender, about 2 minutes. Drain well, stir in garlic, and set aside.

2 Using pastry brush, brush bottom (not sides) of 12-inch skillet with oil. Press and roll dough into 14-inch circle on lightly floured counter. Let dough rest on counter for 5 minutes. Loosely roll dough around rolling pin and gently unroll into skillet. Using fingertips, push dough into corners and up sides of skillet (dough should climb about 1 inch up sides of skillet). Using fork, poke bottom of dough 10 times.

3 Cover and cook over medium heat until bottom of crust is spotty brown, 8 to 12 minutes, checking halfway through cooking and popping any air bubbles with fork. Remove skillet from heat. Spread sauce evenly over dough, leaving ½-inch border. Top evenly with mozzarella, broccoli mixture, and Parmesan. Transfer skillet to oven and broil until crust and cheeses are spotty brown, about 5 minutes. Using spatula, slide pizza onto cutting board and let cool for 5 minutes. Sprinkle with basil before slicing. Serve.

MEAL PREP Pizza can be refrigerated for up to 2 days. Reheat in 400-degree oven.

ONE-PAN SPINACH AND CHEESE ENCHILADAS

Serves 2   **Total Time: 55 minutes**

WHEN TO EAT
› **Post-Workout** Within 2 hours
› **Maintenance**

WORKOUTS
› **Everyday**
› **Endurance** Serve with extra warmed tortillas.
› **Strength or Interval** Serve with Pan-Seared Tofu (page 291).

MAKE IT A SNACK
Eat one and a half enchiladas.

---

1 teaspoon canola oil

1 onion, chopped fine

1 green bell pepper, stemmed, seeded, and chopped fine

2 garlic cloves, minced

1½ teaspoons chili powder

1 teaspoon ground cumin

¾ cup jarred tomatillo salsa

½ cup water

10 ounces frozen chopped spinach, thawed and squeezed dry

2 ounces Monterey Jack cheese, shredded (½ cup), divided

6 (6-inch) corn tortillas

2 tablespoons fresh cilantro leaves

4 radishes, trimmed and sliced thin

—

Cal 440; Total Fat 18g; Sat Fat 6g; Chol 25mg; Sodium 860mg; Total Carb 58g; Dietary Fiber 9g; Total Sugars 12g; Protein 17g

WHY THIS RECIPE WORKS ›› With help from jarred tomatillo salsa, these simple green enchiladas seem to come together in a skillet in no time at all. You will need a 10-inch ovensafe skillet with a tight-fitting lid for this recipe. The recipe can easily be doubled: Prepare sauce in skillet as directed and arrange enchiladas in two rows across width of 13 by 9-inch baking dish.

1 Adjust oven rack to middle position and heat oven to 450 degrees. Heat oil in 10-inch ovensafe skillet over medium heat until shimmering. Add onion and bell pepper and cook until softened, about 5 minutes. Stir in garlic, chili powder, and cumin and cook until fragrant, about 30 seconds. Stir in salsa and water, bring to simmer, and cook until sauce is slightly thickened, 4 to 6 minutes. Season with salt and pepper to taste.

2 Measure out and reserve 1½ cups tomatillo sauce, leaving remaining sauce in skillet. Combine spinach and ¼ cup Monterey Jack in large bowl. Stir in ½ cup reserved tomatillo sauce. Stack tortillas and wrap in damp dish towel. Microwave until pliable, 30 seconds to 1 minute.

3 Working with 1 tortilla at a time, spread 2 tablespoons spinach mixture across center. Roll tortilla tightly around filling and place seam side down in sauce in skillet. Repeat with remaining tortillas and remaining filling, arranging enchiladas side by side in single row. Pour remaining reserved sauce over enchiladas and sprinkle with remaining ¼ cup Monterey Jack.

4 Bake, covered, until cheese is melted, 8 to 10 minutes. Uncover and continue to bake until sauce is bubbling around edges, 3 to 5 minutes. Sprinkle with cilantro and radishes and serve.

MEAL PREP Sauce can be refrigerated for up to 2 days. Baked enchiladas can be refrigerated for up to 2 days.

VEGETABLE MAINS

201

RED LENTIL KIBBEH

Serves 2   **Total Time: 1 hour**

WHEN TO EAT
› **Post-Workout** Within 2 hours
› **Maintenance**

WORKOUTS
› **Everyday**
› **Endurance** Serve with pita bread.
› **Strength or Interval** Top with
  tofu (see page 291), tempeh (see
  page 291), or an egg cooked to your
  liking (see pages 292–295).

MAKE IT A SNACK
Eat half a portion.

---

  4 teaspoons extra-virgin
     olive oil, divided

  1 small onion, chopped fine

 ½ red bell pepper,
     chopped fine

 ½ teaspoon table salt

  1 tablespoon harissa

  1 tablespoon tomato paste

 ½ cup medium-grind bulgur

  2 cups water

 ⅓ cup dried red lentils,
     picked over and rinsed

 ¼ cup chopped fresh parsley

  1 tablespoon lemon juice

 ½ head Bibb lettuce
     (4 ounces), leaves
     separated

 ⅔ cup plain low-fat yogurt

     Lemon wedges

Cal 460; Total Fat 18g;
Sat Fat 3g; Chol 5mg;
Sodium 790mg; Total Carb 62g;
Dietary Fiber 11g;
Total Sugars 10g; Protein 18g

**WHY THIS RECIPE WORKS ›› ** Kibbeh is a popular Middle Eastern dish made from bulgur, minced onions, varying spices, and often ground meat that can be formed into balls, pressed into a pan, and baked or grilled, or served raw like this. Our version uses lentils in lieu of meat as the texture of the two is similar. Red lentils are a vibrant, strong source of protein. Cooking them with tomato paste brings out a sweet, umami quality, and harissa adds deeper flavor. To balance the aromatics, we stir in lemon juice and parsley at the end. This dish is flexible, so spoon it onto Bibb lettuce leaves or eat it alongside pita bread—depending upon your exercise that day. We prefer to use our homemade Harissa (page 302) but you can substitute store-bought. This recipe can easily be doubled.

1 Heat 2 teaspoons oil in large saucepan over medium heat until shimmering. Add onion, bell pepper, and salt and cook until softened, about 5 minutes. Stir in harissa and tomato paste and cook until fragrant, about 1 minute.

2 Stir in bulgur and water and bring to simmer. Reduce heat to low, cover, and cook until bulgur is barely tender, about 8 minutes. Stir in lentils, cover, and cook, stirring occasionally, until lentils and bulgur are tender, 8 to 10 minutes.

3 Off heat, lay clean folded dish towel underneath lid, and let sit for 10 minutes. Add remaining 2 teaspoons oil, parsley, and lemon juice and stir vigorously until mixture is cohesive. Season with salt and pepper to taste. Spoon kibbeh into lettuce leaves and top with yogurt. Serve with lemon wedges.

MEAL PREP Kibbeh can be refrigerated for up to 3 days. Serve warm or at room temperature.

QUINOA TACO SALAD

Serves 2   **Total Time: 1¼ hours**

WHEN TO EAT
› **Post-Workout** Within 2 hours
› **Maintenance**

WORKOUTS
› **Everyday**
› **Endurance** Serve with baked tortilla chips (see page 274).
› **Strength or Interval** Top with tofu (see page 291), tempeh (see page 291), or a hard-cooked egg (see page 294).

MAKE IT A SNACK
Eat half a portion.

½ cup prewashed white quinoa

1 tablespoon extra-virgin olive oil, divided

1 small onion, chopped fine

2 teaspoons tomato paste

1 teaspoon chipotle chile powder

¼ teaspoon ground cumin

⅔ vegetable broth

2 teaspoons lime juice, plus lime wedges for serving

1 small head escarole, trimmed and sliced thin

2 tablespoons chopped fresh cilantro, divided

1 (15-ounce) can black beans, rinsed

4 ounces cherry or grape tomatoes, quartered

½ ripe avocado, cut into ½-inch pieces

1 ounce queso fresco, crumbled (¼ cup)

Cal 510; Total Fat 19g;
Sat Fat 3g; Chol 5mg;
Sodium 770mg; Total Carb 71g;
Dietary Fiber 23g;
Total Sugars 7g; Protein 20g

WHY THIS RECIPE WORKS ›› Spiced quinoa pilaf, which is a complete protein, is a flavorful stand-in for ground beef in this simple, healthy taco salad. Complementary escarole further deepens the flavor, and offers more nutrients and fiber than iceberg. We like the convenience of prewashed quinoa. If you buy unwashed quinoa, rinse it to remove its bitter protective coating (called saponin) and then pat dry. This recipe can easily be doubled.

1 Toast quinoa in large saucepan over medium-high heat, stirring often, until quinoa is very fragrant and makes continuous popping sound, 5 to 7 minutes; transfer to bowl.

2 Heat 1 teaspoon oil in now-empty saucepan over medium heat until shimmering. Add onion and cook until softened and lightly browned, 4 to 6 minutes. Stir in tomato paste, chile powder, and cumin and cook until fragrant, about 30 seconds. Stir in broth and toasted quinoa and bring to simmer. Cover, reduce heat to low, and cook until quinoa is tender and liquid has been absorbed, 18 to 22 minutes, stirring halfway through cooking.

3 Off heat, let sit, covered, for 10 minutes. Spread quinoa onto platter or rimmed baking sheet and let cool completely, 10 to 15 minutes.

4 Whisk remaining 2 teaspoons oil and lime juice together in large bowl. Add escarole and cilantro and toss to combine. Fold in beans, tomatoes, and avocado. Season with salt and pepper to taste. Divide escarole mixture between serving dishes and top with quinoa mixture and queso fresco. Serve with lime wedges.

MEAL PREP Quinoa mixture can be refrigerated for up to 2 days. Serve cold or at room temperature.

FATTOUSH WITH BUTTERNUT SQUASH AND APPLE

Serves 2   Total Time: 40 minutes

WHEN TO EAT
› **Post-Workout** Within 2 hours
› **Maintenance**

WORKOUTS
› **Endurance**
› **Everyday** Serve with tofu (see page 291) or a hard-cooked egg (see page 294).

---

5 teaspoons extra-virgin olive oil, divided

4 teaspoons lemon juice

1 teaspoon ground sumac, plus extra for serving

8 ounces butternut squash, peeled, seeded, and cut into ½-inch pieces (about 1½ cups)

⅛ teaspoon table salt

⅛ teaspoon pepper

3 cups baked pita chips, broken into ½-inch pieces

6 ounces chopped romaine lettuce (4 cups)

1 apple, cored and cut into ½-inch pieces

⅔ cup frozen shelled edamame beans, thawed and patted dry

2 tablespoons chopped fresh parsley

2 scallions, sliced thin

1 ounce feta cheese, crumbled (¼ cup)

WHY THIS RECIPE WORKS ›› Pitas are a mainstay of Mediterranean cuisine, but they can stale quickly, so dishes designed to use them up abound. Pita bread salad, or fattoush, is a common example—and its appeal goes far beyond leftovers. This pita salad with distinctly fall flavors boasts fantastic contrasts in texture and multiple sources of helpful carbohydrates (butternut squash, apples, and pita) to fuel your run or any endurance-intensive workout. When buying pita chips, look for brands that contain no more than 3 grams of fat per 1-cup serving. Or, you can use our homemade Baked Pita Chips (page 274). This recipe can easily be doubled.

1 Adjust oven rack to lowest position and heat oven to 450 degrees. Whisk 4 teaspoons oil, lemon juice, and sumac together in large bowl; set aside.

2 Toss squash with remaining 1 teaspoon oil, salt, and pepper. Spread in even layer on rimmed baking sheet and roast until well browned and tender, 10 to 12 minutes, stirring halfway through roasting. Set aside to cool slightly, about 5 minutes.

3 Add squash, pita chips, lettuce, apple, edamame, parsley, and scallions to bowl with dressing and toss gently to coat. Season with salt and pepper to taste. To serve, top each portion with 2 tablespoons feta and sprinkle with extra sumac.

MEAL PREP Roasted squash can be refrigerated for up to 2 days.

Cal 500; Total Fat 18g;
Sat Fat 4g; Chol 15mg;
Sodium 910mg; Total Carb 70g;
Dietary Fiber 11g;
Total Sugars 17g; Protein 17g

VEGETABLE MAINS

207

RAINBOW SALAD WITH CRISPY TEMPEH

Serves 2   Total Time: 20 minutes

WHEN TO EAT
› **Post-Workout** Within 2 hours
› **Maintenance**

WORKOUTS
› **Everyday**
› **Endurance** Serve with bread.
› **Strength or Interval** Serve with extra Crispy Tempeh.

MAKE IT A SNACK
Eat half a portion.

1 orange

5 ounces (5 cups) baby arugula

3 tablespoons Orange-Ginger Vinaigrette (page 301), divided

1 (15-ounce) can diced beets, rinsed and patted dry

6 ounces cherry tomatoes, halved

½ ripe avocado, cut into ½-inch pieces

4 radishes, trimmed, halved, and sliced thin

2 tablespoons crumbled blue cheese

1 recipe Crispy Tempeh (page 291)

WHY THIS RECIPE WORKS ›› A rainbow of fruits and vegetables on a bed of greens makes a stunning presentation—and a healthful, plant-based meal. For good recovery after exercising, canned diced beets are a great choice because they last awhile, reduce prep time, and are rich in nutrients. Other salad toppings—cherry tomatoes and segmented oranges—offer bright acidity which we balance with buttery avocado and crisp radishes. A generous amount of crispy tempeh is just the crunchy protein addition we need. Blue cheese may be a surprising finish, but it provides small umami bites to contrast the fresh vegetables. If you can't find canned diced beets, substitute canned sliced or whole beets and cut them into ½-inch pieces.

1 Cut away peel and pith from orange. Holding fruit over bowl, use paring knife to slice between membranes to release segments.

2 Toss arugula with 1 tablespoon vinaigrette and season with salt and pepper to taste. Divide arugula between serving bowls, then top with orange segments, beets, tomatoes, avocado, radishes, and blue cheese. Drizzle with remaining 2 tablespoons vinaigrette and sprinkle with tempeh. Serve.

MEAL PREP Salad and vinaigrette can be refrigerated separately for up to 2 days.

Cal 410; Total Fat 21g;
Sat Fat 4g; Chol 5mg;
Sodium 600mg; Total Carb 46g;
Dietary Fiber 8g;
Total Sugars 24g; Protein 14g

VEGETABLE MAINS

BLACK-EYED PEA SALAD WITH PEACHES AND PECANS

Serves 2   Total Time: 20 minutes

WHEN TO EAT
› **Post-Workout** Within 2 hours
› **Maintenance**

WORKOUTS
› **Everyday**
› **Endurance** Increase peaches to 4.
› **Strength or Interval** Serve with tofu (see page 291), tempeh (see page 291), or a hard-cooked egg (see page 294).

MAKE IT A SNACK
Eat half a portion.

- 1 tablespoon extra-virgin olive oil
- ½ teaspoon grated lime zest plus 1 tablespoon juice
- 1 small garlic clove, minced
- ¼ teaspoon table salt
- 2 (15-ounce) cans black-eyed peas, rinsed
- 2 peaches or nectarines, halved, pitted, and cut into 1-inch pieces
- 1 small head frisée or escarole, trimmed and cut into 2-inch pieces (about 3 cups)
- 2 tablespoons finely chopped red onion
- 2 tablespoons coarsely chopped fresh basil or parsley
- 1 tablespoon chopped toasted pecans or almonds
- ½ jalapeño chile, seeded and chopped fine

Cal 420; Total Fat 19g;
Sat Fat 2g; Chol 0mg;
Sodium 850mg; Total Carb 53g;
Dietary Fiber 12g;
Total Sugars 15g; Protein 15g

WHY THIS RECIPE WORKS ›› Highly nutritious black-eyed peas are the base for this athlete-supporting salad; as a complex carbohydrate they help you feel satisfied for longer while providing plenty of fiber. Because they are especially popular in the South, we looked to Southern cuisine for inspiration. Peaches add sweet juiciness, while pecans lend crunch and richness. We felt greens were necessary, so we turned to frisée, a delicate but slightly bitter-tasting lettuce. For a little spice, we add a chopped jalapeño, its seeds removed to mellow the fruity heat. This recipe can easily be doubled.

Whisk oil, lime zest and juice, garlic, and salt together in large bowl. Add beans, peaches, frisée, onion, basil, pecans, and jalapeño and toss to combine. Season with salt and pepper to taste. Serve.

MEAL PREP Salad can be refrigerated for up to 1 day.

FREEKEH SALAD WITH SWEET POTATOES AND WALNUTS

Serves 2   Total Time: 55 minutes

WHEN TO EAT
› **Post-Workout** Within 2 hours
› **Maintenance**

WORKOUTS
› **Endurance**
› **Strength or Interval** Serve
with tofu (see page 291), tempeh
(see page 291), or a hard-cooked
egg (see page 294).

MAKE IT A SNACK
Eat half a portion.

- ¾ cup freekeh
- ½ teaspoon table salt, divided, plus salt for cooking freekeh
- 6 ounces sweet potato, peeled and cut into 1-inch pieces (about 1 cup)
- 1 tablespoon extra-virgin olive oil, divided
- ¼ teaspoon pepper, divided
- ¼ teaspoon ground fenugreek or curry powder
- 2 tablespoons tahini
- 1 tablespoon lemon juice
- 1 tablespoon water
- ½ cup fresh cilantro leaves
- 2 tablespoons walnuts, toasted and chopped

—

Cal 500; Total Fat 21g;
Sat Fat 2.5g; Chol 0mg;
Sodium 620mg; Total Carb 66g;
Dietary Fiber 14g;
Total Sugars 3g; Protein 14g

WHY THIS RECIPE WORKS ›› High-fiber freekeh is a wheat-based grain that deserves a spot in your pantry for its grassy, slightly smoky flavor that's absent from other whole-wheat products. It's a good source of carbs, but freekeh also has three times more protein than brown rice, making it a superfood base for athletes wanting a vegetarian bowl. We top our base with roasted sweet potatoes and season them with fenugreek, a sweet seed with a unique, maple-like flavor. To bring everything together, we stir in a rich yet bright tahini-lemon dressing. You can substitute barley for the freekeh; decrease cook time to 20 to 40 minutes. This recipe can easily be doubled using a large pot and a 10- or 12-inch skillet.

1 Bring 2 quarts water to boil in large saucepan. Add freekeh and ½ teaspoon salt, return to boil, and cook until grains are tender with sligh chew, 30 to 45 minutes. Drain freekeh, spread onto platter or rimmed baking sheet, and let cool completely, 10 to 15 minutes.

2 Meanwhile, microwave potato in covered bowl until tender, 5 to 8 minutes, stirring halfway through microwaving; drain well. Heat 1 teaspoon oil in 8- or 10-inch nonstick skillet over medium heat until shimmering. Add potatoes, ¼ teaspoon salt, and ⅛ teaspoon pepper and cook, stirring occasionally, until golden brown, 4 to 6 minutes. Off heat, stir in fenugreek.

3 Whisk tahini, lemon juice, water, remaining ¼ teaspoon salt, remaining 2 teaspoons oil, and remaining ⅛ teaspoon pepper together in large bowl. Add freekeh, potatoes, cilantro, and walnuts and toss to combine. Season with salt and pepper to taste. Serve warm or at room temperature.

MEAL PREP Salad can be refrigerated for up to 1 day.

ORZO SALAD WITH CUCUMBER, FETA, AND MINT

Serves 2   Total Time: 40 minutes

WHEN TO EAT
> **Pre-Workout** 3 to 4 hours before
> **Post-Workout** Within 2 hours
> **Maintenance**

WORKOUTS
> **Endurance**
> **Everyday** Serve with a hard-cooked egg (see page 294).

MAKE IT A SNACK
Eat half a portion.

⅔ cup orzo

½ teaspoon table salt, plus salt for cooking pasta

2½ teaspoons extra-virgin olive oil, divided

1 tablespoon lemon juice

1 garlic clove, minced

¼ teaspoon pepper

¼ English cucumber, halved lengthwise and sliced thin

1½ ounces feta cheese, crumbled (⅓ cup)

½ small red onion, chopped fine

¼ cup chopped fresh mint

2 scallions, sliced thin

**WHY THIS RECIPE WORKS ›› ** Orzo's firm, chewy texture is a great canvas for an easy salad that transforms just a few ingredients into a refreshing, carb-replenishing dinner. So when you don't have a plan for dinner after the gym, turn to the veggie drawer and prep them while the orzo cooks and cools. Cucumber, red onion, and mint add delicate, grassy flavors and crunchy texture while a simple but effective vinaigrette of olive oil, lemon juice, and garlic dresses everything. Enjoy the second serving as a pre-workout meal the next day. This recipe can easily be doubled using a large pot.

1 Bring 2 quarts water to boil in large saucepan. Add orzo and 1½ teaspoons salt and cook, stirring frequently, until al dente. Drain orzo and transfer to rimmed baking sheet. Toss with ½ teaspoon oil and let cool completely, about 15 minutes.

2 Whisk salt, lemon juice, garlic, pepper, and remaining 2 teaspoons oil together in large bowl. Add cucumber, feta, onion, mint, scallions, and cooled orzo and toss to combine. Season with salt and pepper to taste Serve.

MEAL PREP Pasta can be refrigerated for up to 2 days.

Cal 340; Total Fat 11g;
Sat Fat 4.5g; Chol 20mg;
Sodium 860mg; Total Carb 49g;
Dietary Fiber 1g; Total Sugars 5g;
Protein 12g

ESPINACAS CON GARBANZOS

Serves 2   Total Time: 45 minutes

WHEN TO EAT
› **Post-Workout** Within 2 hours

WORKOUTS
› **Everyday**
› **Endurance** Serve with extra bread.
› **Strength or Interval** Serve with an egg cooked to your liking (see pages 292–295).

---

1 plum tomato, halved lengthwise

1 (15-ounce) can chickpeas, rinsed

¾ cup vegetable or chicken broth

1 (7-inch) piece baguette (4 ounces), cut on bias into 3 pieces

2 tablespoons extra-virgin olive oil, divided

3 garlic cloves, minced

1 teaspoon smoked paprika

½ teaspoon ground cumin

Pinch ground cinnamon

Pinch cayenne pepper

1 small pinch saffron (optional)

2 teaspoons sherry or white wine vinegar, plus extra for seasoning

5 ounces frozen chopped spinach, thawed and squeezed dry

½ cup water

—

Cal 450; Total Fat 18g;
Sat Fat 2.5g; Chol 0mg;
Sodium 870mg; Total Carb 54g;
Dietary Fiber 9g;
Total Sugars 7g; Protein 17g

WHY THIS RECIPE WORKS ›› Substantive and flavorful espinacas con garbanzos has an Arab influence but is a spinach and chickpea dish native to Seville. Briefly simmering canned chickpeas (a convenient option after a workout) in broth tenderizes them and ensures that the flavor of the main ingredient is extra savory. A picada, a paste of garlic and bread cooked in plenty of olive oil, thickens and seasons the sauce like magic—and also provides extra carbs. Cumin, smoked paprika, and cinnamon add warm flavors, while spinach disperses beautifully throughout. This recipe can easily be doubled.

1 Using box grater, shred flesh of tomato into small bowl; discard skin and set bowl aside. Combine chickpeas and broth in large saucepan and bring to boil over high heat. Adjust heat to maintain simmer and cook until level of liquid is just below top layer of chickpeas, 8 to 10 minutes.

2 Meanwhile, tear one baguette piece into 1-inch pieces and process in food processor until finely ground (you should have about 1 cup crumbs). Heat 1 tablespoon oil in 8- or 10-inch nonstick skillet over medium heat until just shimmering. Add bread crumbs and cook, stirring often, until deep golden brown, 3 to 4 minutes. Add garlic, paprika, cumin, cinnamon, cayenne, and saffron, if using, and cook until fragrant, about 30 seconds. Off heat, stir in shredded tomato and vinegar.

3 Stir bread mixture, spinach, and water into chickpeas and bring to simmer over medium heat. Cook, stirring occasionally, until mixture is thick and stew-like, 5 to 10 minutes. Off heat, stir in remaining 1 table-spoon oil. Cover and let sit for 5 minutes. Season with salt and extra vinegar to taste. Serve with remaining bread.

MEAL PREP Chickpea and spinach mixture can be refrigerated for up to 2 days. Serve with fresh bread.

VEGETABLE MAINS

BEET AND CARROT SESAME NOODLES WITH TOFU

Serves 2   Total Time: 30 minutes

WHEN TO EAT
> **Post-Workout** Within 2 hours

WORKOUTS
> **Everyday**
> **Endurance** Serve with baked snack chips (see page 274).
> **Strength or Interval** Serve with extra Pan-Seared Tofu.

---

1 pound beets,
  trimmed and peeled

1 pound carrots,
  trimmed and peeled

½ cup Peanut-Sesame Sauce
  (page 302)

1 tablespoon hot water,
  plus more if needed

2 scallions, sliced thin on bias

Soy sauce

1 recipe Pan-Seared Tofu
  (page 291)

2 tablespoons fresh
  cilantro leaves

1 teaspoon sesame seeds,
  toasted

Lime wedges for serving

WHY THIS RECIPE WORKS ›〉 We're always seeking creative ways to add more vegetables to our diet, and spiralizing them into noodles offers an easy way to fill our plate, and our body. This supercharged mix of raw beet and carrot noodles has bright colors from pigments associated with antioxidant and anti-inflammatory properties and is a great carrier for a creamy sesame dressing. We prefer to spiralize our own vegetables, but you can substitute store-bought spiralized beets and carrots, though they tend to be drier and less flavorful. We prefer unsweetened natural almond or peanut butter (smooth or chunky) in the Peanut-Sesame Sauce, but any style of nut butter can be used. This recipe can easily be doubled.

1 Using spiralizer, cut beets and carrots into ⅛-inch-thick noodles, then cut beet and carrot noodles into 6-inch lengths.

2 Whisk sauce and hot water together in large bowl until mixture has consistency of heavy cream, about 1 minute. (Adjust consistency with extra hot water, 1 tablespoon at a time, as needed.)

3 Add noodles and scallions to sauce and toss to combine. Season with soy sauce to taste. Top each portion with tofu and sprinkle with cilantro and sesame seeds. Serve with lime wedges.

MEAL PREP The cut noodles, tofu, and sauce can be refrigerated separately for up to 2 days. Thin sauce with hot water as needed before tossing with noodles.

Cal 480; Total Fat 20g;
Sat Fat 3g; Chol 0mg;
Sodium 870mg; Total Carb 61g;
Dietary Fiber 15g;
Total Sugars 36g; Protein 21g

SPICY BASIL NOODLES WITH TOFU AND BOK CHOY

Serves 2   Total Time: 50 minutes

WHEN TO EAT
› **Pre-Workout** 3 to 4 hours before
› **Post-Workout** Within 2 hours

WORKOUTS
› **Everyday**
› **Endurance** Increase noodles to 5 ounces.
› **Strength or Interval** Serve with extra Pan-Seared Tofu.

MAKE IT A SNACK
Eat half a portion.

---

4 ounces (⅜-inch-wide) flat rice noodles

1 cup vegetable broth

1½ tablespoons lime juice

1 tablespoon packed brown sugar

2 teaspoons fish sauce

1 Thai chile, stemmed, seeded, and chopped

2 shallots, chopped coarse

3 garlic cloves, chopped coarse

2 teaspoons canola oil, divided

2 heads baby bok choy (4 ounces each), sliced ¼ inch thick and washed thoroughly

½ red bell pepper, sliced thin

1 recipe Pan-Seared Tofu (page 291)

1 ounce sugar snap peas, strings removed, sliced thin

1 cup fresh Thai basil leaves, torn into 1-inch pieces, divided

—

Cal 450; Total Fat 13g;
Sat Fat 1g; Chol 0mg;
Sodium 770mg; Total Carb 69g;
Dietary Fiber 4g;
Total Sugars 13g; Protein 17g

WHY THIS RECIPE WORKS ›› For a sustaining dish to awaken your senses, spicy basil rice noodles are combined with crisp-tender vegetables in a feisty sauce. With lots of fueling carbohydrates, rice noodles are low in fiber (and fat), so you can indulge in these chewy strands on either end of your workout. You can substitute an equal amount of Italian basil for the Thai basil. This recipe can easily be doubled using a large pot.

1 Bring 2 quarts water to boil in large saucepan. Off heat, add noodles and let sit, stirring occasionally, until softened and pliable but not fully tender, about 15 minutes. Drain noodles, rinse well, and drain again; set aside.

2 Meanwhile, whisk broth, lime juice, sugar, and fish sauce together in bowl until sugar has dissolved; set aside. Process chile, shallots, and garlic in blender, adding up to 3 tablespoons water and scraping down sides of blender jar as needed to form smooth paste, 15 to 20 seconds.

3 Heat 1 teaspoon oil in 12-inch nonstick skillet over high heat until shimmering. Add bok choy and bell pepper and cook until crisp-tender and lightly browned, 3 to 4 minutes; transfer to second bowl. Heat remaining 1 teaspoon oil in now-empty skillet over medium-high heat until shimmering. Add processed chile mixture and cook until color deepens, 3 to 5 minutes. Add noodles and broth mixture and cook, tossing gently, until noodles are well coated and tender, about 5 minutes.

4 Off heat, add sautéed vegetables, tofu, snap peas, and ¾ cup basil and toss to combine. Season with salt and pepper to taste. Sprinkle with remaining basil and serve.

MEAL PREP Noodles and vegetables can be refrigerated for up to 2 days.

CHILLED SOBA NOODLE SALAD WITH SNOW PEAS

Serves 2   **Total Time: 25 minutes**

WHEN TO EAT
› **Pre-Workout** 3 to 4 hours before
› **Post-Workout** Within 2 hours

WORKOUTS
› **Endurance**
› **Everyday** Serve with tofu (see page 291), tempeh (see page 291), or an egg cooked to your liking (see pages 292–295).

MAKE IT A SNACK
Eat half a portion.

---

6 ounces dried soba noodles

1 tablespoon mirin

1 tablespoon toasted sesame oil

1 tablespoon water

2 teaspoons white miso

½ teaspoon grated fresh ginger

⅛–¼ teaspoon red pepper flakes

¼ English cucumber, quartered lengthwise and sliced thin

3 ounces snow peas, strings removed, cut lengthwise into matchsticks

2 radishes, trimmed, halved, and sliced thin

2 scallions, sliced thin on bias

1 tablespoon sesame seeds

1 sheet toasted nori, quartered and cut into thin strips

WHY THIS RECIPE WORKS ›› Soba are buckwheat-based noodles that are satiating while being low on the glycemic index, so they'll fuel you up without a crash. We toss the cooked soba with an umami-loaded dressing of miso, ginger, and pepper flakes that clings to and flavors the noodles without overpowering their distinctly nutty taste. The chilled nature of this dish makes for great leftovers so you can look forward to it the next day. You can substitute yellow, red, or brown miso for the white miso and plain pre-toasted seaweed snacks for the toasted nori. This recipe can easily be doubled using a large pot.

1 Bring 2 quarts water to boil in large saucepan. Add noodles and cook, stirring often, until tender. Drain noodles, rinse well, and drain again; set aside.

2 Whisk mirin, oil, water, miso, ginger, and pepper flakes together in large bowl. Add noodles and toss to combine. Add cucumber, snow peas, radishes, scallions, sesame seeds, and nori and toss to combine. Season with salt and pepper to taste. Serve.

MEAL PREP Finished dish can be refrigerated for up to 2 days; add nori just before serving.

Cal 430; Total Fat 10g;
Sat Fat 1g; Chol 0mg;
Sodium 850mg; Total Carb 74g;
Dietary Fiber 3g;
Total Sugars 6g; Protein 16g

CAMPANELLE WITH ROASTED CAULIFLOWER AND GARLIC SAUCE

Serves 2   **Total Time: 45 minutes**

WHEN TO EAT
› **Post-Workout** Within 2 hours
› **Maintenance**

WORKOUTS
› **Endurance**
› **Everyday** Top with a fried or poached egg (see pages 292 and 294).

---

10 whole garlic cloves, peeled

2 tablespoons extra-virgin olive oil, divided

1 pound cauliflower florets, cut into 1-inch pieces

½ teaspoon table salt, plus salt for cooking pasta

¼ teaspoon pepper

⅛ teaspoon sugar

6 ounces 100 percent whole-wheat campanelle pasta

1 tablespoon lemon juice, plus extra for seasoning

¼ cup grated Parmesan cheese

2 tablespoons chopped fresh parsley

⅛–¼ teaspoon red pepper flakes

Cal 510; Total Fat 19g;
Sat Fat 3.5g; Chol 5mg;
Sodium 780mg; Total Carb 70g;
Dietary Fiber 14g;
Total Sugars 6g; Protein 19g

WHY THIS RECIPE WORKS ›› Roasted garlic, which can give simple dishes complex flavor (without adding fat), is low-lift here as you can roast it alongside the cauliflower. After roasting, we mash the garlic into a creamy sauce with olive oil, lemon juice, Parmesan, and some of the pasta cooking water. You can substitute traditional pasta for the whole-wheat pasta. You can also substitute 6 ounces of farfalle or medium shells for the campanelle, but the cup amount will differ. This recipe can easily be doubled using a large pot.

1 Adjust oven rack to lower-middle position and heat oven to 500 degrees. Place garlic cloves in center of 12-inch square of aluminum foil and drizzle with 1 teaspoon oil. Pull sides of foil up around garlic, keeping cloves in single layer, and crimp tightly to seal. Place packet on rimmed baking sheet.

2 Toss cauliflower with 1 tablespoon oil, salt, pepper, and sugar and arrange in even layer on empty portion of baking sheet. Roast until cauliflower is well browned and tender and garlic is soft, 10 to 15 minutes. Carefully open the garlic foil packet, allowing steam to escape away from you, and let cool slightly, about 2 minutes.

3 Meanwhile, bring 2 quarts water to boil in large saucepan. Add pasta and 1½ teaspoons salt and cook, stirring frequently, until tender. Reserve ½ cup cooking water, then drain pasta and return it to pot.

4 Transfer garlic to medium bowl and mash with fork until mostly smooth. Whisk in ⅓ cup reserved pasta water, lemon juice, Parmesan, parsley, pepper flakes, and remaining 2 teaspoons oil. Add garlic sauce and cauliflower to pasta and toss to combine. Adjust consistency with remaining reserved cooking water as needed. Season with salt, pepper, and extra lemon juice to taste. Serve.

MEAL PREP Fully assembled dish can be refrigerated for up to 2 days.

PENNE WITH CHERRY TOMATOES AND CRISPY CAPER CRUMBS

Serves 2   Total Time: 45 minutes

WHEN TO EAT
> **Pre-Workout** 3 to 4 hours before
> **Post-Workout** Within 2 hours
> **Maintenance**

WORKOUTS
> **Endurance**
> **Everyday** Top with a fried or poached egg (see pages 292 and 294).

- ¼ cup panko bread crumbs
- 2 tablespoons capers, rinsed and patted dry
- 1 tablespoon extra-virgin olive oil, divided
- 2 anchovy fillets, rinsed, patted dry, and minced, divided
- 2 tablespoons minced fresh parsley
- ½ teaspoon grated lemon zest
- 6 ounces penne, ziti, or fusilli pasta
- ⅛ teaspoon table salt, plus salt for cooking pasta
- 1 garlic clove, sliced thin
- 1 pound cherry tomatoes
- ⅛ teaspoon sugar
- ⅛–¼ teaspoon red pepper flakes
- ½ cup fresh basil leaves, torn if large
- 2 tablespoons grated Parmesan cheese

Cal 480; Total Fat 12g;
Sat Fat 2g; Chol 10mg;
Sodium 790mg; Total Carb 79g;
Dietary Fiber 6g;
Total Sugars 8g; Protein 18g

WHY THIS RECIPE WORKS ›› This umami-bomb pasta is comforting and quick to enjoy before an intense spin class, or to look forward to after a lengthy run. Surprisingly, cherry tomatoes are the perfect choice for a fast, fresh tomato sauce: Toss them directly into the pan and—thanks to their size—they don't take long to concentrate and thicken into a sauce. Be sure to use cherry tomatoes; grape tomatoes won't break down as much and will result in a drier sauce. This recipe can easily be doubled using a large pot.

1 Stir panko, capers, 1 teaspoon oil, and half the anchovies together in small bowl until evenly combined. Microwave, stirring occasionally, until golden, 2 to 4 minutes; let cool completely. Stir in parsley and lemon zest and season with salt and pepper to taste; set aside.

2 Bring 2 quarts water to boil in large pot. Add pasta and 1½ teaspoons salt to boiling water. Cook, stirring often, until al dente. Reserve ½ cup cooking water, then drain pasta and return it to pot.

3 Meanwhile, heat remaining 2 teaspoons oil, garlic, and remaining anchovies in large saucepan over medium heat. Cook, stirring occasionally, until anchovies break down and garlic is lightly browned, 4 to 5 minutes. Stir in tomatoes, sugar, pepper flakes, and salt. Increase heat to medium-high, cover, and cook, without stirring, for 10 minutes.

4 Add tomato mixture to pasta and stir gently until oil and tomato juices combine to form light sauce, about 15 seconds. Adjust consistency with reserved cooking water as needed. Stir in basil and Parmesan and season with salt and pepper to taste. Top each portion with panko mixture. Serve.

MEAL PREP Pasta can be refrigerated for up to 2 days. Top with panko mixture before serving.

FIDEOS WITH CHICKPEAS AND GOAT CHEESE

Serves 2   Total Time: 50 minutes

WHEN TO EAT
› **Post-Workout** Within 2 hours
› **Maintenance**

WORKOUTS
› **Endurance**
› **Everyday** Increase goat cheese to ½ cup.

4 ounces 100 percent whole-wheat thin spaghetti

4 teaspoons extra-virgin olive oil, divided

1 small onion, chopped fine

2 tomatoes, cored and chopped

2 garlic cloves, minced

1 teaspoon smoked paprika

1½ cups vegetable or chicken broth

1 (15-ounce) can chickpeas, rinsed

¼ cup dry white wine

½ teaspoon pepper

¼ cup crumbled goat cheese

1 tablespoon chopped fresh parsley

Lemon wedges

Cal 530; Total Fat 17g;
Sat Fat 3.5g; Chol 5mg;
Sodium 910mg; Total Carb 73g;
Dietary Fiber 11g;
Total Sugars 10g; Protein 18g

WHY THIS RECIPE WORKS ›› Fideos, a richly flavored and incredibly popular Spanish dish, calls for breaking noodles into small lengths and toasting them before cooking them with seafood and chorizo in a garlicky tomato stock. We thought the base of bold tomatoes and toasted noodles would work well with chickpeas, so we developed our plant-forward, endurance-ready version using the bean. You can substitute traditional spaghetti for the whole-wheat spaghetti. This recipe can easily be doubled using a 12-inch broiler-safe skillet.

1 Break spaghetti into 1- to 2-inch lengths. Toast pasta in 1 teaspoon oil in 10- or 12-inch broiler-safe skillet over medium-high heat, tossing frequently with tongs, until pasta is well browned and releases nutty aroma (pasta should be color of peanut butter), 6 to 10 minutes; transfer to bowl.

2 Heat 2 teaspoons oil in now-empty skillet over medium heat until shimmering. Add onion and cook until softened and lightly browned, 4 to 6 minutes. Stir in tomatoes and cook until softened, 3 to 5 minutes. Stir in garlic and paprika and cook until fragrant, about 30 seconds. Stir in toasted pasta, broth, chickpeas, wine, and pepper and bring to simmer. Cook, stirring gently and often, until liquid is thickened and pasta is just tender, 8 to 10 minutes.

3 Adjust oven rack 6 inches from broiler element and heat broiler. Off heat, sprinkle goat cheese over fideos and drizzle with remaining 1 teaspoon oil. Transfer skillet to oven and broil until surface of pasta is dry with crisped, browned spots, 3 to 5 minutes. Using pot holder, remove skillet from oven, and let sit for 5 minutes. Sprinkle each portion with parsley and serve with lemon wedges.

MEAL PREP Pasta can be refrigerated for up to 2 days.

VEGETABLE MAINS

BULGUR PILAF WITH TOFU, SHIITAKES, AND EDAMAME

Serves 2   Total Time: 50 minutes

WHEN TO EAT
› **Post-Workout** Within 2 hours
› **Maintenance**

WORKOUTS
› **Everyday**
› **Endurance** Serve with bread.
› **Strength or Interval** Increase tofu to 14 ounces.

MAKE IT A SNACK
Eat half a portion.

---

1 tablespoon canola oil

4 ounces shiitake mushrooms, stemmed and sliced thin

1 carrot, peeled and sliced ¼ inch thick

4 scallions, white parts minced, green parts sliced thin on bias, divided

1 tablespoon grated fresh ginger

1 cup medium-grind bulgur, rinsed

1 cup vegetable or chicken broth

½ cup water

1 tablespoon soy sauce, plus extra for seasoning

7 ounces firm or extra-firm tofu, cut into 1-inch pieces

¼ cup frozen shelled edamame beans, thawed and patted dry

2 teaspoons unseasoned rice vinegar

1 teaspoon mirin

Cal 500; Total Fat 14g; Sat Fat 1g;
Chol 0mg; Sodium 880mg;
Total Carb 70g; Dietary Fiber 8g;
Total Sugars 8g; Protein 25g

WHY THIS RECIPE WORKS ›› Rice isn't the only whole grain that takes well to the pilaf method. To bring more diversity to our grain dishes, we swapped out rice for bulgur, a form of wheat grain that's been parboiled and dried so it cooks quickly. We cook the bulgur with earthy mushrooms and carrots, which pair well with the hearty grain. After cooking, we sprinkle low-prep cubed tofu on top of the still-hot pilaf and let it just warm through, perfectly balancing this dish for everyday workouts. You can substitute cremini, oyster, or white mushrooms for the shiitakes. Don't confuse bulgur with cracked wheat, which has a much longer cooking time and will not work in this recipe. The recipe can easily be doubled.

1 Heat oil in large saucepan over medium heat until shimmering. Add mushrooms and carrot and cook until softened, 4 to 6 minutes. Stir in scallion whites and ginger and cook until fragrant, about 30 seconds.

2 Stir in bulgur, broth, water, and soy sauce and bring to simmer. Cover, reduce heat to low, and simmer until bulgur is tender, 16 to 18 minutes.

3 Off heat, sprinkle tofu, edamame, and scallion greens over bulgur. Lay clean folded dish towel underneath lid, and let bulgur sit, covered, for 5 minutes. Gently fluff bulgur with fork, sprinkle with vinegar and mirin, and season with extra soy sauce to taste. Serve.

MEAL PREP Bulgur pilaf can be refrigerated for up to 2 days.

RISOTTO PRIMAVERA

Serves 2   Total Time: 55 minutes

WHEN TO EAT
› **Pre-Workout** 3 to 4 hours before
› **Post-Workout** Within 2 hours

WORKOUTS
› **Everyday**
› **Endurance** Serve with bread.
› **Strength or Interval** Top with a fried or poached egg (see pages 292 and 294).

1¾ cups vegetable or
     chicken broth

½ cup water, plus extra
     as needed

1 tablespoon extra-virgin
     olive oil, divided

3 ounces cremini mushrooms,
     trimmed and sliced thin

½ teaspoon table salt, divided

1 small onion, chopped fine

½ cup arborio rice

3 ounces asparagus,
     trimmed and cut into
     ½-inch pieces

¼ cup frozen peas

¼ cup grated
     Parmesan cheese

2 tablespoons chopped
     fresh basil or parsley

2 teaspoons lemon juice

Cal 340; Total Fat 12g;
Sat Fat 3g; Chol 10mg;
Sodium 870mg; Total Carb 45g;
Dietary Fiber 4g;
Total Sugars 5g; Protein 15g

WHY THIS RECIPE WORKS ›› Most risottos require attentive stirring from start to finish. For busy athletes, we streamlined our vegetable-full risotto so it cooks undisturbed for the first 12 minutes before you break out the wooden spoon. Yet the finished dish is still remarkably creamy. You can substitute oyster, shiitake, or white mushrooms for the cremini. This recipe can easily be doubled.

1 Combine broth and water in 4-cup liquid measuring cup or medium bowl and microwave until simmering, about 5 minutes. Cover to keep warm.

2 Heat 1 teaspoon oil in large saucepan over medium heat until shimmering. Add mushrooms and ¼ teaspoon salt, cover, and cook until mushrooms begin to release their liquid, about 3 minutes. Uncover and continue to cook until liquid has evaporated and mushrooms begin to brown, about 3 minutes; transfer to bowl.

3 Heat remaining 2 teaspoons oil in now-empty saucepan over medium heat until shimmering. Add onion and remaining ¼ teaspoon salt and cook until softened, about 3 minutes. Add rice and cook, stirring constantly, until grains are translucent around edges, about 1 minute. Stir in 1½ cups warm broth and bring to simmer. Reduce heat to medium-low, cover, and simmer until almost all liquid is absorbed, 10 to 12 minutes. Stir in asparagus, cover, and cook for 2 minutes. Add ½ cup warm broth and cook, stirring constantly, until liquid is absorbed, about 3 minutes. Add remaining broth and peas and cook, stirring constantly, until rice is creamy and tender, about 3 minutes.

4 Off heat, stir in mushrooms, cover, and let sit until warmed through, about 2 minutes. Stir in Parmesan, basil, and lemon juice. Adjust consistency with extra warm water as needed. Season with salt and pepper to taste. Serve.

MEAL PREP Risotto can be refrigerated for up to 2 days. Adjust consistency with broth or water as needed when reheating.

BEET-BARLEY RISOTTO

Serves 2   Total Time: 1 hour

WHEN TO EAT
› **Post-Workout** Within 2 hours
› **Maintenance**

WORKOUTS
› **Everyday**
› **Endurance** Serve with bread.
› **Strength or Interval** Top with a fried or poached egg
  (see pages 292 and 294).

1½ cups water, plus extra
   as needed

1 cup vegetable broth

1 tablespoon extra-virgin
  olive oil

1 small onion, chopped fine

½ cup pearl barley

2 garlic cloves, minced

½ teaspoon minced fresh
  thyme or ¼ teaspoon dried

¼ cup dry white wine

1 (15-ounce) can whole
  beets, rinsed, patted dry,
  and shredded

1 ounce (1 cup) baby spinach

1½ ounces Parmesan cheese,
   grated (¾ cup)

2 tablespoons chopped
  fresh parsley

—

Cal 430; Total Fat 15g;
Sat Fat 4g; Chol 15mg;
Sodium 860mg; Total Carb 55g;
Dietary Fiber 11g;
Total Sugars 10g; Protein 17g

WHY THIS RECIPE WORKS ›› Risotto might seem to need arborio rice, however, we found a different grain that yields similar results: nutrient-dense pearl barley. It creates a supple, velvety sauce when simmered, while delivering a boost of vitamins and minerals to replenish after any kind of workout. For even more beneficial properties, canned beets are an easy, nutritious addition that simmers directly in the risotto. Do not substitute hulled, hull-less, quick-cooking, or presteamed barley for the pearl barley. Use the large holes of a box grater to shred the beets. This recipe can easily be doubled.

1 Combine water and broth in 4-cup liquid measuring cup or medium bowl and microwave until simmering, about 5 minutes. Cover to keep warm.

2 Heat oil in large saucepan over medium heat until shimmering. Add onion and cook until softened and lightly browned, 4 to 6 minutes. Add barley and cook, stirring often, until grains are lightly toasted, about 3 minutes. Stir in garlic and thyme and cook until fragrant, about 30 seconds. Stir in wine and cook until fully absorbed, about 2 minutes.

3 Stir in 1 cup warm broth and beets and bring to simmer. Cook, stirring often, until liquid is absorbed and bottom of saucepan is dry, 10 to 15 minutes. Repeat with 1 cup broth.

4 Add spinach and remaining broth and continue to cook, stirring often, until spinach is wilted and barley is cooked through but still somewhat firm in center, 5 to 10 minutes. Off heat, stir in Parmesan and adjust consistency with extra warm water as needed. Season with salt and pepper to taste. Sprinkle each portion with parsley and serve.

MEAL PREP Risotto can be refrigerated for up to 2 days. Adjust consistency with broth or water as needed when reheating.

VEGETABLE MAINS

235

DRINKS & SNACKS

STRAWBERRY ELECTROLYTE REFRESHER

Makes ⅔ cup dry mix, enough for 8 drinks   **Total Time: 15 minutes**

WHEN TO DRINK
› **Pre-Workout** 30 to 60 minutes before
› **Post-Workout** Within 1 hour

WORKOUTS
› **Endurance**

½ cup (½ ounce) freeze-dried strawberries

½ cup sugar

1 teaspoon citric acid

½ teaspoon table salt

½ teaspoon dried mint (optional)

WHY THIS RECIPE WORKS ›› For sports drink lovers, this excitingly easy homemade powdered mix is quickly rehydrated with water for benefits before or after any heart-pumping activity—sans any dyes or artificial flavors. Freeze-dried fruit, blitzed in the blender, is both the drink's coloring and flavoring. Containing valuable electrolytes from salt, which we lose in sweat, and necessary carbs from sugar that provide energy, this great tasting and hydrating refresher can be ready in 15 minutes, with extra mix to make 7 more drinks. You can find citric acid online or with canning supplies in most supermarkets. This recipe can easily be doubled.

1 Process all ingredients in blender until finely ground, about 30 seconds, scraping down sides of blender jar as needed. Using fine-mesh strainer, sift mixture into large bowl; discard any seeds and remaining fruit pieces. Transfer to storage container with tight-fitting lid.

2 To drink, combine 8 ounces water and 1 rounded tablespoon dry mix in 2- to 4-cup beverage container with tight-fitting lid. Seal container and shake vigorously until refresher mix is fully combined (fruit powder will not dissolve), about 30 seconds. Serve.

BLUEBERRY-CINNAMON ELECTROLYTE REFRESHER
Substitute freeze-dried blueberries for strawberries and ¼ teaspoon ground cinnamon for mint.

TART CHERRY–FENNEL ELECTROLYTE REFRESHER
Substitute freeze-dried tart cherries for strawberries and ¼ teaspoon ground fennel seeds for mint.

MEAL PREP Dry mix can be stored in airtight container at room temperature for up to 2 weeks. Break up any clumps before using.

—

Per Drink
Cal 60; Total Fat 0g; Sat Fat 0g;
Chol 0mg; Sodium 150mg;
Total Carb 15g; Dietary Fiber 0g;
Total Sugars 13g; Protein 0g

CHOCOLATE PROTEIN DRINK

Makes 2¼ cups powdered protein mix, enough for 8 drinks   Total Time: 10 minutes

WHEN TO DRINK
> **Pre-Workout** 1 to 2 hours before
> **Post-Workout** Within 1 hour

WORKOUTS
> **Everyday**
> **Strength or Interval**

Dry Mix

- 2 cups (6 ounces) unflavored whey protein isolate powder
- ¼ cup (¾ ounce) unsweetened cocoa powder
- 2 tablespoons sugar
- 2½ teaspoons ground cinnamon (optional)

Drink

- Unsweetened rice or oat milk

WHY THIS RECIPE WORKS ›› Although flavored protein powders are all over the market, having control over your protein source and ingredients puts your health in your own hands. We balance readily available unflavored whey protein isolate with a touch of sugar, spice, and chocolate (or coffee or matcha flavors) for a superlative shake that will be the envy of the locker room. The small amount of sugar and the choice of rice or oat milk give the drink enough carbohydrates for proper fuel before a workout, or for optimizing the protein uptake for muscle rebuilding afterward. Do not substitute whey protein concentrate for the whey protein isolate powder; their protein amounts differ. This recipe can easily be doubled.

1 For the dry mix Whisk whey protein powder, cocoa, sugar, and cinnamon, if using, together in bowl; transfer to storage container with tight-fitting lid.

2 For each drink Combine 8 ounces rice milk and rounded ¼ cup dry mix in 2- to 4-cup beverage container with tight-fitting lid. Seal container and shake vigorously until protein mix has fully dissolved, about 30 seconds. Serve.

MATCHA-CARDAMOM PROTEIN DRINK
Substitute matcha powder for the cocoa powder and ground cardamom for the cinnamon.

SPICED COFFEE PROTEIN DRINK
Substitute espresso powder for the cocoa powder and 2 teaspoons five-spice powder for the cinnamon.

MEAL PREP Dry mix can be stored in an airtight container at room temperature for up to 2 weeks.

Per Drink
Cal 220; Total Fat 4g; Sat Fat 1g;
Chol 0mg; Sodium 90mg;
Total Carb 33g; Dietary Fiber 0g;
Total Sugars 15g; Protein 15g

MELON-LEMON AGUA FRESCA

Serves 2   Total Time: 20 minutes

WHEN TO DRINK
› **Pre-Workout** 30 to
  60 minutes before
› **Post-Workout**
› **Maintenance**

WORKOUTS
› **Everyday**
› **Endurance**
› **Strength or Interval**

---

4 cups (1-inch pieces)
  honeydew melon or
  cantaloupe (1¼ pounds)

1½ cups water

2 tablespoons lemon juice

1 tablespoon honey

Pinch table salt

Ice

WHY THIS RECIPE WORKS ›› Agua fresca, a refreshing
Mexican fruit drink, is made by blending fruits (and sometimes
additional flavorings) with water, citrus juice, and a modest amount
of sugar. This melon version is a great way to hydrate, and its sugars
can provide a quick burst of energy in the immediate pre-workout
phase, especially when food isn't an option. The melon contains
lots of natural sugar so a little honey is all that is needed for
additional sweetness and carbohydrates. And if you make it ahead,
you have a better-than-bottled beverage to grab on the way out of
the house, especially when you're short on time. The agua fresca is
a good pre-workout snack, but it shouldn't take the place of solid
snacks on a more regular basis. This recipe can easily be doubled.

Process melon and water in blender until smooth, about 30 seconds.
Strain mixture through fine-mesh strainer into 1-quart jar or pitcher;
discard solids. Stir in lemon juice, honey, and salt until honey is
dissolved, about 30 seconds. Serve over ice.

MEAL PREP Agua fresca can be refrigerated for up to 3 days; stir to
recombine before serving.

—

Cal 120; Total Fat 0g; Sat Fat 0g;
Chol 0mg; Sodium 80mg;
Total Carb 31g; Dietary Fiber 1g;
Total Sugars 26g; Protein 2g

HIBISCUS-GUAVA AGUA FRESCA

Serves 2   Total Time: 10 minutes, plus 45 minutes steeping

WHEN TO DRINK
› **Pre-Workout** 30 to
  60 minutes before
› **Post-Workout**
› **Maintenance**

WORKOUTS
› **Everyday**
› **Endurance**
› **Strength or Interval**

---

2 hibiscus tea bags

1 cup water, room
  temperature

1 cup guava nectar, chilled

1 tablespoon honey

2 teaspoons lemon juice

  Pinch table salt

  Ice

WHY THIS RECIPE WORKS ›› Tea bags are an excellent, natural way to infuse hydrating drinks with tons of flavor. We chose a fruity combination of hibiscus tea and guava nectar because, on top of being floral and inviting, hibiscus is packed with beneficial antioxidants. The guava nectar brightens the hibiscus tea with a tangy, sweet presence. This energy-packed agua fresca makes a great pre-workout snack if you don't have time to eat, but it shouldn't take the place of solid snacks on a regular basis. Look for hibiscus tea that is 100 percent hibiscus and for guava nectar without added sugars. You can substitute pineapple or mango juice for the guava nectar. This recipe can easily be doubled.

Tie strings of tea bags together (for easy removal), place in 1-quart jar or pitcher, and cover with water. Let steep for 45 minutes, then discard tea bags. Stir in guava nectar, honey, lemon juice, and salt until honey is dissolved, about 30 seconds. Serve over ice.

MEAL PREP Agua fresca can be refrigerated for up to 3 days; stir to recombine before serving.

Cal 90; Total Fat 0g; Sat Fat 0g;
Chol 0mg; Sodium 80mg;
Total Carb 24g; Dietary Fiber 0g;
Total Sugars 22g; Protein 0g

CANTALOUPE-MINT ICED GREEN TEA

Serves 4   **Total Time: 20 minutes, plus 1 hour steeping**

WHEN TO DRINK
> Maintenance

WORKOUTS
> Everyday
> Endurance
> Strength or Interval

½ small ripe cantaloupe, seeded

2 tablespoons loose-leaf green tea

3 cups hot water (175 degrees)

1 cup ice water

3 tablespoons chopped fresh mint

2 tablespoons sugar (optional)

1 tablespoon lemon juice

Ice

WHY THIS RECIPE WORKS ›› When you want something more exciting than water that you can hydrate with anytime, look to interesting iced teas. This green tea is infused with the invigorating combination of cantaloupe and mint and has optional sugar for when you need a little sweetness or an energy boost. Chinese green tea will produce a grassy, floral tea, whereas Japanese green tea will be more savory. You can use caffeinated or decaffeinated tea in this recipe. Three tea bags can be substituted for the loose-leaf tea. This recipe can easily be doubled.

1 Cut cantaloupe into 4 quarters; do not peel. Grasping peel, shred flesh on large holes of box grater to yield 1 cup pulp; set aside. Place tea in bowl. Add hot water and steep for 4 minutes. Add ice water, mint, sugar, if using, lemon juice, and reserved cantaloupe. Stir tea with wooden spoon until sugar is dissolved. Let steep for 1 hour.

2 Strain tea through fine-mesh strainer into 1-quart jar or pitcher (or strain into second bowl and transfer to pitcher); discard solids. Serve over ice.

MEAL PREP Strained tea can be refrigerated for up to 3 days.

Cal 40; Total Fat 0g; Sat Fat 0g;
Chol 0mg; Sodium 15mg;
Total Carb 10g; Dietary Fiber 0g;
Total Sugars 9g; Protein 0g

RASPBERRY-BASIL ICED BLACK TEA

Serves 4   Total Time: 15 minutes, plus 1 hour steeping

WHEN TO DRINK
› **Maintenance**

WORKOUTS
› **Everyday**
› **Endurance**
› **Strength or Interval**

7½ ounces (1½ cups) frozen raspberries, thawed

3 tablespoons chopped fresh basil

2 tablespoons sugar (optional)

2 teaspoons lemon juice

1½ teaspoons loose-leaf black tea

3 cups boiling water

1 cup ice water

Ice

WHY THIS RECIPE WORKS ›› Caffeine is a go-to performance enhancer for athletes, but we wanted something more refreshing than coffee. So we looked to tea as the backbone for an iced drink. The addition of frozen raspberries and fresh basil makes this fruity, hydrating drink feel like summer, anytime of the year. Go ahead and double the batch—it will keep for several days. We prefer frozen raspberries since they are generally less expensive, but you can use fresh, ripe raspberries. You can use caffeinated or decaffeinated tea in this recipe. Two tea bags can be substituted for the loose-leaf tea. For an accurate measurement of boiling water, bring a kettle of water to a boil and then measure out the desired amount.

1 Place raspberries, basil, sugar, if using, and lemon juice in bowl. Using wooden spoon, mash until no whole berries remain. Place tea in second bowl. Add boiling water and steep for 4 minutes. Add ice water and raspberry mixture. Stir tea with wooden spoon until sugar is dissolved. Let steep for 1 hour.

2 Strain tea through fine-mesh strainer into 1-quart jar or pitcher (or strain into third bowl and transfer to pitcher); discard solids. Serve over ice.

MEAL PREP Strained tea can be refrigerated for up to 3 days.

Cal 10; Total Fat 0g; Sat Fat 0g;
Chol 0mg; Sodium 5mg;
Total Carb 3g; Dietary Fiber 1g;
Total Sugars 1g; Protein 0g

KALE-PINEAPPLE SMOOTHIES

Serves 2   Total Time: 10 minutes

WHEN TO DRINK
> **Pre-Workout** 1 to 2 hours before
> **Post-Workout** Within 1 hour
> **Maintenance**

WORKOUTS
> **Everyday**
> **Endurance**
> **Strength or Interval**

1¼ cups plain low-fat yogurt

1 cup baby kale or spinach

¾ cup frozen pineapple chunks

1 small banana, peeled and halved

½ cup natural pineapple juice

½ cup water

2 tablespoons hemp seed hearts

WHY THIS RECIPE WORKS ›› Smoothies are ubiquitous, but achieving a balanced one is no simple task: The ingredients must pack the nutrients you need and the texture must be smooth and not gritty—all while tasting good. For our smoothie, we balance the earthiness of baby kale with chunks of sweet pineapple and a little juice. The frozen pineapple is also a way of getting the consistency we wanted without flavor-diluting ice. Plain low-fat yogurt contributes creaminess while banana gives us more body and bridges the flavors of the kale and pineapple. For a little more protein, we incorporate heart-healthy hemp seed hearts, which blend in beautifully and add bountiful nutrients without flavor. Avoid juices and nectars with added sugars. We like the neutral flavor and color of hemp seed hearts, but you can substitute 4 teaspoons almond or peanut butter.

Add all ingredients to blender in order listed and process on low speed until mixture is combined but still coarse in texture, about 10 seconds, scraping down sides of blender jar as needed. Increase speed to high and process until completely smooth, about 1 minute. Serve.

KALE-MANGO SMOOTHIES
Substitute frozen mango chunks for the pineapple and mango nectar for the pineapple juice.

KALE-ORANGE SMOOTHIES WITH CHOCOLATE
Substitute orange juice for the pineapple juice and cacao nibs or chopped bittersweet chocolate for the hemp seed hearts. Add ¼ teaspoon grated orange zest.

MEAL PREP Smoothie can be refrigerated for up to 1 day. Whisk vigorously to recombine before drinking.

Cal 270; Total Fat 8g; Sat Fat 2g; Chol 10mg; Sodium 120mg; Total Carb 41g; Dietary Fiber 3g; Total Sugars 25g; Protein 13g

STRAWBERRY-BANANA SMOOTHIES

Serves 2   Total Time: 10 minutes

WHEN TO DRINK
› **Pre-Workout** 1 to 2 hours before
› **Post-Workout** Within 1 hour
› **Maintenance**

WORKOUTS
› **Everyday**
› **Strength or Interval**

1¼ cups plain low-fat yogurt

2 cups frozen strawberries

1 small banana, peeled and halved

1 cup water

2 tablespoons hemp seed hearts

WHY THIS RECIPE WORKS ›› You might think every berry can become a smoothie, but if you want a berry boost that works before or after a workout, strawberries are best because they're not too high in fiber. Strawberry-banana is a classic fruit pairing, and we especially love it for athletes because bananas are rich in carbohydrates and potassium, both of which are vital for exercise performance and muscle growth. We like the neutral flavor and color of hemp seed hearts, but you can substitute 4 teaspoons almond or peanut butter.

Add all ingredients to blender in order listed and process on low speed until mixture is combined but still coarse in texture, about 10 seconds, scraping down sides of blender jar as needed. Increase speed to high and process until completely smooth, about 1 minute. Serve.

CHERRY-ALMOND SMOOTHIES
Substitute 2 cups (6½ ounces) frozen cherries for the strawberries and 4 teaspoons almond butter for the hemp seed hearts.

PEACH-VANILLA SMOOTHIES
Substitute 2 cups (6 ounces) frozen peaches for the strawberries and add ¾ teaspoon vanilla extract.

MEAL PREP Smoothie can be refrigerated for up to 1 day. Whisk vigorously to recombine before drinking.

Cal 240; Total Fat 7g; Sat Fat 2g;
Chol 10mg; Sodium 110mg;
Total Carb 36g; Dietary Fiber 5g;
Total Sugars 23g; Protein 13g

CHIA PUDDING CUPS WITH FRESH BERRIES

Serves 2   Total Time: 30 minutes, plus 8 hours soaking

WHEN TO EAT
› **Post-Workout** Within 1 hour
› **Maintenance**

WORKOUTS
› **Everyday**
› **Endurance**

---

1 cup 1 percent low-fat milk, plus extra as needed

¼ cup chia seeds

1 tablespoon maple syrup, plus extra for serving

¾ teaspoon vanilla extract

⅛ teaspoon table salt

1 cup blueberries, raspberries, blackberries, or sliced strawberries

WHY THIS RECIPE WORKS ›› When chia seeds are combined with liquid and left to soak overnight they create a gel, which thickens and produces a filling, no-cook tapioca-like pudding. Chia, a nutritional powerhouse packed with fiber, protein, and omega-3 fatty acids, has a neutral flavor that's the perfect canvas for fruity toppings. Because the pudding can last for a week, double the recipe and store extra portions in the fridge for a wonderful grab-and-go breakfast that only requires topping the pudding to your liking. This recipe takes little effort, just time. The recipe can easily be doubled.

1 Whisk milk, chia seeds, maple syrup, vanilla, and salt together in bowl. Let mixture sit for 15 minutes, then whisk again to break up any clumps. Divide pudding between serving cups or jars. Cover and refrigerate for at least 8 hours or up to 1 week.

2 Adjust consistency of pudding with additional milk as needed. Top each portion with ½ cup fruit. Drizzle with extra maple syrup to taste. Serve.

MEAL PREP Chia mixture prepared through step 1 can be refrigerated for up to 1 week.

Cal 220; Total Fat 8g;
Sat Fat 1.5g; Chol 5mg;
Sodium 200mg; Total Carb 30g;
Dietary Fiber 12g;
Total Sugars 15g; Protein 8g

BANANA-WALNUT MUFFINS

Serves 12 (makes 12 muffins)   **Total Time: 50 minutes**

WORKOUTS
› **Everyday**
› **Endurance**
› **Strength or Interval**

1⅔ cups (9⅛ ounces) bread flour

1 tablespoon baking powder

½ teaspoon baking soda

½ teaspoon table salt

4–5 very ripe large bananas, peeled and mashed (2 cups)

¾ cup (5¼ ounces) plus 1 tablespoon sugar, divided

2 large eggs

⅓ cup canola oil

2 teaspoons vanilla extract

⅓ cup chopped toasted walnuts or pecans

WHY THIS RECIPE WORKS ›› Packed with nutrients from a whopping five bananas, these perfectly portable muffins can also be frozen for reheating at a later date. We use oil instead of butter for muffins that are low in saturated fat. Choose bananas that are very heavily speckled or even black; less-ripe bananas will produce dry muffins with less flavor. You can substitute thawed frozen bananas; be sure to add any juice that is released as the bananas thaw.

1 Adjust oven rack to middle position and heat oven to 425 degrees. Spray 12-cup muffin tin with canola oil spray. Whisk flour, baking powder, baking soda, and salt together in medium bowl.

2 Whisk bananas, ¾ cup sugar, eggs, oil, and vanilla in large bowl until fully combined. Add flour mixture and whisk until fully combined. Stir in walnuts. Divide batter evenly among prepared muffin cups (about ½ cup batter per cup; cups will be very full). Sprinkle evenly with remaining 1 tablespoon sugar.

3 Bake until tops are golden brown and toothpick inserted in center comes out clean, 15 to 20 minutes, rotating pan halfway through baking. Let muffins cool in muffin tin on wire rack for 10 minutes. Remove muffins from muffin tin and let cool for at least 5 minutes. Serve warm or at room temperature.

BANANA MUFFINS WITH MACADAMIA AND COCONUT
Substitute ¼ cup chopped toasted macadamia nuts plus 2 tablespoons toasted unsweetened flaked coconut for the walnuts.

MEAL PREP Muffins can be stored at room temperature for up to 1 day or individually wrapped in plastic, placed in zipper-lock bags, and frozen for up to 1 month. Defrost unwrapped muffins at room temperature for at least 4 hours or in microwave for about 1 minute.

Cal 260; Total Fat 9g; Sat Fat 1g; Chol 30mg; Sodium 270mg; Total Carb 42g; Dietary Fiber 2g; Total Sugars 20g; Protein 5g

SPICED APPLESAUCE MUFFINS WITH PECANS

Serves 12 (makes 12 muffins)   **Total Time: 55 minutes**

WHEN TO EAT
› **Pre-Workout** 1 to 2 hours before

WORKOUTS
› **Everyday**
› **Endurance**
› **Strength or Interval**

¾ cup (3¾ ounces) all-purpose flour

¾ cup (4⅛ ounces) whole-wheat flour

1 teaspoon baking soda

½ teaspoon salt

⅔ cup (4⅔ ounces) sugar

½ teaspoon ground cinnamon

¼ teaspoon ground nutmeg

1 cup unsweetened applesauce

⅓ cup canola oil

¼ cup (2 ounces) apple cider or apple juice

1 large egg

1 teaspoon vanilla extract

6 tablespoons chopped toasted pecans, divided

Cal 200; Total Fat 9g; Sat Fat 1g; Chol 15mg; Sodium 200mg; Total Carb 28g; Dietary Fiber 2g; Total Sugars 14g; Protein 3g

WHY THIS RECIPE WORKS ›› These autumnal treats, light on refined sugar, are a great, energy-dense snack before any workout. Our secret weapon is pantry-friendly unsweetened applesauce, which helps to healthfully maintain moisture while providing binding and a bit of sweetness. Seasonally delicious apple cider contributes further apple flavor (though apple juice will work just as well). By using a mixture of all-purpose and whole-wheat flour we are able to get a fluffy, light texture while also keeping the beneficial nutrients from whole wheat.

1 Adjust oven rack to middle position and heat oven to 375 degrees. Spray 12-cup muffin tin with canola oil spray. Whisk all-purpose flour, whole-wheat flour, baking soda, and salt together in medium bowl.

2 Whisk sugar, cinnamon, and nutmeg together in large bowl. Set aside 2 tablespoons sugar mixture. Add applesauce, oil, cider, egg, and vanilla to remaining sugar mixture in large bowl and whisk until well combined. Add flour mixture and gently stir until just combined and no dry flour remains. Stir in ¼ cup pecans.

3 Divide batter evenly among prepared muffin cups. Sprinkle with reserved sugar mixture and remaining 2 tablespoons pecans. Bake until tops are deep golden brown and toothpick inserted in center comes out clean, 20 to 25 minutes. Let muffins cool in muffin tin on wire rack for 10 minutes. Remove muffins from muffin tin and let cool for at least 5 minutes. Serve warm or at room temperature.

MEAL PREP Muffins can be stored at room temperature for up to 1 day or individually wrapped in plastic, placed in zipper-lock bags, and frozen for up to 1 month. Defrost unwrapped muffins at room temperature for at least 4 hours or in microwave for about 1 minute.

ZUCCHINI BREAD

Serves 10 (makes 1 loaf)   **Total Time: 1¾ hours, plus 30 minutes cooling**

WHEN TO EAT
› **Pre-Workout** 1 to 2 hours before

WORKOUTS
› **Everyday**
› **Endurance**
› **Strength or Interval**

1½ pounds zucchini, shredded

1 cup packed (7 ounces)
   brown sugar

¼ cup canola oil

2 large eggs

1 teaspoon vanilla extract

1½ cups (7½ ounces)
   all-purpose flour

½ cup (2¾ ounces)
   whole-wheat flour

1 teaspoon ground
   cinnamon

1 teaspoon baking powder

1 teaspoon baking soda

¾ teaspoon table salt

½ teaspoon ground nutmeg

WHY THIS RECIPE WORKS ›› This sweet-savory bread uses zucchini as a base, which provide workout-fueling carbohydrates and some extra vitamins and nutrients. By using a pound and a half of moist zucchini we can use a smaller amount of liquid from oil than many baked goods often require. A mix of all-purpose and nutrient-rich whole-wheat flour creates a bread with nutty flavor and a fluffy texture. Use the large holes of a box grater to shred the zucchini. This recipe was developed with a loaf pan that measures 8½ by 4½ inches; if you use a 9 by 5-inch loaf pan, start checking for doneness 5 minutes early.

1 Adjust oven rack to middle position and heat oven to 325 degrees. Spray 8½ by 4½-inch loaf pan with canola oil spray.

2 Place zucchini in center of dish towel. Gather ends together and twist tightly to drain as much liquid as possible, discarding liquid (you should have ½ to ⅔ cup liquid). Whisk brown sugar, oil, eggs, and vanilla together in medium bowl. Fold in zucchini.

3 Whisk all-purpose flour, whole-wheat flour, cinnamon, baking powder, baking soda, salt, and nutmeg together in large bowl. Fold in zucchini mixture until just incorporated. Pour batter into prepared pan.

4 Bake until top bounces back when gently pressed and toothpick inserted in center comes out with few moist crumbs attached, 1 hour 5 minutes to 1 hour 15 minutes. Let cool in pan on wire rack for 30 minutes. Remove bread from pan and let cool completely on wire rack. Serve.

MEAL PREP Zucchini bread can be refrigerated, wrapped tightly in plastic wrap, for up to 3 days. Individual slices can be wrapped in plastic, placed in zipper-lock bags, and frozen for up to 1 month. Defrost unwrapped slices at room temperature for at least 2 hours or in microwave for about 1 minute.

—

Cal 240; Total Fat 7g; Sat Fat 1g;
Chol 35mg; Sodium 360mg;
Total Carb 41g; Dietary Fiber 1g;
Total Sugars 23g; Protein 5g

CHEWY GRANOLA BARS WITH WALNUTS AND CRANBERRIES

Serves 12 (makes 12 bars)   Total Time: 35 minutes, plus 2 hours cooling

WHEN TO EAT
› **Pre-Workout** 1 to 2 hours before
› **Maintenance**

WORKOUTS
› **Everyday**
› **Endurance**
› **Strength or Interval**

⅔ cup (2½ ounces) walnuts

1¼ cups (3¾ ounces) old-fashioned rolled oats

½ cup raw sunflower seeds

½ cup dried apricots

½ cup packed (3½ ounces) brown sugar

¼ teaspoon table salt

2 tablespoons canola oil

2 tablespoons water

¾ cup (¾ ounce) crisped rice cereal

½ cup dried cranberries

WHY THIS RECIPE WORKS ›› These better-than-store-bought bars are made with such wholesome ingredients—nuts, seeds, and fruit. Use moist dried apricots, or the bars will not hold together. Avoid using quick, instant, or extra-thick rolled oats in this recipe. The recipe can easily be doubled using a 13 by 9-inch baking pan.

1 Adjust oven rack to middle position and heat oven to 350 degrees. Make foil sling for 8-inch square baking pan by folding 2 long sheets of aluminum foil so each is 8 inches wide. Lay sheets of foil in pan perpendicular to each other, with extra foil hanging over edges of pan. Push foil into corners and up sides of pan, smoothing foil flush to pan. Spray foil with canola oil spray. Pulse walnuts in food processor until finely chopped, 8 to 10 pulses. Spread walnuts, oats, and sunflower seeds on rimmed baking sheet and bake until lightly browned and fragrant, 10 to 12 minutes, stirring halfway through baking. Reduce oven temperature to 300 degrees.

2 Meanwhile, process apricots, sugar, and salt in food processor until apricots are finely ground, about 15 seconds. With processor running, add oil and water and process until paste forms, about 1 minute; transfer to large bowl. Stir in oat mixture until well coated. Stir in cereal and cranberries. Transfer mixture to prepared pan and spread into even layer. Using lightly greased bottom of dry measuring cup, press firmly on mixture, especially at edges and corners, until level and very compact.

3 Bake granola until fragrant and just beginning to brown at edges, 20 to 25 minutes. Transfer pan to wire rack and let cool for 1 hour. Using foil overhang, lift granola out of pan. Return to wire rack and let cool completely. Discard foil and transfer granola to cutting board. Cut granola in half, then cut each half crosswise into 6 equal pieces. Serve.

MEAL PREP Bars can be stored at room temperature in airtight container for up to 2 weeks.

Cal 210; Total Fat 9g; Sat Fat 1g; Chol 0mg; Sodium 65mg; Total Carb 31g; Dietary Fiber 3g; Total Sugars 20g; Protein 3g

HONEY-NUT CRISPY RICE CEREAL BARS

Serves 12 (makes 12 bars)   Total Time: 20 minutes, plus 1 hour cooling

WHEN TO EAT
› **Pre-Workout** 30 to 60 minutes before

WORKOUTS
› **Everyday**
› **Endurance**
› **Strength or Interval**

¾ cup almond or peanut butter

½ cup honey

½ cup packed (3½ ounces) brown sugar

1 tablespoon vanilla extract

½ teaspoon ground cinnamon

¼ teaspoon table salt

5 cups (5 ounces) crisped rice cereal

WHY THIS RECIPE WORKS ›› You might think that marshmallows are necessary when making rice cereal bars, but you can make a delicious, crispy treat that gives you plenty of pre-workout energy without the candy. For a nourishing take on this beloved classic, we use nut butter, brown sugar, and honey for the sweet glue. Vanilla and a hint of cinnamon provide the toasty flavor of a baked good. This recipe makes 12 totally portable bars, so whip up a batch and take them on the go when you know you'll want a tasty treat with a little boost. We prefer unsweetened, natural almond or peanut butter (smooth or chunky) in this recipe, but any style of nut butter can be used. This recipe can easily be doubled using a 13 by 9-inch baking pan.

1 Combine almond butter, honey, and sugar in Dutch oven. Cook over medium heat, whisking often, until sugar has melted and mixture is smooth and just beginning to simmer, about 2 minutes. Off heat, whisk in vanilla, cinnamon, and salt. Using lightly greased rubber spatula, stir in rice cereal until well combined.

2 Transfer cereal mixture to greased 8-inch square baking pan and spread into even layer. Using lightly greased bottom of dry measuring cup, press firmly on mixture, especially at edges and corners, until level and very compact. Let cool completely, about 1 hour.

3 Run knife around the edge of pan to loosen cereal mixture, then turn out onto cutting board. Cut mixture in half, then cut each half crosswise into 6 pieces. Serve.

MEAL PREP Bars can be stored at room temperature in airtight container for up to 2 weeks.

Cal 230; Total Fat 9g; Sat Fat 1g; Chol 0mg; Sodium 160mg; Total Carb 36g; Dietary Fiber 2g; Total Sugars 22g; Protein 4g

DRIED FRUIT AND SEED ENERGY BITES

Serves 6 (makes 18 bites)   **Total Time: 35 minutes, plus 1 hour chilling**

WHEN TO EAT
> **Pre-Workout** 1 to 2 hours before
> **Post-Workout** Within 1 hour

WORKOUTS
> **Everyday**
> **Endurance**
> **Strength or Interval**

1 cup hot water
  (175 degrees)

1 cup dried apricots, dried
  tart cherries, and/or dried
  cranberries

¼ cup pitted dates, chopped

½ cup unsalted roasted
  sunflower seeds

¼ cup unsalted roasted
  pepitas

3 tablespoons hemp seed
  hearts

¼ teaspoon ground
  cinnamon

¼ teaspoon table salt

WHY THIS RECIPE WORKS ›› Poppable, portable, and super-tasty, these snacks provide energy—literally—in a bite. They're the easiest thing to toss in your bag to cushion your workout at either end with extra fuel. Sweet dried fruits provide the quick carb fix and are a sticky base for nutritious nuts and seeds. Rolling the final balls in more seeds allows the balls to hold their shape without sticking together. Be sure to use dried fruit that is soft and moist or the bites will not hold together well. This recipe can easily be doubled using an 8-inch square pan.

1 Line 8½ by 4½-inch loaf pan with plastic wrap, letting excess hang over sides of pan. Combine water, apricots, and dates in bowl and let sit until fruit has plumped, 5 to 10 minutes. Drain well and pat fruit dry with paper towels.

2 Process sunflower seeds, pepitas, hemp seeds, cinnamon, and salt in food processor until finely ground, about 20 seconds. Transfer ¼ cup processed seed mixture to small bowl; set aside.

3 Add drained fruit to seed mixture in processor bowl and pulse until fruit is finely chopped and mixture starts to clump together, 15 to 20 pulses. Transfer fruit mixture to prepared pan and spread into even layer. Fold excess plastic wrap over top and refrigerate until firm, about 1 hour.

4 Using overhanging plastic wrap, lift chilled fruit mixture from pan and invert onto cutting board; discard plastic wrap. Cut fruit mixture lengthwise into thirds, then cut each third crosswise into 6 pieces (you should have 18 pieces). Using lightly moistened hands, roll mixture into balls, then roll balls in reserved seed mixture until evenly coated. Serve.

MEAL PREP Bites can be refrigerated for up to 1 week.

Cal 210; Total Fat 10g; Sat Fat 1g;
Chol 0mg; Sodium 110mg;
Total Carb 26g; Dietary Fiber 2g;
Total Sugars 18g; Protein 6g

STRAWBERRY FRUIT LEATHER

Serves 6 (makes 6 strips)   Total Time: 5 to 6 hours, plus 30 minutes cooling

WHEN TO EAT
› **Pre-Workout** 30 to 60 minutes before

WORKOUTS
› **Everyday**
› **Endurance**
› **Strength or Interval**

1¼ pounds strawberries, hulled

2 large Granny Smith apples (8 ounces each), peeled, cored, and chopped

¼ cup sugar

WHY THIS RECIPE WORKS ›› Strawberry rolled fruit snacks are a unique, nostalgic way to get portable fuel. And don't worry: This project is largely hands-off. Granny Smith apples have just the right amount of natural pectin to give firm yet tender texture without additives. You can substitute frozen strawberries for the fresh. You will need a rimless baking sheet to ensure even cooking.

1 Draw 14 by 11-inch rectangle on sheet of parchment paper. Flip parchment and place on rimless baking sheet. Spray parchment evenly with oil spray.

2 Pulse strawberries and apples in blender until finely chopped, about 10 pulses. Add sugar and process until very smooth, about 3 minutes, scraping down sides of blender jar as needed. Set fine-mesh strainer over large saucepan. Pour strawberry mixture through strainer into saucepan. Using back of ladle or rubber spatula, stir and press firmly on solids to extract as much liquid as possible; discard solids.

3 Bring strawberry mixture to boil over medium-high heat. Reduce heat to medium-low and simmer, whisking often and lowering heat if mixture begins to splatter, until mixture is thickened and measures 2 cups, about 30 minutes. Carefully pour strawberry mixture onto center of prepared baking sheet. Using icing spatula, spread mixture in even layer to edges of drawn 14 by 11-inch rectangle. Gently jiggle and tap baking sheet on counter to create smooth, even layer.

4 Adjust oven rack to middle position and heat oven to 200 degrees. Bake fruit until center feels dry but slightly tacky to touch and fruit leather peels away from parchment cleanly, 4 to 5 hours. Let fruit leather cool completely, about 30 minutes. Using kitchen shears, cut fruit leather (along with parchment backing) crosswise into six 2-inch-wide strips (trimming away any dry edges as needed). Roll up fruit leather strips. Serve.

MEAL PREP Fruit leather can be stored at room temperature in airtight container for up to 2 weeks.

Cal 100; Total Fat 0g; Sat Fat 0g; Chol 0mg; Sodium 0mg; Total Carb 25g; Dietary Fiber 4g; Total Sugars 19g; Protein 1g

DRINKS & SNACKS

CHEESY VEGGIE CRISPS

Serves 2 (makes 6 crisps)   **Total Time: 45 minutes**

WHEN TO EAT
› **Pre-Workout** 1 to 2 hours before
› **Post-Workout** Within 1 hour

WORKOUTS
› **Everyday**
› **Strength or Interval**

---

1 zucchini (8 ounces), shredded

1 carrot, peeled and shredded

⅔ cup panko bread crumbs

2 large eggs, lightly beaten

1 ounce part-skim block mozzarella cheese, shredded (¼ cup)

½ teaspoon garlic powder

½ teaspoon dried oregano

⅛ teaspoon table salt

**WHY THIS RECIPE WORKS ›› ** Think beyond the box for a savory, cheesy snack that hits the spot—and also helps you reach your workout goals. These veggie crisps are perfect for a busy athlete because they are loaded with the goodness of an entire zucchini and carrot, and you can make them in under an hour. Part-skim mozzarella is the best cheese here because it provides salty flavor and binds without being too high in fat. We love the option to make a big batch and freeze the treats for easy eating at a later date. Use the large holes of a box grater to shred the zucchini and carrot. This recipe can easily be doubled.

1 Adjust oven rack to upper-middle position and heat oven to 425 degrees. Line baking sheet with parchment paper and spray with canola oil spray.

2 Place zucchini in center of clean dish towel. Gather ends of towel together, twist tightly, and squeeze over sink to drain as much liquid as possible. Transfer zucchini and carrot to large bowl. Stir in panko, eggs, mozzarella, garlic powder, oregano, and salt until well combined.

3 Scoop and drop zucchini mixture onto baking sheet in 6 even mounds (about ¼ cup each). Gently press each mound to flatten into 3-inch round.

4 Bake until edges are browned and tops are spotty brown, 14 to 16 minutes. Transfer sheet to wire rack and let cool slightly, about 5 minutes. Serve warm or at room temperature.

MEAL PREP Crisps can be refrigerated for up to 2 days or frozen for up to 1 month. From refrigerator or freezer, microwave until heated through, 30 to 60 seconds.

Cal 250; Total Fat 8g;
Sat Fat 3.5g; Chol 195mg;
Sodium 390mg; Total Carb 29g;
Dietary Fiber 2g;
Total Sugars 5g; Protein 14g

BROWN RICE BALLS WITH SPINACH AND EDAMAME

Serves 2 (makes 8 rice balls)   Total Time: 1 hour

WHEN TO EAT
› **Pre-Workout** 1 to 2 hours before
› **Post-Workout** Within 1 hour
› **Maintenance**

WORKOUTS
› **Everyday**
› **Endurance**
› **Strength or Interval**

---

1 cup water

½ cup short-grain brown rice

½ cup baby spinach

⅓ cup frozen shelled edamame beans, thawed and patted dry

1 scallion, sliced thin

1 sheet toasted nori, crumbled

2 teaspoons toasted sesame oil

½ teaspoon grated fresh ginger or ¼ teaspoon dried

⅛ teaspoon table salt

—

Cal 230; Total Fat 7g;
Sat Fat 0.5g; Chol 0mg;
Sodium 160mg; Total Carb 39g;
Dietary Fiber 5g; Total Sugars 1g;
Protein 8g

WHY THIS RECIPE WORKS ›› A Japanese bento box staple, traditional onigiri are triangular bundles of white rice stuffed with any number of ingredients. We were inspired by these packable bundles for a brown rice snack to eat before or after a workout. Instead of stuffing the rice balls, we pulsed spinach and edamame with the rice in the food processor. This processing step released starch from the rice, which made the mixture easy to shape, and it enabled us to incorporate a good amount of filling. You can substitute plain, pre-toasted seaweed snacks for the toasted nori. This recipe can easily be doubled. Serve with a drizzle of soy sauce or sriracha or a squeeze of lemon or lime juice, if desired.

1 Bring water and rice to boil in large saucepan over high heat. Reduce heat to low, cover, and simmer until rice is tender and water is absorbed, 30 to 35 minutes. Remove saucepan from heat, lay clean folded dish towel underneath lid, and let sit for 10 minutes. Fluff rice with fork and season with salt and pepper to taste.

2 Pulse spinach, edamame, scallion, nori, sesame oil, ginger, and salt in food processor until mixture is finely ground (mixture should not be smooth), about 12 pulses, scraping down sides of bowl as needed. Add rice and pulse until rice is coarsely chopped and mixture is well combined, about 8 pulses.

3 Divide rice mixture into 8 portions (about 2 tablespoons each). Using lightly moistened hands, roll each portion into ball. Serve warm or at room temperature.

MEAL PREP Rice balls can be refrigerated for up to 3 days or frozen for up to 1 month. If frozen, thaw completely in refrigerator. Microwave until heated through, about 20 seconds.

BAKED PITA CHIPS

Serves 4 (makes about 8 cups)   **Total Time: 35 minutes**

WHEN TO EAT
› **Pre-Workout** 30 to
60 minutes before

WORKOUTS
› **Everyday**
› **Endurance**
› **Strength or Interval**

4 (6½-inch) pita breads
Olive or canola oil spray
⅛ teaspoon table salt
⅛ teaspoon pepper

WHY THIS RECIPE WORKS ›› There's no easier way to boost your carbohydrates or round out a meal or snack than by adding a handful of crunchy snack chips (which we do throughout the book). Though store-bought pita chips are readily accessible, we wanted an easy recipe that could be ready in about half an hour that gave us control over the fat and salt amounts. For less fussy preparation, we found that flipping the chips was unnecessary—they baked up evenly crisp and flavorful with just a little bit of movement halfway through. Both white and whole-wheat pita breads will work in this recipe. To enjoy this as a post-workout snack, eat with Sweet Potato Hummus (page 279) or Toasted Corn and Bean Salsa (page 280).

1 Adjust oven racks to upper-middle and lower-middle positions and heat oven to 350 degrees. Using kitchen shears, cut around perimeter of each pita and separate into 2 thin rounds.

2 Working with 1 round at a time, spray rough side evenly with oil spray and sprinkle with salt and pepper. Stack rounds on top of one another, rough sides up. Using chef's knife, cut pita stack into 6 wedges. Spread wedges, rough sides up and in single layer, on 2 rimmed baking sheets.

3 Bake until wedges are golden and crisp, 10 to 15 minutes, stirring occasionally and switching and rotating sheets halfway through baking. Transfer sheets to wire rack and let chips cool slightly, about 10 minutes. Serve warm or at room temperature.

BAKED CORN TORTILLA CHIPS
Substitute 8 (6-inch) corn tortillas for the pitas. Increase baking time to 20 to 25 minutes.

MEAL PREP Chips can be stored in airtight container at room temperature for up to 1 week.

Cal 170; Total Fat 0g; Sat Fat 0g;
Chol 0mg; Sodium 390mg;
Total Carb 33g; Dietary Fiber 0g;
Total Sugars 0g; Protein 5g

SEEDED PUMPKIN CRACKERS

Serves 8 (makes 48 crackers)   Total Time: 2 hours, plus 5½ hours cooling and freezing

WHEN TO EAT
› **Pre-Workout** 1 to 2 hours before

WORKOUTS
› **Everyday**
› **Endurance**
› **Strength or Interval**

---

1 cup (5 ounces)
  all-purpose flour

1 teaspoon baking powder

¼ teaspoon baking soda

1 cup canned unsweetened
  pumpkin puree

1 teaspoon baharat

½ teaspoon table salt

¼ cup (1¾ ounces) sugar

5 teaspoons canola oil

2 large eggs

1 tablespoon grated
  orange zest

⅓ cup dried
  apricots, chopped

⅓ cup sesame seeds

⅓ cup shelled pistachios,
  toasted and chopped

2 tablespoons coarse sea salt

—

Cal 230; Total Fat 9g;
Sat Fat 1.5g; Chol 45mg;
Sodium 210mg; Total Carb 32g;
Dietary Fiber 3g;
Total Sugars 14g; Protein 6g

WHY THIS RECIPE WORKS ›› These savory-sweet crackers are delicious fuel to have on hand. Freezing the loaves after the first bake ensures that you can slice the crackers thin for the second bake—so slice any amount you want to eat. You can substitute a combination of ½ teaspoon ground cumin, ¼ teaspoon pepper, ¼ teaspoon ground coriander, pinch ground cinnamon, and pinch ground clove for the baharat. Crackers will crisp as they cool.

1 Adjust oven rack to middle position and heat oven to 350 degrees. Grease two 5½ by 3-inch loaf pans. Whisk flour, baking powder, and baking soda together in large bowl; set aside. Combine pumpkin puree, baharat, and table salt in 10-inch skillet. Cook over medium heat until reduced to ¾ cup, 6 to 8 minutes; transfer to medium bowl. Stir in sugar and oil and let cool slightly, about 5 minutes.

2 Whisk eggs and orange zest into pumpkin mixture then fold into flour mixture until combined (some small lumps may remain). Fold in apricots, sesame seeds, and pistachios. Scrape batter into prepared pans and smooth tops. Bake until skewer inserted in center comes out clean, 45 to 50 minutes, switching and rotating pans halfway through baking. Let loaves cool in pans on wire rack for 20 minutes. Remove loaves from pans and let cool completely on rack, about 1½ hours. Transfer cooled loaves to zipper-lock bag and freeze until firm, about 3 hours.

3 Heat oven to 300 degrees and line rimmed baking sheet with parchment paper. Using serrated knife, slice each frozen loaf crosswise, about ¼ inch thick. Arrange slices in single layer on prepared sheet and sprinkle with sea salt. Bake until dark golden, 25 to 30 minutes, flipping crackers and rotating sheet halfway through baking. Transfer sheet to wire rack and let crackers cool completely, about 30 minutes. Serve.

MEAL PREP Loaves prepared through step 2 can be frozen for up to one month. Crackers can be stored in airtight container at room temperature for up to 3 days.

DRINKS & SNACKS

SWEET POTATO HUMMUS WITH PITA CHIPS

Serves 6 (makes about 2 cups)   **Total Time: 35 minutes**

WHEN TO EAT
› **Pre-Workout** 1 to 2 hours before

WORKOUTS
› **Everyday**
› **Endurance**
› **Strength or Interval**

---

1 pound sweet potatoes, unpeeled

3 tablespoons tahini

2 tablespoons extra-virgin olive oil, divided

¾ cup water

2 tablespoons lemon juice

1 garlic clove, minced

1 teaspoon paprika

¾ teaspoon table salt

½ teaspoon ground coriander

¼ teaspoon ground cumin

¼ teaspoon chipotle chile powder

6 cups baked pita chips or tortilla chips

Cal 230; Total Fat 9g;
Sat Fat 1.5g; Chol 0mg;
Sodium 340mg; Total Carb 33g;
Dietary Fiber 3g;
Total Sugars 5g; Protein 5g

WHY THIS RECIPE WORKS ›› While we love traditional chickpea hummus, vegetables can just as easily be used to make a sweet, earthy take on the creamy dip. Switching out the legumes for high-carb (without so much fiber) sweet potatoes is a smooth move for athletes: We simply microwave the potatoes until softened before blending them with the traditional hummus ingredients, plus some spices that balance the sweet. Enjoy the hummus (with chips, of course) in the hours before any workout to ensure you're fueled and focused. When buying pita chips, look for brands that contain no more than 3 grams of fat per 1-cup serving. Or, you can use our homemade Baked Pita Chips (page 274).

1 Prick sweet potatoes several times with fork, place on plate, and microwave until very soft, about 12 minutes, flipping potatoes halfway through microwaving. Let potatoes cool for 5 minutes. Combine tahini and 1 tablespoon oil in small bowl.

2 Slice potatoes in half lengthwise and scoop flesh from skins; discard skins. Process sweet potato, water, lemon juice, garlic, paprika, salt, coriander, cumin, and chile powder in food processor until completely smooth, about 1 minute, scraping down sides of bowl as needed.

3 With processor running, add tahini mixture in steady stream and process until hummus is smooth and creamy, about 15 seconds, scraping down bowl as needed. Season with salt and pepper to taste. Transfer hummus to serving bowl or storage container. Drizzle each ⅓-cup portion hummus with ½ teaspoon oil and serve with 1 cup pita chips.

MEAL PREP Hummus can be refrigerated for up to 5 days; stir in warm water (1 tablespoon at a time) to loosen as needed before serving.

TOASTED CORN AND BEAN SALSA WITH TORTILLA CHIPS

Serves 4 (makes about 2 cups)   **Total Time: 20 minutes**

WHEN TO EAT
› **Pre-Workout** 1 to 2 hours before

WORKOUTS
› **Everyday**
› **Endurance**
› **Strength or Interval**

1½ tablespoons extra-virgin olive oil, divided

1 cup frozen corn, thawed and patted dry

1 red bell pepper, stemmed, seeded, and chopped fine

¾ cup canned black beans, rinsed

½ jalapeño chile, seeded and minced

1 scallion, sliced thin

2 garlic cloves, minced

2 tablespoons lime juice, plus extra for seasoning

2 tablespoons minced fresh cilantro

½ teaspoon ground cumin

¼ teaspoon table salt

⅛ teaspoon pepper

4 cups baked corn tortilla chips or pita chips

WHY THIS RECIPE WORKS ›› Instead of traditional tomato salsa, we thought corn would be an excellent base for a pre-workout snack because it's a good source of carbohydrates and calories—the cornerstones of fuel. Frozen corn is extra convenient, and all it needs is a little toasting in a pan to become golden. Familiar flavors of jalapeño, lime juice, cilantro, and cumin bring the salsa to life, while stirring in black beans adds hearty texture and supporting protein. When buying tortilla chips, look for brands that contain no more than 3 grams of fat per 1-cup serving. Or, you can use our homemade Baked Corn Tortilla Chips (page 274).

1 Heat 1½ teaspoons oil in 10-inch nonstick skillet over medium-high heat until shimmering. Add corn and cook, stirring occasionally, until golden brown, about 4 minutes.

2 Transfer corn to serving bowl or storage container and stir in remaining 1 tablespoon oil, bell pepper, beans, jalapeño, scallion, garlic, lime juice, cilantro, cumin, salt, and pepper. Season with extra lime juice to taste.

3 Serve each ½-cup portion salsa with 1 cup tortilla chips.

MEAL PREP Salsa can be refrigerated for up to 3 days; bring to room temperature before serving.

Cal 200; Total Fat 7g;
Sat Fat 0.5g; Chol 0mg;
Sodium 190mg; Total Carb 29g;
Dietary Fiber 4g;
Total Sugars 2g; Protein 5g

CHAPTER 8

SUPPLEMENTS

The word "supplements" in conjunction with working out suggests enhancing your routine with helpful additions; here, it's with food, of course. These stand-alone recipes for ultra-nutritious carbohydrate bases, proteins, and vegetables work to enhance and round out your workout meals.

The recipes can be made independently and stored so you have components on hand for easy-to-prepare mix-and-match bowls combining a base with a protein, vegetable, and simple sauce or dressing. Their benefits are built in: Combine a serving of one recipe per category and you'll get a meal with roughly the 3:1 carbohydrate-to-protein ratio you need to accompany everyday workouts. Trust them to fuel you; no need to do math.

These supplements are also called upon throughout the book when we suggest adding more grains, say, when eating for an endurance workout, or boosting the protein when eating for a strength or interval exercise. Having cooked ingredients ready in your fridge allows for last-minute modifications to support your day. Like most supplements, these are good for your body—and good for your lifestyle, too.

CARBOHYDRATE BASES

When you're choosing carbohydrates to pair with exercise,
grains and noodles give you a
great energy bang for your buck.
They make a versatile base for
a variety of toppings and can
also add heft to an existing meal.
Best of all, they are easy to cook,
and you can make them ahead
and reheat for quick pre- or
post-workout options. Endurance
athletes might particularly want
grains and noodles cooked and on
hand to boost the carbohydrates
in their recipes when necessary.

LONG-GRAIN WHITE RICE PILAF

Makes about 2 cups, enough for 2 servings

When you need an easy base for a bowl or plate, or you're looking for an energy-dense addition to your plate, white rice pilaf is nice to have on hand as its mild flavor mingles with a variety of proteins. You can use conventional long-grain white, jasmine, or basmati rice here. Rice can be refrigerated for up to 3 days.

    1 teaspoon extra-virgin olive oil
    1 cup long-grain white rice, rinsed
1½ cups water
⅛ teaspoon table salt

1 Heat oil in large saucepan over medium heat until shimmering. Stir in rice and cook until edges of grains are translucent, about 2 minutes. Stir in water and salt and bring to boil. Reduce heat to low, cover, and simmer until rice is tender and liquid is absorbed, 16 to 18 minutes.

2 Off heat, lay clean folded dish towel underneath lid, and let sit for 10 minutes. Fluff rice with fork and season with salt and pepper to taste.

STEAMED SHORT-GRAIN WHITE RICE

Makes about 2 cups, enough for 2 servings

For rice that is soft and sticky to soak up savory sauces, turn to steamed short-grain rice. Having this rice ready to go makes enjoying meals such as Stir-Fried Chicken and Broccoli (page 124) as easy as reheating. Short-grain rice varieties (except for glutinous rice) such as Arborio work well here. Rice can be refrigerated for up to 3 days.

    1 cup water
    1 cup short-grain white rice, rinsed
⅛ teaspoon table salt

Bring water, rice, and salt to boil in large saucepan over medium-high heat. Reduce heat to low, cover, and simmer until water is absorbed, about 10 minutes. Off heat, let rice sit until fully tender, about 15 minutes.

SIMPLE BOIL METHOD FOR GRAINS

To cook the grains, bring 2 quarts water to boil in large saucepan. Stir in 1 cup grain and ½ teaspoon table salt and cook until tender, following the times indicated. Drain well.

All grains make about 2 cups, enough for 2 servings. Grains can be easily doubled using 4 quarts water and 1 teaspoon salt in a large pot. Cooked grains can be refrigerated for up to 3 days.

To reheat grains, microwave in covered bowl until hot throughout, fluffing with fork halfway through microwaving (timing will vary depending on the quantity and type of grain used). Season with salt and pepper to taste.

GRAIN	IDEAL FOR	COOKING TIME
Pearl barley	Post-Workout, Maintenance	20 to 40 minutes
Medium- or coarse-grind bulgur	Post-Workout, Maintenance	5 minutes
Farro	Pre-Workout	15 to 30 minutes
Long-grain white rice	Pre-Workout	10 to 15 minutes
Long-grain brown rice	Pre-Workout	25 to 30 minutes
Oat berries (groats)	Post-Workout, Maintenance	40 to 50 minutes

HANDS-OFF BAKED BROWN RICE
Makes about 2 cups, enough for 2 servings

Having a rice option with fiber and beneficial nutrients after exercise is a boon. Brown rice cooks most evenly in the oven, so this hands-off method frees you to focus on making your meal. For an accurate measurement of boiling water, bring a full kettle of water to a boil and then measure out the desired amount. Rice can be refrigerated for up to 3 days.

1⅔ cups boiling water
  1 cup long-grain or short-grain brown rice, rinsed
  1 teaspoon extra-virgin olive oil
⅛ teaspoon table salt

1 Adjust oven rack to middle position and heat oven to 375 degrees. Combine boiling water, rice, oil, and salt in 8½ by 4½-inch loaf pan. Cover pan tightly with double layer of aluminum foil. Bake until rice is tender and liquid is absorbed, 45 to 55 minutes.

2 Remove pan from oven and fluff rice with fork, scraping up any rice that has stuck to bottom. Lay clean folded dish towel over pan, re-cover loosely with foil, and let sit for 10 minutes. Season with salt and pepper to taste.

QUINOA PILAF
Makes about 2½ cups, enough for 2 servings

Quinoa is a gluten-free grain (well, actually, it's a seed) that's referred to as a "supergrain" because it's a nutritionally complete protein. It has a faint crunch with mineral flavor. If you buy unwashed quinoa (or if you≈are unsure if it's been washed), be sure to rinse it before cooking to remove its bitter protective coating. Quinoa can be refrigerated for up to 3 days.

  1 cup prewashed white quinoa
1¼ cups water or broth
⅛ teaspoon table salt

1 Cook quinoa in large saucepan over medium-high heat, stirring frequently, until very fragrant and making continuous popping sound, 5 to 7 minutes. Stir in water and salt and bring to boil. Reduce heat to low, cover, and simmer until quinoa is tender and water is absorbed, 18 to 22 minutes, stirring once halfway through cooking.

2 Off heat, let sit for 10 minutes. Fluff quinoa with fork and season with salt and pepper to taste.

PEARL COUSCOUS PILAF

Makes about 2 cups, enough for 2 servings

Pearl couscous, a chewy pasta with larger grains than regular couscous, takes well to being dressed with a light sauce (see pages 300–303). Couscous can be refrigerated for up to 3 days.

> 1 teaspoon canola oil
> 1 cup pearl couscous
> 1¼ cups water
> ⅛ teaspoon table salt

1 Cook oil and couscous in large saucepan over medium heat, stirring frequently, until about half the grains are golden brown, about 3 minutes. Stir in water and salt and bring to boil. Reduce heat to low, cover, and simmer until couscous is tender and water is absorbed, 9 to 12 minutes.

2 Off heat, let sit for 10 minutes. Fluff couscous with fork and season with salt and pepper to taste.

SIMPLE BOIL METHOD FOR PASTA AND NOODLES

For 2 servings of noodles, bring 2 quarts water to boil in large pot. Add 1½ teaspoons table salt to boiling water for dried pasta; do not salt water for noodles. Add 4 ounces dried pasta, soba noodles, or udon noodles and cook, stirring often until tender; drain well.

To make ahead, rinse cooked pasta or noodles with cold water to halt the cooking process and shake to remove excess water. Toss noodles with 1 teaspoon canola or olive oil (to prevent sticking) and refrigerate for up to 2 days. Serve noodles chilled or at room temperature.

Sirloin Steak Tips and Farro with Tomatoes, Asparagus, and Chimichurri Sauce

PROTEINS

Eating a moderate amount of protein is essential to building and repairing muscle. Protein can be especially helpful for athletes who focus on strength or interval training. We focus on good-for-you lean proteins, which are helpful for times of the day when you want to keep fat content moderate. These robust, simple proteins are great to prep in advance and keep on hand as they're just as good cold or at room temperature as they are reheated. It's easy to change up the profiles of simple proteins by rubbing them with your favorite spice blend.

SIMPLE POACHED CHICKEN
Serves 2

This poaching method gives you moist meat for a protein that works in nearly any dish. If you need a quick lunch, slice the breast thin, pair it with a grain, and top with your favorite sauce. Or, shred the meat and stir into a number of our soups (see pages 64–89) for a protein boost. You will need an 8- or 10-inch skillet with a tight-fitting lid for this recipe. The recipe can easily be doubled using a 12-inch skillet. Chicken can be refrigerated for up to 3 days.

- 1 (6-ounce) boneless, skinless chicken breast, trimmed
- ⅛ teaspoon table salt
- ⅛ teaspoon pepper
- 1 teaspoon canola oil

1 Pat chicken dry with paper towels and sprinkle with salt and pepper. Heat oil in 8- or 10-inch skillet over medium heat until just smoking. Add chicken and cook until well browned on first side, about 3 minutes. Flip chicken, add 2 tablespoons water, and cover skillet. Reduce heat to low and continue to cook until chicken registers 160 degrees, about 3 minutes.

2 Transfer chicken to cutting board, let cool slightly, then slice, chop, or shred as desired.

PAN-SEARED PORK CHOP
Serves 2

Pork chops are a surprisingly lean, deeply flavored protein—perfect to keep on hand for simple, filling dinners. You will need an 8- or 10-inch skillet with a tight-fitting lid for this recipe. The recipe can easily be doubled using a 12-inch skillet. Pork can be refrigerated for up to 3 days.

- 1 (6-ounce) boneless pork chop, ¾ to 1 inch thick, trimmed
- ⅛ teaspoon table salt
- ⅛ teaspoon pepper
- 1 teaspoon canola oil

1 Pat chop dry with paper towels and sprinkle with salt and pepper. Heat oil in 8- or 10-inch skillet over medium-high heat until just smoking. Add chop and cook, turning occasionally, until well browned on both sides and pork registers 140 degrees, 8 to 10 minutes, reducing heat as needed if skillet begins to scorch.

2 Transfer chop to cutting board, let rest for 5 minutes, then slice or chop as desired.

SIRLOIN STEAK TIPS
Serves 2

Sirloin tips, a leaner cut of beef, are high in protein and rich in iron for recovery. Toss them with Chimichurri (page 302) and your favorite cooked vegetable to top a grain bowl for a fast yet delectable dinner. Steak tips, also known as flap meat, can be sold as whole steaks, cubes, or strips. To ensure evenly sized pieces, we prefer to buy whole steaks and cut them ourselves. This recipe can easily be doubled using a 12-inch skillet. Steak tips can be refrigerated for up to 3 days.

- 6 ounces sirloin steak tips, trimmed and cut into 2-inch pieces
- ⅛ teaspoon table salt
- ⅛ teaspoon pepper
- 1 teaspoon canola oil

1 Pat steak tips dry with paper towels and sprinkle with salt and pepper. Heat oil in 8- or 10-inch skillet over medium-high heat until just smoking. Add steak tips and cook, turning occasionally, until well browned on all sides and beef registers 120 to 125 degrees (for medium-rare) or 130 to 135 degrees (for medium), 7 to 10 minutes, reducing heat as needed if skillet begins to scorch.

2 Transfer steak tips to plate and let rest for 5 minutes.

Pan-Seared Tofu, Brown Rice, Broccoli, and Mushrooms with Orange-Ginger Vinaigrette

PAN-ROASTED SALMON
Serves 2

Salmon is rich in omega-3 fatty acids, which support a healthy heart and promote anti-inflammatory activity in the body. Flake leftovers on top of a salad or a bowl composed of a base, dressing, and your choice of vegetables. It is important to keep the skin on during cooking to prevent the fish from falling apart. If using wild salmon, cook the fillets until they register 120 degrees (for medium-rare). This recipe can easily be doubled using a 12-inch skillet. Salmon can be refrigerated for up to 2 days.

    1 (6-ounce) skin-on salmon fillet,
       1 to 1½ inches thick
    ⅛ teaspoon table salt
    ⅛ teaspoon pepper
    1 teaspoon canola oil

1 Pat salmon dry with paper towels and sprinkle with salt and pepper. Heat oil in 8- or 10-inch nonstick skillet over medium-high heat until shimmering. Cook salmon, skin side up, until well browned, 3 to 5 minutes. Flip and continue to cook until salmon is still translucent when checked with tip of paring knife and registers 125 degrees (for medium-rare), 3 to 5 minutes.

2 Transfer salmon to plate and let cool slightly, about 2 minutes. Divide fillet into 2 portions. If desired, flake salmon into rough 1- or 2-inch pieces; discard skin.

PAN-SEARED SHRIMP
Serves 2

Shrimp have a high protein yield for their minimal amount of calories. You will need an 8- or 10-inch skillet with a tight-fitting lid for this recipe. The recipe can easily be doubled using a 12-inch skillet. Shrimp can be refrigerated for up to 2 days.

- 12 ounces extra-large shrimp (21 to 25 per pound), peeled and deveined
- ⅛ teaspoon table salt
- ⅛ teaspoon pepper
- 1 teaspoon canola oil

Toss shrimp with salt and pepper. Heat oil in 8- or 10-inch skillet over high heat until just smoking. Add shrimp in single layer and cook until spotty brown and edges begin to turn pink, about 1 minute. Off heat, flip shrimp, cover, and cook second side using residual heat of skillet until shrimp are opaque throughout, 1 to 2 minutes.

PAN-SEARED TOFU
Serves 2

Athletes looking for an extra boost of protein can certainly find it from plant-powered sources. Tofu is naturally low in fat and can slide seamlessly into a number of dishes, from udon soup (see page 76) to taco salad (see page 204). This recipe can easily be doubled using a 12-inch skillet. Tofu can be refrigerated for up to 2 days.

- 7 ounces soft, firm, or extra-firm tofu, cut into ¾-inch pieces
- ⅛ teaspoon table salt
- ⅛ teaspoon pepper
- 1 teaspoon extra-virgin olive oil

1 Spread tofu over paper towel–lined baking sheet and let drain for 20 minutes. Gently press tofu dry with paper towels and sprinkle with salt and pepper.

2 Heat oil in 8- or 10-inch nonstick skillet over medium-high heat until shimmering. Add tofu and cook until lightly browned on all sides, 6 to 8 minutes.

CRISPY TEMPEH
Serves 2

Tempeh crumbles have a similar texture to ground beef and can function as a plant-based substitute in many protein-based dishes. It can also take on any flavor you desire—so try it as a taco filling instead of beef or pork, or use to top vegetable-based main dishes (see pages 202–212) when you want crunchy protein. This recipe can easily be doubled.

- 4½ teaspoons soy sauce
- 4 ounces tempeh, crumbled into ¼-inch pieces
- ⅓ cup peanut or canola oil, for frying

1 Bring 2 cups water and soy sauce to boil in large saucepan. Add tempeh, return to boil, and cook for 10 minutes. Drain tempeh well and wipe saucepan dry with paper towels.

2 Line large plate with paper towels. Heat oil in now-empty dry saucepan over medium-high heat until shimmering. Add tempeh and cook until golden brown and crisp, about 12 minutes, adjusting heat as needed if tempeh begins to scorch. Using wire skimmer or slotted spoon, transfer tempeh to prepared plate to drain. Season with salt and pepper to taste.

INCREDIBLE EGGS:
EASY PROTEIN 4 SIMPLE WAYS

Eggs are a widely available, super protein option for athletes that can be prepared numerous ways. We often rely on them in this book because they can be ready in a matter of minutes.

Hard-cooked, scrambled, poached, or fried eggs can be your versatile go-to for fast fuel.

FRIED EGGS
Makes 1–4 eggs

A fried egg is an easy yet luxurious way to elevate a meal—and its protein content. For a post-workout or maintenance meal for a strength or interval exercise, and when you can be more lenient with fat, top our Risotto Primavera (page 232) or Campanelle with Roasted Cauliflower and Garlic Sauce (page 224) with a fried egg. You will need a nonstick skillet with a tight-fitting lid for this recipe. We recommend using an 8- to 10-inch skillet when cooking 1 or 2 eggs and a 10- to 12-inch skillet when cooking 3 or 4 eggs.

  1–4 large eggs
½–2 teaspoons canola or extra-virgin olive oil

Crack each egg into small bowl or teacup. Heat ½ teaspoon oil for each egg in nonstick skillet over medium-high heat until shimmering. Pour eggs into skillet, one at a time, cover skillet, and cook for 1 minute. Remove skillet from heat and let sit, covered, 15 to 45 seconds for runny yolks, 45 to 60 seconds for soft but set yolks, and about 2 minutes for medium-set yolks. Season with salt and pepper to taste.

SCRAMBLED EGG WHITES

Serves 1

Scrambled egg whites are the perfect example of
a beneficial protein, especially before a workout,
because they are low in fat (and cholesterol) and
have a high protein content. Follow visual cues when
cooking the eggs; your skillet's thickness will affect
the cooking times. To dress up the eggs, add 1 teaspoon minced fresh parsley, chives, dill, basil, or
cilantro after reducing the heat. This recipe can
easily be doubled using a 10- or 12-inch skillet.

2 large egg whites
1 teaspoon water
 Pinch table salt
 Pinch pepper
1 teaspoon canola oil

Using fork, beat eggs, water, salt, and pepper in bowl
until thoroughly combined; do not overbeat. Heat oil
in 8- or 10-inch nonstick skillet over medium-high
heat until shimmering. Add egg mixture and, using
rubber spatula, constantly and firmly scrape along
bottom and sides of skillet until eggs begin to
clump and spatula leaves trail on bottom of skillet,
30 to 60 seconds. Reduce heat to low and gently
but constantly fold egg mixture until clumped and
just slightly wet, 30 to 60 seconds. Transfer eggs to
plate and season with salt and pepper to taste.

SCRAMBLED EGGS

Substitute 2 whole large eggs for the 2 egg whites.

POACHED EGGS
Makes 1–4 eggs

While poaching may seem intimidating, our foolproof method gives you easy eggs—with a delicate texture and runny yolks—that you can add to any meal. They are an ideal addition (especially to pre-workout breakfasts) because they don't need any oil to cook. Putting vinegar in the water increases the acidity, which helps the egg whites set up. You will need a 10- or 12-inch skillet with a tight-fitting lid for this recipe; use a 12-inch skillet if cooking 3 or 4 eggs.

1–4 large eggs
  2 tablespoons distilled vinegar

Fill skillet nearly to rim with water, add vinegar, and bring to boil over high heat. Remove skillet from heat. Crack eggs into small bowls or teacup (up to 2 eggs in each). Gently tip bowls so eggs slide into hot water, cover skillet, and let sit for 4 minutes for medium-cooked yolks. (For firmer yolks, let eggs stand in water, checking every 30 seconds, until eggs reach desired doneness.) Using slotted spoon, gently lift each egg from water and let drain over skillet. Season with salt and pepper to taste.

EASY-PEEL HARD-COOKED EGGS
Makes 1–6 eggs

Cooking eggs in advance is an incredibly easy way to add tasty, foolproof protein to a meal. Simply cook, then store in the fridge for peeling and eating at a later date. Enjoy them plain alongside many of our breakfast options (see pages 34–63), or use to top soups, salads, and vegetable dishes. Try soft-cooked eggs (great with grain dishes or for breakfast) and jammy eggs (excellent in certain soups and on salads) for more easy options. Be sure to use large eggs that have no cracks and are cold from the refrigerator. You can use this method to cook up to 12 eggs at once; just be sure to use a pot and a steamer basket that are large enough to hold the eggs in a single layer. Hard-cooked eggs can be refrigerated, peeled or unpeeled, for up to 3 days.

1–6 large eggs

1 Bring 1 inch water to rolling boil in medium saucepan over high heat. Place eggs in steamer basket and transfer basket to saucepan. Cover, reduce heat to medium-low, and steam eggs for 13 minutes.

2 When eggs are almost finished cooking, combine 2 cups ice cubes and 2 cups cold water in bowl. Using tongs or slotted spoon, transfer eggs to ice bath and let sit for 15 minutes. Peel before using.

EASY-PEEL JAMMY EGGS

This method will yield eggs with medium-set yolks and fully set whites.

Cook over medium-high heat in step 1, and decrease cooking time to 8 minutes. In step 2, submerge eggs in ice bath just until cool enough to handle, about 30 seconds.

EASY-PEEL SOFT-COOKED EGGS

This method will yield eggs with runny yolks and fully set whites.

Cook eggs over medium-high heat in step 1, and decrease cooking time to 6½ minutes. In step 2, submerge eggs in ice bath just until cool enough to handle, about 30 seconds.

Soba Noodles and Pan-Seared Shrimp with Snap Peas, Radishes, and Peanut-Sesame Sauce

VEGETABLES

Our plate ratios guidelines (see page 16) refer to the ratio of carbohydrates to protein that optimizes athletic performance. But the thing that makes for great balanced plates, giving them identity and interest, is a vegetable component. Adding vegetables introduces nutrients, flavor, color, and appealing contrasts in texture. Even simple seasonings on your vegetables—garlic, citrus, herbs—can bring layers of complexity to a finished plate. Having precooked or prepped vegetables on hand makes throwing together a lunch or adding heft to a dinner that much simpler. When you're looking to build a complete meal, select two portions of vegetables.

QUICK GO-TO VEGETABLES

We love raw vegetables because they are a quick and easy way to get your nutrients. But blanching vegetables is also a nice option, making them perfectly crisp-tender (and great for advance preparation). Raw or blanched, they can be seasoned however you prefer just before eating. We listed our serving preferences in the chart below.

To quickly blanch vegetables, bring 4 quarts water and 1½ tablespoons table salt to boil in large saucepan over high heat. Cook vegetables, 1 variety at a time, until slightly softened but still crunchy at core. Transfer blanched vegetables immediately to bowl of ice water and let sit until completely cool, then drain and pat dry. (Blanched vegetables can be refrigerated for up to 3 days.)

VEGETABLE	PREP	RAW OR BLANCHED	SERVING SIZE
Asparagus	trim and cut into 2-inch lengths	blanched	4 ounces
Green beans	trim and cut into 2-inch lengths	blanched	4 ounces
Broccoli	cut into 1½-inch florets	raw/blanched	4 ounces
Carrots	peel and slice thin on bias	raw/blanched	2 ounces
Cauliflower	cut into 1½-inch florets	raw/blanched	4 ounces
English cucumber	slice thin	raw	4 ounces
Snap peas	remove strings	raw/blanched	2 ounces
Radishes	trim and quarter	raw	4 ounces
Baby spinach	none	raw	2 ounces
Cherry or grape tomatoes	none or halve	raw	3 ounces

1 Adjust oven rack to middle position and heat oven to 400 degrees. Wrap beets individually in aluminum foil and place on rimmed baking sheet. Roast until beets can be easily pierced with paring knife, 45 minutes to 1 hour, removing beets individually from oven as they finish cooking.

2 Open foil packets to allow steam to escape and let cool slightly. Once beets are cool enough to handle, rub off the skins using paper towels. Slice or chop beets as desired and season with salt and pepper to taste.

ROASTED SWEET POTATOES

Makes 1 cup, enough for 4 servings

Roasting sweet potatoes maximizes their caramelized flavor so you get delicious, toasty-tasting potatoes that are packed with nutrients. Choose potatoes that are as even in width as possible; trimming the small ends prevents them from burning. We like the texture that unpeeled potatoes add to our bowls; just be sure to scrub them well before prepping. Or you can peel the potatoes if you prefer. This recipe can easily be doubled. Sweet potatoes can be refrigerated for up to 2 days.

8 ounces sweet potatoes, halved lengthwise then sliced crosswise ¼ inch thick
1 teaspoon extra-virgin olive oil or vegetable oil
¼ teaspoon table salt
⅛ teaspoon pepper

Adjust oven rack to middle position and heat oven to 400 degrees. Toss potatoes, oil, salt, and pepper together in bowl, then spread in even layer on rimmed baking sheet. Roast until potatoes are tender and lightly browned, 15 to 20 minutes, flipping slices halfway through roasting. Let potatoes cool for 5 minutes then season with salt and pepper to taste.

ROASTED BEETS

Makes 3 cups, enough for 6 servings

Beets are a beloved vegetable for more than their earthy-sweet taste—they may actually benefit athletic performance. Their rich nitrate content may improve blood flow and lung function and strengthen muscle contractions. Roasting the beets concentrates their sweet flavor and gives them a more tender, potato-like texture. The recipe can easily be doubled. Beets can be refrigerated for up to 1 week.

1 pound beets, trimmed

SAUTÉED MUSHROOMS

Makes 1½ cups, enough for 2 servings

Mushrooms are a low-calorie source of fiber and antioxidants (and some protein!) that easily absorb any flavor added to them to go with the meal of your choice. Use a single type of mushroom or a combination, but prep (and yields) will vary: Stem and halve portobellos and cut each half crosswise into ½-inch pieces. Trim white or cremini mushrooms; quarter if large or medium, and halve if small. Trim oyster mushrooms and tear into 1- to 1½-inch pieces. Stem shiitake mushrooms, then quarter large caps and halve small caps. Mushrooms can be refrigerated for up to 2 days.

    12 ounces mushrooms
     2 tablespoons water
     2 teaspoons extra-virgin olive oil or vegetable oil

Cook mushrooms and water in 12-inch nonstick skillet over high heat, stirring occasionally, until skillet is almost dry and mushrooms begin to sizzle, 4 to 8 minutes. Reduce heat to medium-high. Add oil and toss until mushrooms are evenly coated. Continue to cook, stirring occasionally, until mushrooms are well browned, 4 to 8 minutes longer. Season with salt and pepper to taste.

Poached Chicken and Rice Salad with Roasted Beets, Baby Spinach, and Pomegranate-Honey Vinaigrette

DRESSINGS AND SAUCES

Don't buy the bottle: Homemade dressings and sauces aren't intimidating. They're often made with pantry ingredients, and they can stay in your refrigerator for at least a few days to brighten up your meals throughout the week. A well-placed drizzle of sauce adds moisture and additional flavor to a dish, and can tie together the basic recipes in this chapter to create elevated meals.

POMEGRANATE-HONEY VINAIGRETTE

Makes about 1 cup, enough for 8 servings

Fruit juice makes an easy, sweet-tart vinaigrette base. For a clingy texture, we reduced pomegranate juice to thicken it. Toss the vinaigrette with a grain, some poached chicken, and vegetables of your choosing for a simple and satisfying meal. Be sure to use tart juices as reducing sweetened drinks such as cranberry cocktail renders them cloying. To avoid off-flavors, make sure to reduce the juice in a nonreactive stainless-steel saucepan. Vinaigrette can be refrigerated for up to 1 week; whisk to recombine before using.

- 2 cups pomegranate juice
- 1 tablespoon honey
- 3 tablespoons red wine vinegar
- 2 tablespoons extra-virgin olive oil or vegetable oil
- 1 tablespoon minced shallot
- ½ teaspoon table salt
- ½ teaspoon pepper

Bring pomegranate juice and honey to boil in small saucepan over medium-high heat. Reduce to simmer and cook until thickened and juice measures about ⅔ cup, 15 to 20 minutes. Transfer syrup to medium bowl and refrigerate until cool, about 15 minutes. Whisk in vinegar, oil, shallot, salt, and pepper until combined.

APPLE CIDER–SAGE VINAIGRETTE

Substitute apple cider for pomegranate juice and cider vinegar for red wine vinegar. Add ½ teaspoon minced fresh sage to syrup with vinegar.

ORANGE-GINGER VINAIGRETTE

Substitute orange juice for pomegranate juice and lime juice for red wine vinegar. Add 1 teaspoon grated fresh ginger to syrup with lime juice.

CREAMY AVOCADO DRESSING

Makes about 1 cup, enough for 8 servings

Avocado gives this dressing a creamy, sturdy texture that holds up to tossing and doesn't slide off ingredients. Dressing can be refrigerated for up to 5 days; whisk to recombine before using.

- ½ ripe avocado, cut into ½-inch pieces
- 3 tablespoons water
- 2 tablespoons honey
- 1 tablespoon extra-virgin olive oil
- 1 teaspoon grated lemon zest plus 3 tablespoons juice
- 1 garlic clove, minced
- ½ teaspoon table salt
- ¼ teaspoon pepper

Process all ingredients in food processor until smooth, about 30 seconds, scraping down sides of bowl as needed. Season with salt and pepper to taste.

CHIMICHURRI

Makes about 1 cup, enough for 8 servings

This punchy and herbaceous sauce is an Argentinian accompaniment that comes together quickly in a food processor and pairs well with meats and grains. Chimichurri can be refrigerated for up to 3 days.

      1 cup fresh parsley leaves
    ¼ cup water
      2 tablespoons extra-virgin olive oil
      2 tablespoons honey
      1 tablespoon red wine vinegar
      2 garlic cloves, minced
    ½ teaspoon dried oregano
    ½ teaspoon table salt
    ¼ teaspoon red pepper flakes

Pulse all ingredients in food processor until coarsely chopped, about 10 pulses, scraping down sides of bowl as needed. Season with salt and pepper to taste.

PEANUT-SESAME SAUCE

Makes about ¾ cup, enough for 6 servings

Chunky peanut butter helps this Asian-inspired sauce turn rich and creamy once processed. We love the way the thick sauce clings to noodles and vegetables. Sauce can be refrigerated for up to 3 days; add warm water as needed to loosen before using.

    ¼ cup boiling water, plus extra as needed
      3 tablespoons chunky peanut butter
      2 tablespoons toasted sesame seeds
      1 tablespoon soy sauce
  1½ tablespoons rice vinegar
  1½ tablespoons packed light brown sugar
  1½ teaspoons grated fresh ginger
      1 garlic clove, minced
    ¾ teaspoon hot sauce

Process all ingredients in blender until smooth and mixture has consistency of heavy cream, about 1 minute (adjust consistency with extra boiling water, 1 tablespoon at a time, as needed). Season with salt and pepper to taste.

HARISSA

Makes about ½ cup, enough for 8 servings

Harissa is a Tunisian chile paste that is great for flavoring chicken and grains, or even for spreading on a sandwich when you want a spicy condiment instead of mayo. Try it in our chicken and barley salad (see page 105) or our lentil kibbeh (page 202). If you can't find Aleppo pepper, you can substitute ¾ teaspoon paprika plus ¾ teaspoon finely chopped red pepper flakes. Harissa can be refrigerated for up to 4 days.

      6 tablespoons extra-virgin olive oil
      6 garlic cloves, minced
      2 tablespoons paprika
      1 tablespoon ground coriander
      1 tablespoon ground dried Aleppo pepper
      1 teaspoon ground cumin
    ¾ teaspoon caraway seeds
    ½ teaspoon table salt

Combine all ingredients in bowl and microwave until bubbling and very fragrant, about 1 minute, stirring halfway through microwaving. Let cool completely.

KALE AND SUNFLOWER SEED PESTO
Makes about 1 cup, enough for 8 servings

This pesto has a nutrient-dense twist: We add hearty baby kale to the traditional basil, and use sunflower seeds, which are lower in fat than the traditional pine nuts. Pesto can be refrigerated with plastic wrap pressed flush to surface for up to 3 days.

    2½ ounces baby kale (2½ cups)
    ½   cup fresh basil leaves
    3   tablespoons roasted sunflower seeds
    ¼   cup water
    2   garlic cloves, minced
    ⅛   teaspoon table salt
    ¼   cup extra-virgin olive oil
    2   tablespoons grated Parmesan cheese

Process kale, basil, sunflower seeds, water, garlic, and salt in food processor until smooth, about 30 seconds, scraping down sides of bowl as needed. With processor running, slowly add oil until incorporated. Transfer mixture to bowl, stir in Parmesan, and season with pepper to taste.

YOGURT SAUCE
Makes about 1 cup, enough for 8 servings

Yogurt is a great way to create a creamy sauce with lower-fat ingredients. The base can be flavored in endless ways—we provide a few to get you started with our variations. Spread any iteration on our Spiced Cauliflower Burgers (page 197), or use with any bowl combination you come up with when you need a cool and contrasting sauce to tie everything together. Sauce can be refrigerated for up to 4 days.

    1   cup plain low-fat yogurt
    1   teaspoon grated lemon zest plus
        2 tablespoons juice
    1   garlic clove, minced
    ½   teaspoon table salt

Whisk all ingredients together in bowl. Cover and refrigerate until flavors meld, at least 30 minutes. Season with salt and pepper to taste.

CHIPOTLE YOGURT SAUCE
Substitute lime zest and juice for lemon zest and juice. Add 1 tablespoon minced canned chipotle in adobo sauce.

HERB YOGURT SAUCE
Add 2 tablespoons minced fresh cilantro and 2 tablespoons minced fresh mint.

TAHINI YOGURT SAUCE
Add ¼ cup tahini.

CONVERSIONS & EQUIVALENTS

Some say cooking is a science and an art. We would say that geography has a hand in it, too. Flours and sugars manufactured in the United Kingdom and elsewhere will feel and taste different from those manufactured in the United States. So we cannot promise that the loaf of bread you bake in Canada or England will taste the same as a loaf baked in the States, but we can offer guidelines for converting weights and measures. We also recommend that you rely on your instincts when making our recipes. Refer to the visual cues provided. If the dough hasn't "come together in a ball" as described, you may need to add more flour—even if the recipe doesn't tell you to. You be the judge.

The recipes in this book were developed using standard U.S. measures following U.S. government guidelines. The charts below offer equivalents for U.S. and metric measures. All conversions are approximate and have been rounded up or down to the nearest whole number.

Example

1 teaspoon	=	4.9292 milliliters, rounded up to 5 milliliters
1 ounce	=	28.3495 grams, rounded down to 28 grams

VOLUME CONVERSIONS

U.S.	METRIC
1 teaspoon	5 milliliters
2 teaspoons	10 milliliters
1 tablespoon	15 milliliters
2 tablespoons	30 milliliters
¼ cup	59 milliliters
⅓ cup	79 milliliters
½ cup	118 milliliters
¾ cup	177 milliliters
1 cup	237 milliliters
1¼ cups	296 milliliters
1½ cups	355 milliliters
2 cups (1 pint)	473 milliliters
2½ cups	591 milliliters
3 cups	710 milliliters
4 cups (1 quart)	0.946 liter
1.06 quarts	1 liter
4 quarts (1 gallon)	3.8 liters

WEIGHT CONVERSIONS

OUNCES	GRAMS
½	14
¾	21
1	28
1½	43
2	57
2½	71
3	85
3½	99
4	113
4½	128
5	142
6	170
7	198
8	227
9	255
10	283
12	340
16 (1 pound)	454

CONVERSIONS FOR COMMON BAKING INGREDIENTS

Baking is an exacting science. Because measuring by weight is far more accurate than measuring by volume, and thus more likely to produce reliable results, in our recipes we provide ounce measures in addition to cup measures for many ingredients. Refer to the chart below to convert these measures into grams.

INGREDIENT	OUNCES	GRAMS
Flour		
1 cup all-purpose flour*	5	142
1 cup cake flour	4	113
1 cup whole-wheat flour	5½	156
Sugar		
1 cup granulated (white) sugar	7	198
1 cup packed brown sugar (light or dark)	7	198
1 cup confectioners' sugar	4	113
Cocoa Powder		
1 cup cocoa powder	3	85
Butter†		
4 tablespoons (½ stick or ¼ cup)	2	57
8 tablespoons (1 stick or ½ cup)	4	113
16 tablespoons (2 sticks or 1 cup)	8	227

* U.S. all-purpose flour, the most frequently used flour in this book, does not contain leaveners, as some European flours do. These leavened flours are called self-rising or self-raising. If you are using self-rising flour, take this into consideration before adding leaveners to a recipe.

† In the United States, butter is sold both salted and unsalted. We generally recommend unsalted butter. If you are using salted butter, take this into consideration before adding salt to a recipe.

OVEN TEMPERATURES

FAHRENHEIT	CELSIUS	GAS MARK
225	105	¼
250	120	½
275	135	1
300	150	2
325	165	3
350	180	4
375	190	5
400	200	6
425	220	7
450	230	8
475	245	9

CONVERTING TEMPERATURES FROM AN INSTANT-READ THERMOMETER

We include doneness temperatures in many of the recipes in this book. We recommend an instant-read thermometer for the job. Use this simple formula to convert Fahrenheit degrees to Celsius:

Subtract 32 degrees from the Fahrenheit reading, then divide the result by 1.8 to find the Celsius reading.

Example

"Roast chicken until thighs register 175 degrees."

To convert:

$175°F - 32 = 143°$

$143° \div 1.8 = 79.44°C$, rounded down to 79°C

INDEX

Note: Page references in *italics* indicate photographs.

D

E

P

T

U